THE ECONOMICS OF RATIONALITY

The concept of the rational economic agent is at the heart of modern economics. Mainstream economic theory seems unable to develop without the assumption that agents proceed by finding the optimal means to a well-defined end. Yet despite its centrality many economists find this concept of rationality of little use when trying to explain a wide range of economic phenomena.

This volume contains a number of critical perspectives on the treatment of rationality in economics. They are drawn from a variety of subdisciplines within economics. Insights from such diverse areas as game theory, experimental economics, psychology, post-Keynesian and institutional economics cast considerable doubt on whether a unitary conception of rationality within economics is possible or indeed desirable.

Bill Gerrard is a Lecturer in Economics at the University of York. He has previously held positions at the Universities of Leeds and Manitoba and at Unilever plc. He has written in a number of key areas of economics: methodology, macroeconomics, the economics of J. M. Keynes and industrial economics. His publications include *The Theory of the Capitalist Economy* (Blackwell 1989) and a co-edited collection of essays on Keynes.

THE ECONOMICS OF RATIONALITY

Edited by
Bill Gerrard

ROUTLEDGE

London and New York

First published 1993
by Routledge
11 New Fetter Lane, London EC4P 4EE

Simultaneously published in the USA and Canada
by Routledge
29 West 35th Street, New York, NY 10001

Typeset in Times by J&L Composition Ltd, Filey, North Yorkshire
Printed and bound in Great Britain by
T.J. Press (Padstow) Ltd.
Padstow, Cornwall

British Library Cataloguing in Publication Data

A catalogue reference for this book is available from the British Library

ISBN 0-415-06875-4

Library of Congress Cataloging in Publication Data has been applied for.

ISBN 0-415-06875-4

CONTENTS

List of figures vii
List of tables ix
Contributors xi
Preface xiii
Acknowledgement xv

1 INTRODUCTION 1
Bill Gerrard

2 RATIONALITY IS AS RATIONALITY DOES 6
John D. Hey

3 DEVELOPMENTS IN UTILITY THEORY AS A PARADIGM LANGUAGE GAME 22
Paul Anand

4 CALCULATION, HABITS AND ACTION 36
Geoffrey M. Hodgson

5 BEYOND THE LOGICAL THEORY OF RATIONAL CHOICE 52
Bill Gerrard

6 POST-MODERNITY AND NEW CONCEPTIONS OF RATIONALITY IN ECONOMICS 68
Shaun Hargreaves Heap

7 KEYNES ON RATIONALITY 91
Ted Winslow

8 PUBLIC CHOICE, STABILITY AND SOCIAL RATIONALITY 123
David Mayston

9 DISPARITIES BETWEEN HEALTH STATE MEASURES: IS THERE A RATIONAL EXPLANATION? 149
Graham Loomes

10 BOUNDED RATIONALITY IN ACTION: THE GERMAN SUBMARINE CAMPAIGN, 1915–18 179
Avner Offer

Index 203

FIGURES

3.1 The immunization game tree 30
6.1 The centipede game 82
8.1 Single-peaked preferences 134
8.2 Extremal restrictedness 137
8.3 Path dependency 141
8.4 Ordinal individual preferences 143
9.1 Non-linear relationship between *C*/*V* and *T*/*S* 153
9.2 Choice matrix for time trade-off method 158

TABLES

8.1 Non-transitivity in collective choice 124
8.2 The prisoner's dilemma: the case of overfishing 131
9.1 Visual analogue scores and standard gamble indices 166
9.2 Measures of disparities – selected cases 170

CONTRIBUTORS

Paul Anand, Templeton College, University of Oxford, Oxford, UK

Bill Gerrard, Department of Economics and Related Studies, University of York, Heslington, York, UK

Shaun Hargreaves Heap, School of Economic and Social Studies, University of East Anglia, Norwich, UK

John D. Hey, Department of Economics and Related Studies, University of York, Heslington, York, UK

Geoffrey M. Hodgson, Department of Economics and Government, University of Northumbria, Newcastle upon Tyne, UK

Graham Loomes, Department of Economics and Related Studies, University of York, Heslington, York, UK

David Mayston, Department of Economics and Related Studies, University of York, Heslington, York, UK

Avner Offer, Nuffield College, University of Oxford, Oxford, UK

Ted Winslow, Division of Social Science, York University, North York, Ontario, Canada

PREFACE

The concept of rationality lies at the foundation of modern economic theory. Yet the form of its conceptualization remains problematic. The nature and limitations of the treatment of rationality in economics is the subject matter of this volume. The contributions are mostly new papers written for an interdisciplinary seminar series 'Deconstructing Rationality' held at the University of York and hosted by the Group for Alternative Perspectives. Thanks are due to the Department of Economics and Related Studies, the Department of Philosophy and the Institute for Research in the Social Sciences at the University of York for jointly providing the financial support for the seminar series. Thanks are also due to Joanna Hodge as co-organizer of the seminar series and to Helen Hawksby for all her efforts in the preparation of the manuscript. Finally, the advice and editorial assistance of Alan Jarvis at Routledge has been invaluable.

ACKNOWLEDGEMENT

The editor and Routledge wish to thank Professor Graeme Snooks, editor of the *Australian Economic History Review*, for permission to reprint the article by Avner Offer which appears as Chapter 10 in this volume. This article was originally published under the title 'Economic interpretation of war: the German submarine campaign, 1915–1918' in the *Australian Economic History Review*, vol. 24 (March 1989), pp. 21–41.

1

INTRODUCTION

Bill Gerrard

The notion of the rational agent is the basic building block of modern economics. Economic theorists invariably presuppose that economic behaviour consists of the actions of agents seeking to optimize with respect to some well-defined objective function. Rationality in economics is viewed in instrumentalist terms: the choice of the optimal means to achieve some given ends. Yet, despite its axiomatic status, the conception of rationality in economics is not without criticism. In particular its empirical relevance is seen by many as open to question in all but the very simplest choice situations. This volume is a contribution to the debate on the appropriate conception (or conceptions) of rationality required in economics. The essays represent a number of different perspectives. Many of the authors broadly agree that there is a need to adopt some notion of bounded rationality and to give greater prominence to the effects of uncertainty on decision-making. But this view is by no means universal. The debate continues.

The first essay, by John Hey, attempts to clarify the nature and function of the concept of rationality in economics. Hey defines rational behaviour as people trying to do what they perceive as best for them to do. He considers the different roles that rationality plays in economics. In normative economics rationality is the assumption that agents ought to optimize. As such, rationality is relative to the aspiration of the agent. It requires only that the agent has a well-defined objective function. Different objective functions lead to different rationalities. In positive economics rationality is the maintained hypothesis of consistency, necessary in any predictive science. Rationality provides the structure for meaningful empirical investigation. It cannot be proved or disproved. If any particular form of the maintained hypothesis is discredited by the empirical evidence, an alternative form of rationality must be proposed.

Paul Anand considers the debates on rationality in utility theory in game-theoretic terms. He views these debates as a series of games involving two different language communities. On the one side there is the mathematical language community with its emphasis on precision and tractability. On the other side there is the natural language community with its concern with the vaguer aspects of human behaviour. Anand discusses the reasons for the dominance of the mathematical language utility theory. In particular he focuses on the various immunizing stratagems that have been adopted to protect axiomatic utility theory from apparent anomalous empirical evidence. These immunizing stratagems include reinterpreting the evidence as well as the claim that it is only the degree of rationality of an agent which is testable, not rationality itself.

The next essay, by Geoffrey Hodgson, deals with the two arguments usually employed to justify the orthodox conception of rationality. First, it may be contended that agents do actually have the motivation and abilities to be rational in the global sense of searching out the optimal solution. Alternatively it is argued that there is some form of Darwinian evolutionary dynamic at work ensuring convergence towards optimizing behaviour. Hodgson considers neither of these arguments to be tenable. He is particularly critical of the use of the Darwinian analogy in economics. It may be appropriate in the context of competition between firms but elsewhere its relevance is a matter of some doubt. In what way, for example, would non-rational consumers be eliminated by rational consumers? Also the ability to survive need not imply optimizing behaviour. Hodgson argues for a wider conception of rationality to include habitual and routine behaviour. A viable notion of human action needs to involve a bounded and multilevelled process of monitoring and deliberation with different degrees and levels of consciousness.

In my own essay I argue for the need to encompass the standard logical theory of rational choice within a more general framework. The logical theory provides theoretical and empirical tractability but its explanatory power is problematic. It can give realistic explanations of behaviour only in very simple choice situations. It can retain explanatory power despite its non-realistic assumptions in more complex situations if there is a strong validation process in the form of learning or competition to ensure convergence to some optimum. The logical theory is of limited use in complex situations with no strong validation process. There is a need, therefore, for a more general theory of economic behaviour. Two specific contributions are discussed as starting points for a more general approach: Simon's notion of procedural rationality and Keynes's analysis of the investment decision in which he emphasizes the role of conventional assumptions, confidence and the precautionary motive in behaviour under uncertainty.

The importance of uncertainty emerges also in the essay by Shaun Hargreaves Heap. He attempts to draw parallels between the literature on post-modernism and economics. In both he finds an emphasis on doubt and uncertainty. In post-modernism the denial of objectivist and positivist presuppositions has produced an open-endedness in which the role of human creativity becomes focal. Hargreaves Heap sees the same sort of open-endedness in economics, particularly in the theory of rational expectations, in game theory and in experimental economics. The problem of underdetermination in these areas of economics illustrates the inadequacy of instrumental rationality. Hargreaves Heap argues for a conception of the economic agent as socially located, capable of open-ended and creative actions.

The essay by Ted Winslow provides an account of the changing conceptions of human behaviour to be found in the writings of John Maynard Keynes. The early thought of Keynes resulted in *A Treatise on Probability* in which Keynes developed a logical theory of probability. Keynes considered probability as the rational degree of belief in a non-conclusive argument given the available evidence. After the *Treatise* Keynes gave much greater attention to the irrationality of human behaviour, abandoning his belief in the essential rationality of human nature. In his ethical thought Keynes came to argue for the customary morals and conventions as the means by which civilization can protect itself from irrationality. This is in stark contrast to Keynes's earlier Bloomsbury philosophy which rejected the constraints imposed by customary morals and conventions. Winslow argues that Keynes's acceptance of the irrationality of human behaviour is also reflected in Keynes's economics in the analysis in the *General Theory* of the psychological propensities which underlie consumption, investment and liquidity preference.

David Mayston's essay is concerned with the rationality of group behaviour, specifically the difficulties of establishing a well-defined objective function for a group. These difficulties are enshrined in Arrow's impossibility theorem. Mayston shows how the notion of rationality at the group level breaks down once one moves away from a world of single peaked individual preferences over a unidimensional policy variable. The breakdown of rationality at the group level can have serious consequences, including social instability and the threat of dictatorship. Mayston proposes a solution involving the abandonment of Arrow's requirement of the independence of irrelevant alternatives as well as the use of additional information on individual preferences.

The essay by Graham Loomes considers a specific problem that has arisen in the application of rational choice models in the area of health policy. Practical applications require measurement of the preferences of agents. In the case of health state measures it is found that different methods of valuation lead to systematic and persistent inconsistencies. These disparities also arise if only a single method of valuation is used. Such anomalies raise questions about the validity of the assumption that agents are rational. They undermine the economist's ability to contribute to policy appraisal. Loomes argues that the disparities in health state measures need not be seen as evidence of irrationality. He shows that they can be explained within the framework of regret theory. However, this is not the complete story, as is shown by the fresh evidence reported in the essay.

The final essay, by Avner Offer, analyses the rationality of the German submarine campaign during the First World War. Offer adopts a framework of bounded rationality and provides a detailed discussion of the arguments within the German Admiralty for the submarine campaign. He shows that the problem lay not in the lack of evidence but in the perceptual framework used. Offer describes the German Admiralty as becoming stuck in a degenerating research programme immunized against counter-evidence. They employed a military rationality which stressed willpower, fighting spirit and acceptance of sacrifice as the means of prevailing in the face of superior material forces. Offer argues that this military rationality is an appropriate response to limited resource endowment but was inappropriate in the context of the submarine campaign. He concludes that economic rationality, an assessment of political and economic costs and benefits, would have been more appropriate in that specific situation, but not universally so as evidenced by American experience in the Vietnam War.

2

RATIONALITY IS AS RATIONALITY DOES[1]

John D. Hey

Some time after I foolishly agreed to give a seminar in the series 'Deconstructing rationality', I decided that I ought to discover what I had let myself in for. Accordingly, I trotted along to the library and tried first to find out what the first word in the title meant. I could not find the word in any normal dictionary, and the only volume in the library with the word 'deconstructing' in the title was alarmingly called *Deconstructing Marxism*. I began to panic at this stage. However, things were rather different with the word 'rationality'. This *did* appear in various dictionaries and in the titles of numerous volumes in the library. Indeed, there was almost an embarrassment of riches, with several shelves groaning with books devoted to rationality. On closer inspection, unfortunately, they all turned out to be philosophy books, full of words and virtually no maths. I did select a few at random and take them out of the library, but they looked even worse when I got them home. True, there was one by Martin Hollis, *The Cunning of Reason*, which started off promisingly, but it did not seem to get anywhere, even though it was a refreshing change to read some good English prose.

I decided then that this was all a fiendish put-up job by the seminar organizers to try and get Old Hey educated. But I was damned if I was going to read all those boring words. I'd get my own back by trying to define at least one of the two words in the series title myself. To hell with the other; it probably doesn't mean anything anyhow.

This got me thinking about a recent article by Amartya Sen on equality that I had read only a few weeks back. Sen spent the first half of the paper asking the question 'equality of what?'; the second half being devoted to asking the rather more usual question 'why equality?'. The analogy is not 100 per cent complete, but it stimulates the question in *our* context: 'why are we interested in the issue of rationality?'.

I do not want to get bogged down in a fruitless semantic discussion: what is love? What is a banana? What is yellow? (A banana is a banana because we call it that; it's yellow because we call it that. How do you know what I call a banana is the same thing that you call a banana? How do you know that what looks yellow to you also looks yellow to me? and so on. As if anyone cared.) But I fear that my conclusions, as well as my title, may end up with a rather semantic air. Let us see.

Why then are we, as economists, interested in rationality? In order to begin to formulate an answer to this question, I think we need to distinguish carefully between whether we are doing *normative* or *positive* economics. Suppose, to get the ball rolling, that we are interested in the former: we are using economics to tell somebody, or some bodies, how they *ought* to be behaving. They *ought*, in common parlance, to behave rationally. But why? And why do we advise them that they ought to behave rationally? Presumably, because it would appear to us that there is some gain for them by doing so: they would be better off in some sense behaving rationally than not behaving rationally. This line of argument immediately gets us into the *optimization* story beloved of economists. I will return to this shortly.

Now consider the situation of *positive* economics in which case we are trying to describe (and thence predict) economic behaviour. Why do we worry about rationality here? In my opinion, this is a quite different kettle of fish. What we need rationality for here is to imbue our economic agents (whose behaviour we are trying to describe and predict) with some behavioural *consistency*. Any predictive theory requires some consistency somewhere, even those theories arising in the natural sciences. How does a scientist 'know' that the sun will rise tomorrow? Because it has risen every day in the past and the scientist assumes that this behaviour is consistent. This is, of course, a particularly simple type of consistency, but the same requirement applies in more complicated situations. The economist, when predicting, for example, aggregate savings behaviour, will estimate a relationship using past observations, and use this relationship to predict future observations. So he or she is assuming that the relationship remains constant and that the behaviour on which it was constructed will be consistent in the future with what it was in the past.

What I would appear to be arguing is that rationality used in positive economics is simply the assumption of consistency (or constancy? – we shall see); and we need this in order to use the past to predict the future. In any area of scientific discourse, the scientist must, of necessity, take *something* as given. It is simply not possible to carry out any kind of empirical test or empirical investigation without so doing. For instance, the physicist carrying out an experiment in the laboratory will control for those factors that he or she thinks are relevant, but will, of necessity, ignore those factors that are considered irrelevant. When asked to justify this procedure there will follow, if the scientist is honest, an embarrassed silence. When carrying out, say, a test of Boyle's Law will the physicist control for the time of day, or for the race and sex of the laboratory assistants or for the weather on the other side of the globe? Of course not. But how is this justified? How does the physicist *know* that the sex of the laboratory assistant does not influence the outcome of the laboratory test? How does the physicist *know* that the colour of the desks in the laboratory does not affect the outcome of the test? The simple and honest answer is that he or she does not *know*. Possibly, however, the reply might be that on some previous occasion the physicist concerned had carried out a carefully controlled pair of experiments, identical in all respects except that one was carried out by female assistants, the other by male assistants, with no perceptible differences in the results. But note the phrase 'carefully controlled' – what controls had been enforced in this previous experiment? Had control been exercised over the colour of the desks? Had control been exercised over the race of the assistants?

Clearly there is an infinite regress problem here. However much prior testing has been done, there can be no guarantee that those factors considered irrelevant to a particular problem are actually so. In this sense then, even 'proper' science is religion; it is an act of faith that certain things are irrelevant.

We have a similar religious problem in economics. The economist takes certain things as given, but there can be no guarantee that those things are actually given. Some would argue, but I do not want to get involved in this argument here, that one can always decide whether something is *not* given. But this is slippery ground: how do we know, for example, that an individual's income *is* relevant to that individual's saving decision? Just because we have observed some correlations in the past? But how were we led to estimating those particular correlations? Because our theorizing told us that certain *other* things, such as the length of hair of the prime minister of Australia, were irrelevant to Joe Soap's saving decision. But how did we know that?

It is the same point really: the economist takes certain things as given, but there can be no guarantee that those things are actually given. But, like the 'proper' scientist, we need to do this in order to carry out any empirical investigation. In particular we take rationality as given. I have almost gone full circle: rationality is simply consistency, when we are doing positive economics.

Rationality is therefore something rather flexible: like the 'proper' scientist, we work within some maintained hypothesis (that is, we work with a particular set of givens) while generating testable hypotheses. These we test. The outcome of the test is either acceptance or rejection of the hypothesis (or more realistically partial acceptance or partial rejection of the hypothesis), and if the test suggests to us that there appears to be something badly lacking in our maintained hypothesis, we then grudgingly go back to it and reappraise it.

This has been happening *par excellence* in my own field – decision-making under uncertainty. Some years ago (despite the mutterings of Maurice Allais in the 1950s) the maintained hypothesis in the field of decision-making under uncertainty was subjective expected utility (SEU) theory. This generated numerous testable hypotheses which people went out and tested. Gradually, sufficient evidence accumulated (after translation in some instances) to convince many that SEU theory was not a particularly good maintained hypothesis for a large portion of human behaviour. This generated a new generation of theories of decision-making under uncertainty: prospect theory, regret theory, disappointment theory, weighted utility theory, implicit utility theory, generalized expected utility theory and so on. On the surface the move from the partially disgraced SEU theory to these theories was intimately tied up with an ongoing debate about rationality. Were the SEU axioms correct as characterizations of rational behaviour? Were other sets of (weaker) axioms more correct?

Yet, on one interpretation, certainly *my* interpretation as far as positive economics is concerned, this was not a debate about rationality *per se* but rather a debate about the nature of the maintained hypothesis. Strike out the word 'rational' and replace it by 'consistent' or 'reasonable' or some other name and nothing changes. The debate was simply about the maintained hypothesis.

At this point one might want to bring in some consideration of the role of *theory* in economics; if one is not careful – or even if one is – the above process of maintained hypothesis / hypothesis formation / hypothesis testing / reformulation of the maintained hypothesis could simply degenerate into empiricism. I say 'degenerate' as most economists would defend the use of theory and would argue against 'pure' empiricism. But why? This is where one is on very slippery ground, particularly, but not necessarily only, as far as economics is concerned. What *is* the role of theory in economics? Why do most economists like it?

There seem to be a number of possible legitimate responses. First, and perhaps *ex ante*, theory gives the economist a framework in which to work and in which to formulate the hypotheses to be tested; it gives some structure in which to conduct further analyses; it suggests, indeed determines, the relevant endogenous and exogenous variables in the subsequent empirical analyses. Second, and possibly *ex post*, it gives some apparent generality to any positive, or negative, findings that emerge from the analysis. If one does, say, a consumption study using aggregate time-series data for the UK for the post-war period, then it gives one a certain licence to generalize these findings and to suggest that they also apply to other countries and to other time periods, most crucially in the future. But why? Logically, one can at most conclude that these particular findings apply to the UK for the post-war period. It is only because one is assuming that the maintained hypothesis is correct that one can generalize to other times and other countries. The use of theory apparently gives one the authority so to do, but it is a very dubious form of authority: one not based on logic nor indeed on empirical evidence. How does one *know* that one's maintained hypothesis is correct? Which brings us back to where we started.

Possibly a more hopeful alternative is to argue that one's maintained hypothesis, one's axioms if you like, have some kind of moral authority. That is, I think, the reason why 'rationality' is so important: not only rationality itself but the very word. What would be the moral authority if we used 'consistent' or 'reasonable' or some other name? On this line of argument, then, one might be tempted to conclude that the use of the word 'rationality' in positive economics is a simple con-trick designed to fool the easily fooled and, indeed, even the not-so-easily fooled. I do not think that one can *logically* argue against this conclusion.

Perhaps we should move away from arguments which are based on logical correctness or otherwise as I think they are fruitless. For reasons that I have already discussed one cannot *know* that the sun will rise tomorrow. Yet at the same time, most people in the world would be happy to bet a large sum of money on the proposition that it *will* rise tomorrow. So most of us are happy to base our behaviour on the supposition that the sun will rise tomorrow. True, there are a handful of fruitcases who would argue that the sun is *not* going to rise tomorrow – for the End of The World is Nigh – but they are in a minority. One cannot say that these fruitcases are wrong – at least not until tomorrow, by which time it may be too late! – and certainly one cannot *prove* that they are wrong. Nor indeed can one use the fact that most of the people in the world think they are wrong as a basis for arguing that they are wrong.

This reminds me of a conversation that I had with an eminent economist at a distinguished English university a year or so ago after I had given a seminar there. We were discussing the goodies and the baddies in the faculty there – the goodies being the eminent economist's small band of neoclassical colleagues, and the baddies being the dreaded M*rx*sts. The baddies are a great force for reaction in the faculty, and the eminent economist was complaining how he found them a permanent millstone round his neck. I remarked something to the effect: 'Why doesn't the fact that you and your band are doing lots of good work and getting it published in good journals, while the M*rx*sts are doing nothing of any value at all and publishing at best in second-rate journals, not help in the political process of decision-making in your University? Surely everyone knows that they have to take you seriously and dismiss the claims of the lefties because it is you that brings in all the Brownie Points for Economics at this University?'

The eminent economist replied that the M*rx*sts did not accept that the fact that they published in 'second-rate' journals while the eminent economist's band published in *Econometrica* and the *Review of Economic Studies* was any kind of evidence that they were bad and the neoclassicists good. On the contrary, this was just evidence of a counter-revolutionary plot against the true scientific research that the M*rx*sts were doing. Meanwhile, the rest of the faculty, who were sitting round politely listening to this debate, being good middle-class intellectuals, declared the M*rx*sts the winners on the grounds that the eminent economist had not proved his point. Which was indeed true (even if morally disastrous).

So what is the moral of this little story? If you insist on logical proofs of propositions you end up with an economics department with a lower research ranking? Possibly. And if you insist on some logically defensible definition of rationality you waste lots of time in seminars rather than doing serious work. Let me put it more bluntly: I do not think that you can get a logically defensible definition of rationality that holds for all people for all time and in all situations.

So why bother with theory? And why bother with theories that start from some notion of rational behaviour on the part of the people whose behaviour is being studied? Here we get back once again to religion. We *believe* that people act in some kind of systematic way and that by discovering what that systematic way is we can improve the art (science?) of positive economics. Why do we believe this? Because theories based on this line of argument have achieved *more* success in the past than theories based on alternative arguments: whether you like it or not, economists are better than most other people (statisticians and chancellors of the exchequer alike) at predicting (and perhaps, by implication, explaining) economic behaviour.

There is also an argument – which I think is a side argument, but I can't make up my mind – which says that the general notions of rationality that economists use are a good thing because they are general. They provide general guiding rules for economic behaviour which can be used in myriads of situations. Anyone who has used SEU theory knows that this is indeed true, that the SEU handle can be cranked in a whole variety of different contexts – saving theory, search theory, demand theory, marriage theory, etc. – and countless journal articles can thereby be produced. So it must be a good thing! More seriously, it suggests that human behaviour itself is in some sense internally consistent, that individuals are applying the same analytical apparatus to solve their savings problems as to solve their search problems as to solve their demand problems. But note that this is once again a consistency argument. If it is valid it means that we can not only generalize the findings of a study of consumption behaviour based on post-war UK data to other countries and other times but we can also generalize them to other decision areas such as search and demand. It therefore has much the same status as the earlier arguments in favour of consistency; it provides a maintained hypothesis which will be of use until it is discredited and replaced by an alternative maintained hypothesis. True, economics derives much of its strength, cohesion and alleged superiority over other social science disciplines by its almost overriding use of the single theoretical structure but there appears to be no logically defensible argument for this. The conclusion, therefore, seems no different from the general conclusion of my arguments in relation to the use of rationality in even a localized setting.

To summarize: economists like to have some kind of 'theory', just like scientists like to have some kind of theory. In essence, the economists' theory, like the scientists' theory, is simply there to provide a maintained hypothesis. It will stay until discredited or even later, if you take a cynical view of progress in economics. But why a particular kind of theory and why one based on some notion of 'rational behaviour' by economic agents? You could argue that this was entirely semantic, which is tempting, if only to avoid the tedious attacks raised by the logicians. But let me meet the issue head on: I *believe* that some theoretical bases are better than others. I *believe* that neoclassical economics is better than Marxist economics for the explanation of certain phenomena. I *believe* that neoclassical economics is particularly bad at explaining other phenomena. I can point to the volume of evidence in favour of this point of view; others could point to the volume of evidence against it. I could argue that the former was heavier, in all ways, than the latter. But I *know* that I could not prove my belief. Similarly, I *believe* that God exists and that Christ is the Son of God, but I know that I cannot prove this belief. Neither can you disprove it.

Having got to this point, I can now happily go my own way without further justification. I can *assert* certain propositions about human behaviour; I can justify these to myself, and to an audience if they care to listen, by the analysis of empirical evidence of one kind or another. I *believe* that progress in economic understanding will be achieved by extending the analysis in certain directions but I relieve myself of the necessity of having to justify these beliefs.

I find the notion that one can logically argue in favour or against a particular form of behaviour as being rational or otherwise as being bizarre in the extreme, though I will point to the weight of empirical evidence apparently in favour or against.

Rationality in positive economics is, therefore, simply a maintained hypothesis. If it is discredited by empirical evidence then one needs to replace the maintained hypothesis by an alternative; one needs to replace 'rationality' by some other 'rationality' or 'consistency' or 'reasonableness' or whatever. How does one do this? How should one do this? These are two different questions. It should be apparent by now that I think there is no answer to the second, though I would happily give you advice on the first. Let me do this now; and at the same time say more on my beliefs about economic behaviour.

I start with an apparent tautology which defines what I mean by 'rationality'. *Rational behaviour is people trying to do what they perceive as best for them to do.* That wasn't too painful was it? Perhaps, though, it wasn't painful enough? It almost sounds as if it has no testable implications and is therefore worthless. I fear that that is inevitable because what people perceive as being in their best interests almost inevitably changes over time. So we cannot have a *specific* rule that is true for all space and for all time. Instead, we have an almost untestable *meta-rule*.

But all is not lost. Just because we cannot prove that a particular (testable) implication of the meta-rule will hold in a particular time and a particular place does not mean that it *cannot* hold. Indeed, the very fact that economists are successful in 'explaining' and predicting a whole range of economic behaviour, suggests that it often does.

So what about 'rationality' in economics? As I have demonstrated, this is merely a maintained hypothesis which one cannot prove or disprove. But, though once again one cannot prove or disprove this, there are 'good' maintained hypotheses and 'bad' maintained hypotheses. They are 'good' in two senses: the first empirical and the second intuitive. When trying to theorize about economic behaviour, the economist, being a human being, will tend to introvert about the motives behind human behaviour. This leads to the identification of a set of axioms of varying plausibility. Let me illustrate with reference to the field of economic decision-making under risk and uncertainty. Consider the usual starting point: the discussion of one-off decision-problems under risk.

Obviously, this is a totally unrealistic situation as it asks one to imagine an individual in a situation of having to choose one from a number of choice alternatives, with the outcome being decided by some random device conditional on the individual's decision. Then, presumably, the individual dies (having, of course, experienced the outcome). All very convenient. The individual may, in actuality, have lived before this particular choice problem, but this is excluded by the analysis since, as shall be seen, it might well bring in problems raised by dynamic decision-making under risk, which in turn might imply that history matters. So the individual's life is assumed to consist of just this one decision-problem.

It is supposed that the complete list of possible outcomes that might be experienced as a result of this decision-problem can be drawn up by the individual and that the individual can rank the outcomes in order of desirability or, less demandingly, that the individual can identify the best and the worst outcomes (which, in turn, implies the existence of some kind of ranking of the set of outcomes). We then consider the set of all gambles over these outcomes, and try and build up some axioms of behaviour that are 'rational' or 'reasonable' or 'consistent' or whatever. Naturally, the economic theorist is not stupid and therefore tries to find axioms which he or she finds reasonable as sensible descriptions of other people's behaviour or indeed of his or her own behaviour. After all, the economist is trying to describe that behaviour.

A starting point might be the following: if G_1 and G_2 are two gambles over the set of final outcomes, and if $M \equiv [G_1,G_2;p,1-p]$ is a gamble (a mixture) between G_1 and G_2 with respective probabilities p and $(1-p)$, then it seems reasonable to assert that:

Axiom 1 (Betweenness): If $G_1 \sim G_2$ then $G_1 \sim G_2 \sim M$, where '$\sim$' denotes indifference.

Axiom 1 seems harmless indeed: if our individual does not care whether he or she 'gets' G_1 or G_2 then he or she should not mind if some random device decides which he or she is to get. But whether it appears harmless or not, it is still an assertion about rationality; one cannot in any sense *prove* that it is a requirement of rationality. For an individual could ('quite rationally') not mind which of G_1 and G_2 he or she gets but 'would be damned if some infernal machine were to decide which I got'. Note, too, that Mark Machina's generalized expected utility theory does not require betweenness. His theory does impose some restrictions on behaviour in order to provide testability but betweenness is not one of them.

Equally well, there will be many people who would be quite happy to go along with betweenness, not only as a reasonable proposition but also as a description of their own behaviour. So let's stay with them for a little longer. Now what about:

> *Axiom* 2 (Independence): If $G_1 \sim G_2$ and if G_3 is any other gamble then $[G_1,G_3;p,1-p] \sim [G_2,G_3;p,1-p]$.

This seems harmless too, though perhaps not equally harmless. If our individual does not care whether he or she gets G_1 or G_2 then why should he or she feel any different if outcome G_1 in any gamble is replaced by G_2 in that gamble? But, once again, whether it appears harmless or not, it is still an assertion about rationality; one cannot in any sense *prove* that it is a requirement of rationality. For an individual could ('quite rationally') prefer the certainty of G_1 to a gamble between G_1 and G_2 even though he or she was indifferent between G_1 and G_2 for reasons already discussed. Independence is, in one sense, a generalization of betweenness.

Consider the classic example: suppose an individual says he prefers £3,000 with certainty to a gamble which yields £4,000 with probability 0.8 and £0 with probability 0.2, but that he also prefers a gamble which yields £4,000 with probability 0.2 and £0 with probability 0.8 to a gamble which yields £3,000 with probability 0.25 and £0 with probability 0.75. Both preferences/choices are supposed to be in the one-off choice context posited earlier. As is well-known, this pattern of preference/choice violates independence. One would explain this to the individual as follows: according to your second pair of choices you prefer a gamble which yields £4,000 with probability 0.2 and £0 with probability 0.8 to a gamble which yields £3,000 with probability 0.25 and £0 with probability 0.75; yet suppose you chose the latter instead and you got the £3,000 then this would be preferred by you to having a gamble which yielded £4,000 with probability 0.8 and £0 with probability 0.2; so the latter should be preferred by you to a gamble which yields £4,000 with probability 0.2 (that is, 0.25 times 0.8) and £0 with probability 0.8; yet this is precisely *the opposite* of what you have just said.

That is the SEU theory story. What do we say if the individual says 'So what? Your arguments are completely irrelevant to my one-off choice problem. If it is genuinely a one-off choice problem then your attempts to interpret a one-off choice as a multi-stage gamble are out of court: you cannot give me the outcome and then replace it by some other gamble at the same time. I am not convinced by your logic.'

He is quite correct: one *cannot* argue that it is rational (or consistent or reasonable or whatever) to obey the independence axiom. It is not the same kind of proposition that 'one plus one equals two'; there is no logical necessity about it. It is simply an assertion about human behaviour. Or, to use my earlier terminology, it is simply a maintained hypothesis. If it does not appear to be a particularly good maintained hypothesis then we, as economists, ought to go out and find a better one.

How might we find a better one? (Indeed what do we mean by a 'better one'?) This brings us back to empiricism – and religion. I believe that the vast majority of human beings like to live by some rules which govern their behaviour. Those rules, I *believe*, have some motivational force behind them, which suggests that observed behaviour might well be consistent with what the economist might like to describe as rational behaviour. But this does not pin us (*qua* economists or *qua* human beings) to a *particular* set of rules. I *personally* have a rather general maintained hypothesis about human behaviour – the one mentioned above – which helps me in my search for rules (or axioms) which govern behaviour. This rather general maintained hypothesis includes the proposition that, given sufficient learning and given a sufficiently simple decision-problem (of the one-off type discussed above), most human beings will tend to behave in the manner prescribed by the relevant economic theory if only for the very simple reason that it is in the individual's own interest so to do.

Which brings me back to *normative* economics. In this, we are telling/advising/recommending what some 'one' *ought* to do. This, as I said earlier is a different kettle of fish. The word 'ought' helps us enormously; indeed it almost reduces the economist's problem to the trivial or, at least, to the technical. The word 'ought' implies an objective; without such an objective the word is undefined. In this sense the word is similar to 'equality' or 'fairness' or 'just' or 'big' or 'satisfactory' – meaningless words unless some framework of reference is given.

As far as the 'ought' in normative economics is concerned I have always presumed that it is *not* the economist's job to define the framework of reference; instead this is to be done by the some 'one' to whom the economist will offer subsequent advice. So when this some 'one' asks the economist 'how should I behave?', the economist quite legitimately first responds with the counter-question 'what is your objective?'. Only when this has been answered in a satisfactory fashion can the economist advise on how the some 'one' *ought* to behave. 'In order to achieve such-and-such you *ought* to do so-and-so.'

Almost explicit in the question, if it is a meaningful one, 'how *should* I behave?' is an assumption that the objective is well-defined. In economists' jargon the some 'one' has a well-defined objective function. If that were not the case then advice could not be given – or, at least, it would be conditional. So if the some 'one' is a government which says that it prefers more equality to less and that it prefers more wealth to less but makes no comment about the trade-off between wealth and equality (assuming one exists), it cannot be given unequivocal advice; at best it can be given advice of the form: 'for a given level of wealth you *should* (to meet your equality objective) do such-and-such; for a given level of equality you *should* (to meet your wealth objective) do such-and-such'. To give unconditional advice a well-specified trade-off between wealth and equality would need to be given. Or, as I stated above, a well-defined objective function would need to be specified.

This objective function – in normative economics – defines rationality. Almost tautologically, it must provide a set of rules of behaviour which must be internally consistent, for otherwise, the well-defined objective function would not exist. It must also be complete, for much the same reason. Given these requirements there is no necessity for the behaviour so prescribed to be rational in any *a priori* sense (whatever that means).

A rather trivial digression suggests itself at this point: by implication, the above (normative) 'definition' of rationality cannot support internal inconsistencies. For example, an individual who says he or she (in a pairwise choice context) prefers G_1 to G_2 while at the same time saying that he or she prefers G_2 to G_1, is behaving in a fashion which denies the existence of a well-defined objective function (defined over pairwise choices); thus inconsistencies and well-defined objective functions are incompatible. But this would appear to be of precious little value when trying to define rationality.

Going back to my main theme – I have reached the conclusion that, for example, regret behaviour cannot be considered irrational even in a normative context. But suppose someone who had a regret-type objective function asked my advice: 'Am I being irrational? I note your criticism of the regret story. Should I do something else? Should I behave in accordance with SEU theory? Indeed, perhaps I ought to be a risk-neutral expected utility maximizer for it is clearly those that will do the best in the long run?' Unfortunately, I would have to answer all these questions in the negative: no, it is not irrational to have a regret-type objective function. No, it is not the most rational to be a risk-neutral expected utility maximizer. Whilst I myself am an expected utility maximizer, I cannot impose my preferences on you.

It is a simple question of taste. I like beer; I find it difficult to understand why people like gin and tonic. I intensely dislike coconut, and cannot begin to fathom the mentality of those who like it. (I am convinced that God put a particularly thick shell on a coconut specifically to stop people trying to eat it.) But try as I may I cannot *logically* argue that drinking gin and tonic, or eating coconut is wrong or irrational (or inconsistent, or unreasonable, or whatever). I might try to dissuade people from indulging in these repulsive habits but usually have to admit defeat.

It is similar with notions of rationality in normative economics. While I may personally feel that SEU behaviour is 'better' than regret behaviour (in the same sense that I feel that drinking beer is 'better' than drinking gin and tonic), and while I may try and persuade people to that effect, I may not always be successful. (Actually, it is very rare that I am; it may be something to do with my diplomatic skills.) Sometimes, however, it does work – perhaps where the other person is persuaded by my arguments, or perhaps where I have introduced some new ideas into the other person's thought processes, or perhaps where I have exposed them to some new experiences. But even after I have persuaded my mother-in-law to switch from her bottle of Gordon's to a bottle of Sam Smith's, I cannot *prove* that she is better off than she was. Neither can she. Nor that she would be better off not switching. Or whatever.

Of course, I am excluding from discussion the case of those individuals who have mis-specified their objective functions for one reason or another. But such individuals exist, even though economics would have us believe otherwise. And they will benefit from being straightened out. A good example is the famous case of Savage who was 'caught out' by the dreaded Allais back in the legendary 1953 Conference; and who went to bed that night rather peeved – but awoke refreshed, thanked Allais for pointing out the error of his earlier judgements and resolved to be better in future.

In normative economics, then, rationality is simply a well-defined objective function. As it cannot be proved that one well-defined objective function is any better or worse than any other, then it follows that one set of (consistent) axioms for rational behaviour cannot be considered any more or less rational than any other set of (consistent) axioms for rational behaviour. But there is some kind of relationship between axiom sets and objective functions. This *may* help the economist in his or her quest for a set of useful axioms (the maintained hypothesis) to be used in *positive* economics, for if the economist has some kind of idea of the objectives of the individual whose behaviour he or she is trying to describe (and hence predict) this may be helpful in the search for the 'best' axiom set (the 'best' maintained hypothesis).

Inevitably, the immediate objective function (the one relevant to a particular decision-problem) will vary from problem to problem. Some problems will be relatively simple and relatively familiar and perhaps be reasonably close to the static one-off scenario described above for the objective function to be close to the SEU one (though, once again, this is ultimately an empirical question). Other problems will be relatively complex and relatively unfamiliar and relatively light-years away from this scenario, so that the objective function may well be essentially undefined. In such problems individual behaviour may be close to white noise, and the axiom sets with which we are familiar will almost certainly be unhelpful in terms of describing and predicting behaviour. In such cases the theorist will be forced to fall back on my rather broad definition of rationality: *rational behaviour is people trying to do what they perceive as best for them to do*. Note the implicit (but rather tautological) invocation of the concept of an objective function.

In such instances even the notion of perception has its difficulties: when wandering around in thick fog it is often difficult to disentangle what is real from what is illusory; what has substance from what has not; what is good from what is bad. And the 'objective' test of an action which is perceived by the individual to be in the individual's best interest – whether it is actually so or not

– is fraught with difficulties. The analogy with the problem of trying to decide whether someone is sane or not comes to mind. The problems for the positive economist are immense. At best, just a few forms of 'clearly absurd' behaviour can be eliminated, with many alternative (rational) forms of behaviour still left as contenders. But perhaps that is as it should be.

As one moves from this latter extreme to the former extreme, one hopes – indeed suspects – that the fog continually lifts; and that rationality (as identified through empirical investigation) becomes more and more specific. But that is merely a conjecture.

So let me conclude. As far as positive economics is concerned, rationality is simply a euphemism for the maintained hypothesis. Natural scientists have a similar concept; they call it theory. So do we in some of our moods. In this respect, therefore, we are no better or worse off than the natural scientist. We, like them, like to have a maintained hypothesis (a paradigm if you prefer) in which to work. This paradigm is partly supported by empirical findings, partly by consensus, but mainly by religion. That is as it should be.

In normative economics, things are different. Here, rationality is simply a well-specified objective function. Just as there are different objectives so there are different rationalities. That is as it should be.

As I said at the beginning: rationality is as rationality does. There is now no need for any more chapters in this volume!

NOTE

1 My thanks to the seminar participants for their comments. My especial thanks to Graham Loomes, my Co-Director of the Centre for Experimental Economics at the University of York, whose confused thinking has often clarified mine. Finally, my thanks to Karlie Milford, godson of the legendary Popper, whose comments raised the blood pressure of both of us.

3

DEVELOPMENTS IN UTILITY THEORY AS A PARADIGM LANGUAGE GAME[1]

Paul Anand

INTRODUCTION

Economists and social scientists share the hope that decision theory will furnish them with a theory of rational action. Such an account would underpin both the positive theories applied to situations where agents are acting rationally and the normative theories by whose lights social scientists and philosophers propose we be guided. Even if no one were rational there would, therefore, be demand for a theory which outlined what being rational entails.

Until the end of the 1970s, and notwithstanding the quips about economists never reaching a conclusion, many academic members of the profession were in substantial agreement as to the meaning of rationality. The rational agent was an optimizer whose choices could be described *as if*[2] they were produced by the maximization of some function $u(\ldots)$ with arguments in consequences and probabilities represented as real numbers and elements of the unit interval respectively. Moreover, the maximization of u could be shown to be compatible with adherence to certain constraints on action which, because of their intuitive appeal, came to be known as axioms. The theorems establishing the links between the axioms and maximization of u are known as representation and uniqueness theorems. They show that behaviours consistent with the axioms can be given a maximizing representation and they establish the nature of the scales used to describe preferences and beliefs. Beliefs are measured as probabilities whilst the utilities describing preference are measured on an interval scale; that is, one which is unique only up to positive linear transforms. These components, which constitute a small part of what in mathematics is called measure theory, combined with their decision-related interpretation, constitute the basic elements of what we now call subjective expected utility theory (SEU). The maximization of u was rational because it was derived from the axioms which are necessary conditions of rational choice.

Axioms, therefore, are key to the economic understanding of rational action. There are many versions of SEU (Fishburn 1981) and each offers a slightly different axiomatization of the functional u. A number of assumptions are of technical interest only but three are always taken as possessing substantive content. First, preferences are assumed to be complete, so that you either prefer a to b or you prefer b to a, or you are indifferent between them. Second, it is postulated that preferences are transitive so that if you prefer a to b, and b to c then you prefer a to c. The third and final requirement is an independence assumption, closely related to the expectation operator used in statistics. Put simply, this requires that if a lottery (with two outcomes: win and lose) is enhanced by doubling (a factor of n) the probability of winning, the lottery becomes twice (n times) as attractive. Most researchers would prefer theories without completeness but many accepted the normative interpretation of transitivity and independence.

Much of what counts as decision theory is related to SEU and to the axioms of transitivity and independence. Broadly the related work falls into three categories. First, there are a number of experimental tests by psychologists and economists which show violations of both axioms indicating that they are, on a *positive* level, falsified. Second, there are many accounts both of utility maximization and of the economic analysis derived from it, which prove (in the strict sense) that the assumptions are not required for *technical* reasons. Third, there are theoretical arguments (of a philosophical nature) which undermine the *normative* case made on their behalf. The position might be summarized as saying that the face of decision theory is turned against SEU as an account of anything.

None of this is quite so churlish and destructive of the past as it perhaps sounds to some, but I cannot demonstrate that here. My aim instead is to understand how it was that economics was willing to support a view of decision-making which theorists now wish to reject. To do this, I shall sketch an account of the paradigm dynamics in utility theory over the past fifty years. A new theory of paradigm change, based on an elementary and informal application of game-theory to scientific activity, will be proposed. Attempted defences of expected utility theory will be characterized as strategies in an 'immunization game' and the normative interpretation of SEU theory's axioms will be presented as a position of last defence: normative reasons why these strategies fail will be presented.

THE LANGUAGE GAME

Science as a language game

Kuhn (1962) must be acknowledged for first giving voice to the thought that what scientists do and what they say they do are not always the same thing. To be sure, explicit rules for doing science are not adequate for explaining how science is done and Kuhn's analysis of paradigms and how they change provides the first non-normative theory of scientific endeavour to be widely accepted. Most research is what Kuhn calls normal science: it deals with the articulation of theory, the determination of significant facts and the matching of facts to theory. The development of paradigms leads researchers to formulate 'world views' which can be contradicted as scientific activity progresses. Ultimately the anomalous contradictions become so numerous or irresistible that an intellectual revolution takes place in which prevailing theory is rejected for a new paradigm, at which point normal science is resumed.

Subsequently, similar ideas have been pursued by other writers. In his analysis of the scientific research programme Lakatos (1976) emphasizes the importance and value of competition between competing paradigms. Laudan (1977) on the other hand suggests that problem-solving is of central importance and that paradigms should be evaluated in terms of the puzzles they solve, weighed by their importance.

Without diminishing the achievements of Kuhn (and his followers), the need for new theories of (economic) science is all too evident. Some criticisms of the early work relate to Kuhn's theory itself, others to its bearing on economics (Pheby 1988). In an analysis of Kuhn's use of the word 'paradigm', Masterman (1970) found that his original text employed the term in twenty-two different ways. Kuhn's work was grounded in the sociology of physics which differs markedly from economics. For one thing, physics has a long tradition of experimental work which is absent from economics. Conversely, the prescriptive objectives which are important in economic analysis have no direct counterpart in physics. And as Kunin and Weaver (1971) point out, economic institutions change in ways that subatomic particles do not.

Apart from the criticisms of the existing theories by Kuhn and others, there are considerations in the literature on utility theory which suggest a slightly different picture of scientific progress. To say whether this view is particular to utility theory or to economics is beyond the scope of this paper, but the view I wish to sketch is that developments in what non-economists would prefer to call decision theory can be understood as moves in a series of language games.

The players in the games that will be discussed are members of communities which are distinguished by the balance of linguistic competencies that their members have. In general, the language skills that members have are either *formal*, that is to do with methods of argument that they favour, or *application related*, that is concerned with the substantive areas in which the formal linguistic skills are applied. Formal language skills as defined here are closely related to the methods that researchers use, and perhaps what McCloskey (1983) calls rhetoric. Preferences for experimentation, mathematical modelling, verbal argument will, in part, determine the language community to which a researcher belongs. However, the researcher's reference group[3] will also be determined by their application-related skills. An econometrician working in agriculture might, for instance, identify more closely with agricultural economists using non-econometric methods.

Researchers promote the interests of their reference group(s) for two reasons. In economic terms their own interests will usually be positively correlated with the fortunes of the communities to which they belong. Whilst it is less easy to make psychological generalizations, it seems reasonable to suggest that the need for a positive self-image will also be related to the success of the reference group (see for instance Turner 1991). Our theory is made intergenerational by thinking of each group as comprising two cohorts. The senior cohort has as its primary objective the reproduction of the way its members think. This it does by observing and controlling the behavioural correlates, in this case mainly the things people say or write. It does this by selecting potential entrants and promoting members of the junior cohort who have similar language skills to those of their patrons. Both because cognitive skills decline and human capital increases with age, junior members have the most flexible language skills. Nevertheless, it is most important for members of the senior cohort to select according to the language skill, which it is harder to change. This maximizes the prospect that a junior will come to share the language competencies of the senior cohort. There is a biological analogy which is obvious though it cannot be explored here. The model of a language game just sketched nevertheless provides a backdrop against which we can interpret various positions taken in the literature. Such interpretations are examined in the following sections.

The persuasion game

Though many statisticians, philosophers and natural scientists still question the legitimacy of subjective probabilities, most economists espouse a view of decision theory in which they are not just acceptable but are entities on which the rational agent is bound to act. This was not always the case and earlier this century there was a view (see Knight 1921) that uncertainty should be handled using subjective probabilities but that this practice was not terribly *pukka*.

The earliest version of subjective probability theory was proposed by Frank Plumpton Ramsey in 1926 though it was first published posthumously in 1931. That account concentrated on providing a questioning procedure from which an agent's probabilities and utilities could be inferred. There are no axioms as such and the reason appears to be given in characteristically elliptical fashion: 'I have not worked out the mathematical logic of this in detail, because this would, I think, be rather like working out to seven places of decimals a result only valid to two' (Ramsey 1990: 76).

However, the accounts of utility theory normally referred to are those by Savage (1954) (in mathematical economics) and by von Neumann and Morgenstern (1944) (in most other areas of economics). It must be admitted that there are all manner of reasons why originators of ideas are not always properly acknowledged and Ramsey's untimely death might be taken as adding to them. However, it is not impossible to think that the relative priority given to later writers has something to do with the persuasiveness of the axiomatic accounts they provided, particularly in a profession where deductive modelling was, after Ricardo, so highly valued as a method of study.

Theory use

The provision of an axiomatic account of utility puts the theory very clearly into the mathematical domain. At that point the mathematical community (Player M) had the choice of using the theory or not, whilst those who preferred their analysis in natural language (Player N) could either tolerate or reject such an approach.

		Player N			
		Tolerate		Reject	
Player M	Use	a,	$-a$	$a-\varepsilon$,	$-a+\varepsilon$
	Ignore	0,	0	0,	0

At the same time under consideration, the vast majority of economists conducted their analysis predominantly in natural language terms so that anything M did was likely to have little impact on N's payoffs. If M had ignored the opportunity that the axiomatic account of utility theory provided, there would have been no relative change to the payoffs to M or N. The best situation for M appears to be use of the theory matched by a tolerant attitude on the part of N. Because it was assumed that opportunities (academic posts and journal outlets) are relatively fixed in the short run, the game is zero sum and M's gain, a, is N's loss. However, because the number of members in N, n, was greater than the number in M, m, the expected gain for a member of M, (a/m), would have provided a stronger incentive than the expected loss for a member of N, $(-a/n)$. We should, according to this analysis, have expected to see enthusiasm from M matched by the faint resistance of N. Although rejection seems to be a weakly dominant strategy for N, the results of clawing back some of the benefit which might otherwise accrue to M, in this case ε, are unlikely to be as great as a and, as already noted, are spread over a wider constituency. Indeed if the per capita expected benefit of rejection, ε/n, is small, then members of N might find it less than the individual cost of pursuing such a strategy, and therefore prefer to tolerate the new approach.

Over the long term the dynamics would seem to depend on those economists who could, with some bootstrapping, shift camps. To model the decision-making of this group, it will be useful to partition N into two subsets, the potentially bilingual, player P, and the rest ¬P.

		Player ¬P			
		Accept		Reject	
Player P	Bootstrap	b,	0	$b - \varepsilon'$,	0
	Do nothing	0,	0	0,	0

Here we assume that in the 1950s, P was small relative to ¬P. Over the long haul, there seems little reason to suppose the payoffs to economists are fixed – university budgets during all but the end of the recent period were expanding, new journals proliferate, budgets can be wrestled from other departments and so on. The only group who could receive a payoff from investing in bootstrapping are the members of P. At worst their efforts might only be appreciated by members of M but if N tolerates the approach, for the same reasons as before, then the benefit will be greater. Assuming that anyone who becomes bilingual can mitigate any backlash effects by reverting to type, then it would seem reasonable to suppose that their expected pay off will be positive. Bootstrapping then would appear to be the dominant strategy for P.

The games outlined above do not constitute a complete theory of the mathematization of economics though they indicate some of the key stakeholder groups and some of the forces to which they were subject. The preference for those with similar language skills and the incentive to build up benefits accruing to such groups makes this very much like a game-theoretic account of racial or sexual discrimination (if it exists). However, there are bounds on the similarities also. For one thing most observers would say that the once minority group, M, is not only now in the majority but is poised to eliminate the use of natural language as an acceptable method of analysis. In that regard, the growth of members of M is like the virtual extinction of the UK's native red squirrel population by its American cousin, the grey squirrel. It is also worth noting that the process of mathematization can be seen as one in which a group has captured the linguistic totems of an entire subject and given them new meaning. The utility function is now a measure of attitude to risk, not a record of the marginal utility of wealth. New issues, like preference for risk, have become important whilst older ones, such as how we should distribute wealth, have been left unanswered – in this context at least. The parallel between this and the Christian adoption of pagan festivals to which radically new meanings were assigned is a tempting one to draw.

THEORY EVALUATION

Falsification

Until relatively recently, utility theory suffered from a kind of confounding of positive and normative issues. It was not that researchers confused what Hume's 'is–ought' distinction separated, but rather that it was thought, or at least hoped, that one theory would meet all the criteria of concern to scientists.[4] The justification of axioms in von Neumann and Morgenstern could not be described as overly extensive, and on the face of it seems ambiguous. However, it not only suggests a grounding in logic but also an expectation that postulates like those proposed would be approximated for reasonable individuals. This suggests the possibility that axiomatic utility might be evaluated according to the empirical validity of its initial assumptions.

The possibility of empirical testing suggests that we might think of another player O representing observers. Despite the Friedman (1953) view that assumptions should not be tested, there is, in utility theory, a long tradition of experimental work by psychologists and economists aimed at testing the axioms of subjective expected utility.

In a Popperian world, O's interest is in falsification but in general it is just in having a theory to test. Since the path-breaking experiments of economics Nobel laureate, Allais (1953), utility theory has been tested almost *ad nauseam* and none of the surveys (Schoemaker 1982; Machina 1983; Baron 1988) give any reason to suppose that utility theory is the correct answer to the positive question about how humans choose. That it is a false theory has not prevented a number of rescue attempts and it is these that constitute the strategies of the Kuhnian immunization game. Four such strategies can be identified (see Fig. 3.1).

Strategy 1: Require alternative theory (RAT)

One response to falsifying evidence is to suggest that mere facts, however damning, are of a lower order than the theories to which they relate and therefore cannot of themselves remove a theory.

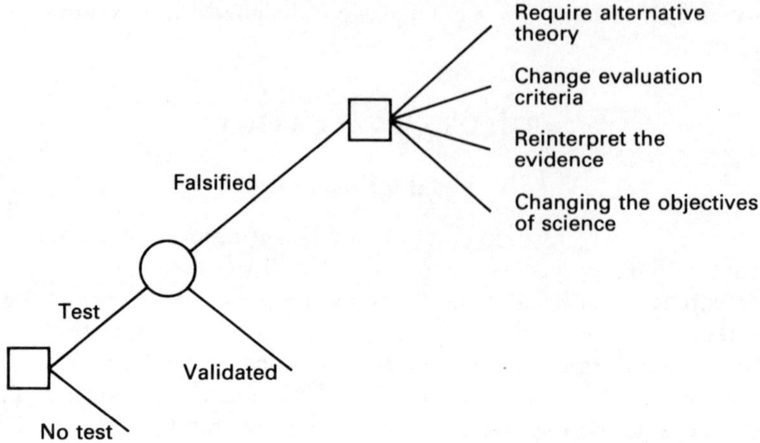

Figure 3.1 The immunization game tree

Only an alternative theory can do that. On the surface this is a strange claim for a person to make, particularly if they claim to be doing positive science. It is more intelligible if it is taken to be a claim about the trumping of theories with theories only of the same kind (i.e. other axiomatic or mathematically interesting theories). If this were the case, one would expect the discovery of more general theories of utility and probability measurement to be accompanied by a decline in the use of the RAT defence.

Strategy 2: Change evaluation criteria

An alternative attempt to deal directly with empirical counter-evidence can be found in attempts to argue that only 'systematic' violations should count against the axioms. This argument amounts to a view that statistical testing of a particular kind can be applied to *universal* propositions, which in turn requires that their universality is dispensed with at the moment of testing.

The doctrine of 'systematic errors' can lead to worse. Consider the experiments on preference reversal which find bets preferred to others which subjects value less. These experiments have been described as tests of transitivity, independence and completeness, but whichever axiom they test they serve to illustrate the paradoxes which the doctrine generates.

		Preference	
		$	*p*
Valuation	$	1	99
	p	99	0

Typically in such experiments, subjects are asked to appraise gambles by giving a numerical, monetary valuation and a preference ranking. Comparing the preferences elicited by each method it is possible to determine the number of times the preference ranking is consistent or not with the ranking implied by the valuations. Gambles frequently used in such experiments are $ (dollar bets) with high money payoffs, and *p* (probability bets) with a high chance of winning.

If an experiment produced the results as shown above, one would intuitively want to reject any theory that predicted the two measures should be consistent (utility theory is one such theory[5]).

However the doctrine of systematic errors forces one to look at the pattern of the off diagonals. The errors are evenly distributed according to the two kinds of violation possible, and so there are no grounds (in systematic errors) for rejecting any theory of which the results are a test. The reason for this *reductio ad absurdum* is that more important in judging theories even than systematic errors, is the total number of errors that a theory leads one to make. In general we prefer less to more and the use of the R^2 statistic is a formal recognition of that. In any case, the evidence is that the violations of utility theory are both systematic and numerous.

Strategy 3: Reinterpret the evidence

A third line of defence for utility theory has been to reinterpret the purported evidence of axiom violation. Some critics, particularly those new to the experimental literature, have tried to undermine the evidence by pointing to weaknesses in the incentive compatibility of payoffs for experimental subjects. The issue is indeed an important one but what counts is that the subjects are motivated to answer the questions in the way the experimenter intends. 'Incentive-compatible' compensation schedules may appear to give a suitable audit trail for readers and referees to follow, but the evidence is that response-contingent rewards have little impact on the incentives as perceived by subjects (Anand

1990a; Bolle 1990). A classic piece of work by Grisley and Kellogg (1983) shows subjects following experimenter's instructions in spite of high real maximum payoffs (a month's wages) which would have led participants to behave quite differently.

A second, and more interesting approach to the reinterpretation of evidence has accepted the validity of experimental evidence but argued that violations demonstrate that the primitives over which a subject is choosing must be redefined. Two tickets to the theatre when the other prize was a booby are not the same as a pair of tickets instead of a fortnight for two in some sun-drenched Pacific island. Counterfactual sensitivity (to use Amartya Sen's term) – that is, concern for what otherwise would have been – may easily be used to suggest that violations of axioms were not tests of them at all (see, for instance, Broome 1991).

Such defences are often made by advocates of expected utility theory who also claim that its axioms have observable behavioural content. This may seem like an almost irrefutable defence but it turns out that reinterpretation of primitives and behavioural content are not compatible. The following theorem states the result formally:

A translation theorem

All intransitive behaviours can be redescribed in such a way that transitivity is not violated and all transitive behaviours can be redescribed in such a way that transitivity is violated.

Proof (see Anand 1990b).

The implication of this result is that whether an axiom is violated or not depends on the linguistic conventions being used. Allowing such reinterpretation saves utility from transitivity violations but at the cost of behavioural content – a price which most economists would not want to pay.

Strategy 4: Change the objectives of science

The fourth and final defence of utility which can be viewed as an attempt to immunize the theory arises from the claims that though scientific, the theory is normative and intended to prescribe how agents should behave if they happened to be rational. There is no *a priori* reason to suppose that any such agents exist and therefore no reason for the theory to kowtow to the evidence of empirical data.

The claim that science is prescriptive rather than predictive or explanatory constitutes an attempt to define science in a way that most Anglo-Saxon speakers would not recognize. More significantly the 1980s have witnessed a number of attempts to evaluate the normative claims made on behalf of utility theory's two substantive axioms, transitivity and independence. Without detailing them, it is worth listing a number of arguments against the normative interpretation of transitivity. First, the idea that transitivity is required for consistency can be shown to be incorrect if consistency is taken to mean logical consistency. Second, the analogy between preference and length which is a transitive measure can be challenged by providing non-transitive analogies (e.g. pairwise competition between teams). Third, intransitive agents need not necessarily be prone to money-pumping if they reserve their intransitive preferences from use in the context of dynamic choices. Fourth, intransitive preferences need not be undecidable if they are context dependent. Fifth, it is not the case that intransitive choices are unrationalizable (i.e. not explainable) because considerations of regret and multiple criteria provide examples of explanations of such behaviour.

A detailed case for arguments against transitivity is reviewed elsewhere (Anand (1987), Bar-Hillel and Margalit (1988)) and similar critiques of independence can be found in McClennen (1983) and Machina (1989). There are as yet no counter-defences to such criticisms. Indeed if my claim that developments in utility theory are determined by the competitive pressures between language groups then we should not expect to see any counter-attacks from the mathematical community, as these would not serve to justify the generation of more general theories of utility.

CONCLUDING REMARKS

Though space has prevented me from a detailed examination of the arguments, it has been claimed that none of the strategies designed to immunize utility against the falsification of its axioms are successful *even on their own terms*. There is no mathematical, philosophical, psychological or technical need for SEU theory and the hold that it has had over economics over the past fifty years is, therefore, worthy of explanation. The hypothesis proposed here is that this curious state of affairs can be understood if we accept that utility theory was a major battlefield in a contest between two different linguistic communities. The immunization theme proposed in Kuhn's account is maintained though certain differences exist also. Instead of distinguishing between normal and revolutionary scientific progress, emphasis was placed on the satisfaction of scientists' personal objectives, the most important of which is the promotion of group interests related to linguistic preferences and competencies. Unlike Lakatos's advocacy of competition, there is no reason to think that different groups are not determined to attain complete dominance. Similarly, the theory proposed here suggests that problem-solving is not as important as Laudan suggests. If anything, the scientific agenda – that is, what problems are worthy of solution – is determined by what problems members of different language communities think they can solve.

NOTES

1 I wish to acknowledge Bill Gerrard for comments on a previous draft and discussions with members of the economics, philosophy and psychology seminar group at the University of York, Avner Offer in particular. The work was funded by a Royal Economics Society post-doctoral fellowship.
2 The simile is due to Friedman (1953).
3 Very roughly, psychological theory holds a distinction between a reference group by which one compares oneself and from which one takes values and attitudes and a membership group to which one belongs in some objective sense.
4 This is evident from the criteria listed at the end of the review in Stigler (1950).
5 See Fenn (1987) for an alternative view.

REFERENCES

Allais, M. (1953) 'Le comportment de l'homme rational devant le risque, critiques des postulates et axiomes de l'école Américaine', *Econometrica* 21: 503–46.

Anand, P. (1987) 'Are the preference axioms really rational?', *Theory and Decision* 23: 189–214.

—— (1990a) 'Analysis of uncertainty as opposed to risk: an experimental approach', *Agricultural Economics* 4: 145–63.

—— (1990b) 'Interpreting axiomatic (decision) theory', *Annals of Operations Research* 23: 91–101.

—— (1991) 'The nature of rationality and the *foundations of statistics*', *Oxford Economic Papers* 43: 199–216.

Bar-Hillel, M. and Margalit, A. (1988) 'How vicious are cycles of intransitive choice?', *Theory and Decision* 24: 119–45.
Baron, J. (1988) *Thinking and Deciding*, Cambridge: Cambridge University Press.
Bolle, F. (1990) 'High reward experiments without high expenditure for the experimenter?', *Journal of Economic Psychology* 11: 157–67.
Broome, J. (1991) *Weighing Goods*, Oxford: Blackwell.
Fenn, P. (1987) 'Evaluating irreplaceable loss', *Geneva Papers on Risk and Insurance* 12: 158–67.
Fishburn, P. C. (1981) 'Subjective expected utility', *Theory and Decision* 13: 139–99.
Friedman, M. (1953) 'The methodology of positive economics', in *Essays in Positive Economics*, Chicago: University of Chicago Press.
Grisley, W. and Kellogg, E. D. (1983) 'Farmers' subjective probabilities in Northern Thailand', *American Journal of Agricultural Economics* 65: 74–82.
Knight, F. H. (1921) *Risk, Uncertainty and Profit*, Boston: Houghton Mifflin.
Kuhn, T. S. (1962) *The Structure of Scientific Revolutions*, Chicago: University of Chicago Press.
Kunin, L. and Weaver, F. S. (1971) 'On the structure of scientific revolutions in economics', *History of Political Economy* 3: 391–7.
Lakatos, I. (1976) *The Methodology of Scientific Research Programmes*, Cambridge: Cambridge University Press.
Laudan, L. (1977) *Progress and its Problems*, London: Routledge & Kegan Paul.
Machina, M. J. (1983) 'The economic theory of individual behaviour toward risk', unpublished manuscript.
—— (1989) 'Dynamic consistency and non-expected utility models of choice under uncertainty', *Journal of Economic Literature* 27: 1622–94.
Masterman, M. (1970) 'The nature of a paradigm', in I. Lakatos and A. Musgrave (eds) *Criticism and the Growth of Knowledge*, Cambridge: Cambridge University Press.
McClennen, E. F. (1983) 'Sure-thing doubts', in B. P. Stigum and F. Wenstop (eds) *Foundations of Utility and Risk Theory with Applications*, Dordrecht: Reidel.
McCloskey, D. N. (1983) 'The rhetoric of economics', *Journal of Economic Literature* 21: 481–517.
von Neumann, J. and Morgenstern, O. (1944) *Theory of Games and Economic Behaviour*, Princeton: Princeton University Press.
Pheby, J. (1988) *Methodology and Economics*, London: Macmillan.
Ramsey, F. P. (1931) *The Foundations of Mathematics and other Logical Essays*, London: Kegan Paul.
Savage, L. J. (1954) *The Foundations of Statistics*, New York: Dover.
Schoemaker, P. J. H. (1982) 'The expected utility model', *Journal of Economic Literature* 20: 529–63.
Simon, H. A. (1976) *Administrative Behaviour*, New York: Free Press.
Stigler, G. (1950) 'The development of utility theory', *Journal of Political Economy* 50: 373–96.
Turner, J. C. (1991) *Social Influence*, Milton Keynes: Open University Press.

4

CALCULATION, HABITS AND ACTION

Geoffrey M. Hodgson

Clearly, the assumption of maximizing behaviour, or individual rationality, has come to dominate economic theory even to the extent that for many it defines the subject. Especially since Lionel Robbins's famous (1935) tract, economics is typically defined in terms of its methodology and basic assumptions. This is unusual for a science, to define itself not in terms of its appropriate object of analysis – in this case the economy – but by its chosen box of theoretical tools. Amongst these, rationality has pride of place, along with the associated techniques of equilibrium analysis under constrained maximization.

Consequently, anyone who has the gall to question the standard notion of rationality risks being described as a non-economist. Leaving aside the question of the legitimacy of any individual claim to the contrary, this is hardly a satisfactory state of affairs. If the other sciences had followed such an example then it would still be taught that the Earth was at the centre of the universe and that the material world consisted simply of the four elements of earth, water, air and fire.

Although it has often been praised for its combination of simplicity with formal analytical utility, the central assumption of rationality is not without its problems. On reflection it would seem that in order to be 'rational', agents would have to be capable of continuous and global deliberative behaviour, involving vast amounts of data, in order to make decisions and to monitor their own acts.

In an attempt to overcome this problem, orthodox economic theory has sometimes assumed that agents are 'selected' as optimizers through some supposedly Darwinian process of 'survival of the fittest'. Agents are deemed to be rational because rational units are presumed to be more efficient, and efficient elements are assumed to have a greater capacity to survive.

It is argued in this paper that both these alternatives are untenable, and that a more viable notion of rationality and human action involves an imperfect, bounded and multilevelled process of monitoring and deliberation, in which habit and social conditioning are incorporated.

In the first section of this essay the problem of computational limitations is examined, along with a review of the seminal contributions of Herbert Simon in this area. The second section examines the 'evolutionary' argument for optimization, as found in the work of Milton Friedman and others, and explores its limitations. The third section calls for an alternative analytical approach to that of maximizing rationality, based on the role of habits and routine. Ironically, such a framework is better-adapted for the incorporation of evolutionary ideas in social science and for the development of an alternative to constrained maximization. The fourth section concludes the essay.

BOUNDED RATIONALITY AND INFORMATION OVERLOAD

It would be misconceived to presume that the central issue involved in examining 'economic man' is simply whether or not the assumption of the rational agent is 'realistic'. Indeed, as Milton Friedman (1953) pointed out in a well-known paper, all theories must involve simplification, and none can possibly include all the complex features of the real world. Indeed, long ago John Stuart Mill (1844: 139) defended the use of the assumption of maximizing or rational behaviour whilst accepting that 'no political economist was ever so absurd as to suppose that mankind are really thus constituted'. Clearly, major simplifications have to be made before any theory can be built. Thereby, Friedman and the majority of economists today seem happy to accept theories built upon standard assumptions of rationality.

It is reasonable to point out, however, that whilst the theorist has no choice but to simplify and to disregard some details, the very same problem confronts the agent as well. The economic theorist cannot conceptualize everything, so why should we expect the economic agent to be different? By suggesting that the economic theorist has to simplify and be selective, Friedman is alluding to problems of limited information and bounded analytical capabilities. However, such problems likewise affect the agent, thus undermining Friedman's own argument for global rationality.

This problem of the agent being unable to deal with all the information available has created perennial unease. John Hey (1979: 232) expressed it well when he wrote: 'the optimization problems that . . . agents are supposed to be solving . . . are so complicated that the economic theorist . . . probably spent several months finding the solution. . . . The "as if" methodology is stretched to breaking point. . . . Have we not gone wrong somewhere?' The key point being raised here is the problem of the limited computational capacity or ability to make optimal decisions, even if sufficient relevant information is available.

Primarily, of course, this problem is associated with the work of Herbert Simon (1955, 1957, 1959, 1962, 1983). From the outset, his behavioural research programme has emphasized the limited computational capacity of the human brain, as well as the weight of uncertainty and incompleteness of crucial knowledge that bears upon decision-making.

A key feature of Simon's work is that he rejects the global maximization hypothesis but retains a notion of 'bounded' rationality. Thus, for example, agents may not be able to gather and process all the information for reaching global maximization decisions, but they can make a 'rational' decision within a small set of possibilities. Consequently, it is suggested by Simon that firms and consumers are not maximizing, but 'satisficing', i.e. simply trying to attain acceptable minima.

Contrary to some neoclassical interpreters, Simon is not simply proposing that agents are faced with additional 'costs', nor even that information is a problem because it is scarce, but there is a central problem of computational limitations for the decision-making agent. Essentially, rationality is 'bounded' in the sense that there is too much information to compute or assess. The adjective 'bounded' refers not to the quantity of information available, but to the limited capacity of the human mind to deal with all accessible data.

It should be emphasized that bounded rationality refers primarily to this matter of computational capacity and not to additional 'costs'. Hence 'satisficing' does not amount to cost-minimizing behaviour. Clearly, the latter is just the dual of the standard assumption of maximization. If 'satisficing' was essentially a matter of minimizing costs then it would amount to maximizing behaviour of the orthodox type and Simon's main contribution would be of little significance.

Faced with information overload, Simon suggests that agents utilize comparatively simple 'rules of thumb'. This is illustrated by his analytical work on the game of chess. Here are examples of 'satisficing' behaviour which do not arise simply because of inadequate information, but also because it would be too difficult to perform the calculations even if the relevant information was available. In principle, the chess players have all the information with which to calculate an optimal strategy – one leading to a win or at least a draw. However, the game-theoretic analysis is so complex that it cannot be completed even with a mammoth computer. Significantly, existing computer algorithms to play chess do not attempt to derive the optimal solution but to obtain one which is 'good enough' (Simon 1976).

Chess algorithms compensate for limited computational capacity and analytical shortcomings by searching incompletely through the immense tree of move possibilities, with criteria for selecting a viable move. The tree is far too large to be searched exhaustively by even the largest and fastest computer, hence the technique is to search for a satisfactory, rather than an optimal strategy. Algorithms differ partly according to their computational capacity, but also according to their menus of choice criteria.

There are important parallels with Ronald Heiner's (1983) work on the origin of rules, norms and 'predictable behaviour'. Heiner stresses the 'competence-difficulty gap' in his treatment of decision-making. Like the work of Simon, one of its features is its stress on the difference between computational capacity or ability, on the one hand, and the complexity of everyday choices and problems in economic life, on the other.

Analogous to Simon's example of chess, Heiner (1983: 563–4) uses the puzzle of Rubic's Cube. Apparently, there are over 43 trillion possible initial positions from which to unscramble the cube. However, the data required in any attempt to find out the quickest way of doing this are readily available by observing the scrambled patterns on the faces of the puzzle. The globally rational agent is supposed to be capable of using all this data and finding the best way of unscrambling the cube. A logical or mathematical agility is assumed that would lead directly to the solution.

Of course, such optimal procedures are too difficult to determine. Thus cube analysts have developed simple procedures which can be used to unscramble the cube (Heiner 1983: 564). These follow a hierarchical sequence and are largely independent of the initial scrambled position. But they are all sub-optimal in that they do not use the minimum number of moves. Instead, their advantage lies in their relative simplicity and operational utility.

In sum, just as the proponents of rationality ask that we should ignore much detail and take a simplified view of the world in adopting their model of rationality, the problem of computational limitations suggests that real-world agents in fact do the same. The unavoidable methodology of theoretical simplification and abstraction thus sits uneasily with the proposition of a global and deliberative rationality which encompasses all facts and details.

Studies of complex decision-making problems suggest that in practice, agents simplify the task by adopting sets of relatively unsophisticated and sub-optimal decision rules. As in the case of most rule systems, some of the rules have priority over others, thus creating a hierarchical algorithm for decision and choice.

EVOLUTIONARY ARGUMENTS FOR MAXIMIZING BEHAVIOUR

In 1950 Armen Alchian published his famous argument that maximizing behaviour by economic agents does not have to be justified in terms of their explicit or implicit objectives, but by the 'evolutionary' contention that maximizing and thus 'fit' firms and individuals are the ones more likely to survive and prosper. Friedman (1953) went one step further and argued that this 'evolutionary' argument constituted a justification of the maximization hypothesis, whether or not firms and individuals deliberately maximized. This seemed to sidestep neatly the problem of computational limitations.

Nevertheless, three problems are immediately apparent. First, although the 'evolutionary' conception of rationality seems to rescue the idea from its critics, it seems to abandon the idea of deliberation and choice which Robbins and others had earlier made central. This is because in orthodox biology at least, evolution is a blind and unintentional process.[1]

Second, the question is left open as to whether this 'evolutionary' argument is applicable to consumers as well as to firms. Friedrich Hayek (1982, vol. 3: 75) seems to accept both possibilities, and in general terms he argues that 'competition will make it necessary for people to act rationally to maintain themselves . . . a few relatively more rational individuals will make it necessary for the rest to emulate them in order to prevail'.

If 'evolutionary' selection hinges on the question of survival or non-survival, then it can ostensibly be applied to the firm, simply because some firms endure and others go out of existence. In contrast, it is more difficult to attach such a notion to the supposedly 'rational' consumer, as 'non-rational' consumers do not go extinct in the same way. If 'non-rationality' simply means inconsistent preferences, there is no obvious reason to assume that a 'rational' consumer will have a superior survival value in socio-economic evolution.

Third, an evolutionary process cannot be an optimizing one, at least in a strict and global sense, because for evolution to work there must always be a variety of forms from which to select. Indeed, without variety there would be no evolutionary selection. Logically, for selection to work there must be rejection, and the process must thus involve ceaseless error-making as well. Optimization implies finality and the attainment of equilibrium. In contrast, the modern biological idea of evolution involves variety, change, process and an open-ended conception of unfolding time.

Evidently, the 'evolutionary' argument for rationality has serious limitations at the outset. Nevertheless, given the durability and widespread acceptance of the idea, it is worth pursuing it in more detail.

In several respects, versions of the evolutionary analogy in the manner of Friedman and Hayek are similar to the earlier applications of evolutionary ideas to social theory by Herbert Spencer. In his hands the idea of 'survival of the fittest' became an explicit justification of *laissez-faire*.

Notably, Spencerian and other similarly apologetic abuses of the evolutionary metaphor fail to specify any plausible and detailed mechanism for the evolution of societies. Consequently, Spencer's theory has to fall back onto some quasi-religious notion of a universal and unknowable motive force to explain its operation. Thus David Wiltshire (1978: 207) sees in Spencer's theory of social evolution an 'inaccessible Ultimate Cause'.

Likewise, Friedman's and Hayek's versions of the evolutionary process fail to specify a sufficiently detailed mechanism for the evolutionary selection of rational behaviour. More specifically, as Sidney Winter (1964) has made clear in his critique of Friedman, there is no clear mechanism to show how a firm that happens to be maximizing profits will continue to do so through time, and how other firms are to acquire this behavioural characteristic. Some writers follow Alchian by suggesting that other firms will 'imitate' the profit maximizers. Not only does this contradict the Alchian–Friedman view that intentional behaviour has to be disregarded in the theoretical explanation, but also it leaves open the non-trivial question as to how other firms know what characteristics to look for and to imitate.

An explication of the evolutionary mechanism is provided by Winter himself, and in collaboration with Richard Nelson. They argue (Nelson and Winter 1982) that the habits and routines to be found in the firm have a genetic quality, in that they have the capacity to pass on their characteristics, albeit imperfectly, through time and to other organizations. This element thereby provides the basis for some Lamarckian notion of economic evolution. Thus, whilst Nelson and Winter criticize Friedman for his abuse of the evolutionary analogy, their emphasis on habit and routine provides the requisite mechanisms and units of selection for a more rigorous evolutionary theory. Nelson and Winter's formulation, however, involves satisficing rather than maximizing behaviour by agents. The nature of habits and routines is discussed later.

Having indicated a viable evolutionary mechanism, we return to the question of the Spencerian quality of the Friedman–Hayek type of argument. Another major error in Spencer's manner of thought, which Charles Darwin himself made occasional attempts to avoid, is the assumption that evolution always means increasing progress and efficiency: as if the evolutionary process means a beneficent journey from the lower to the higher form of organization or life, and from the inferior to the superior (Gould 1978: 34–8).

Like Spencer, Friedman takes it for granted that survival means efficiency. However, Edna Ullmann-Margalit (1978) shows that this is generally invalid. Strictly, in order to explain the existence of a structure it is neither necessary nor sufficient to show that it is efficient. Inefficient structures do happen to exist and survive, and many possible efficient structures will never actually be selected in the evolutionary process.

Although Darwin was persuaded to adopt Spencer's 'survival of the fittest' phrase in later editions of *The Origin of Species*, it has proved to be misleading. As Theodosius Dobzhansky *et al.* (1977: 98) point out, natural selection does not lead to the superlative fittest, only the tolerably fit. In any case, evolution is not necessarily a grand or natural road leading generally towards perfection.

'Survival of the fittest' is additionally an ill-conceived slogan. Indeed, the mechanism of natural selection in modern biology does not even necessarily lead to survival. Consider, for instance, the evolution of tendencies to either 'selfish' or 'altruistic' behaviour. Whilst universal altruism may be most beneficial for all members of the species, the possible existence of a 'prisoner's dilemma' – where individual selfishness is the best one-off individual response to prevailing cooperation – can lead to the breakdown of the arrangement of universal altruism with its advantages for all. Thus there is not necessarily any universal mechanism 'by which natural selection tends to favour the survival of the species or the population. The population, in fact, may "improve itself to extinction"' (Elster 1983: 54). Thus the mere fact of survival, even to a numerous and sustained extent, need not always imply efficiency at all.

Similar conclusions are reached by Stephen Jay Gould and Richard Lewontin (1979), undermining the idea of natural selection as a universally optimizing agent. As they point out, there are alternatives to immediate adaptation for the explanation of form, function and behaviour. For example, the phenomenon of genetic drift (Kimura 1983) involves no adaptation and no selection at all. Furthermore, selection and adaptation could be decoupled, as in the case of a mutation which doubles the fecundity of individuals. As natural selection always favours greater fecundity, a gene promoting it would sweep through a population rapidly, but it need not imply greater survival value.

Gould and Lewontin (1979) also give examples of adaptation without selection, and of adaptation and selection with 'multiple adaptive peaks'. In the latter case we often have no reason for asserting that one solution is better than another. Indeed, because of past events the population may be clustered at a local and sub-optimal peak. The solution followed is path dependent: a result of history.

It has been common in the past to bestow upon natural selection the status of a kind of driving force toward some moral or eternal absolute, whereas in fact it is an unfolding process involving regress as well as progress, and incorporating complex two-way interaction with the environment.

A number of biologists have argued convincingly that the selection process is not necessarily in accord with some absolute standard of 'fitness'. As Ernst Mayr (1963: 296) asserts, a given gene can confer high fitness in one environment and be lethal in another. What is true for a gene in biology is true for a given type of organization, relation or structure in a socio-economic system. What is 'fit' is always relative to an environmental situation. Thus in the economic case, even if the 'selected' firms were the 'fittest' then they would be so in regard to a particular economic, political and cultural environment only; they would not be the 'fittest' for all circumstances and times.

Finally, and most importantly, in biology the environment in which selection proceeds includes not simply the climate, soil, etc., but also other species and even sometimes the 'social relations' or 'culture' of the subject species itself. Consequently, as pointed out by Conrad Waddington (1975: 170), behaviour is not simply a result of environmental change but also in part its cause. Consider a favourable adaptation that may take place in relation to a given environmental situation. Further adaptations take place along similar lines. However, whilst the first few adaptations may be favourable for the units concerned, the accumulation of such adaptations may alter the environment itself, and the result may be that the same adaptation no longer yields beneficial results for any individual unit.

Take the example of a firm finding a market niche involving the manufacture of a new type or variety of product. Initially, the firm may make large profits from the venture. However, if a large number of other firms perceive and grasp the same opportunity the market may become flooded and the product may no longer be profitable. The 'environment', i.e. the state of market demand, itself may alter as other firms seek out buyers. What was profitable for one or a few alone may not be profitable for many together.

This important possibility, deriving from cybernetic or 'feedback' relationship between a unit and its environment, is significant in both economic and biological evolution. Here is another example of the 'fallacy of composition': it is wrong to presume that the selection of fitter individuals always leads to the selection of fitter populations. The repetition of this type of error in economics can likewise have damaging consequences for economic theory and policy.

HABITS, HIERARCHIES AND ECONOMIC EVOLUTION

The normal assumption of global rationality is equivalent to the adoption of a single-valued utility function. We can leave on the side the question whether such mechanical functions can truly represent consciousness, choice and intentionality.[2] The main point here is that the utility analysis takes the level of consciousness and deliberation as the same for all types of action, be they reflexes, habits or major strategic choices.

In some cases it is assumed that this level corresponds to a high degree of deliberation. For instance, Alfred Marshall (1920) and Philip Wicksteed (1910) insist that habits must directly or indirectly emanate from deliberate choice. In other words, habitual acts are regarded as being as intentional as full-flown calculations.

Some neoclassical theorists have tried to model habitual behaviour, including decision-making processes, at more than one level (Pollak 1970; Winston 1980; Thaler and Shefrin 1981). In these models habitual acts are regulated by a secondary preference function, but they are also governed by a primary preference function to which habitual preferences gradually adjust through time. Whilst such a two-level approach removes the implication that habits are activated in precisely the same manner as higher-level decisions, low-level choices over habitual acts are still made as if with a full calculation of benefits and costs. Whether or not such preference functions represent purposeful behaviour, it is clear that all actions thus determined are on the same level of intentionality. Although some notion of habitual or reflex action can be accommodated, this is deemed to result from utility maximization just like anything else.

The ability of neoclassical preference functions to encompass different levels of consciousness and deliberation is thus brought into question. Philosophically, the problem is fundamental. Frequently, in economics and elsewhere, a Cartesian and dualistic view is taken. The realm of thoughts and intentions is partitioned from the physical and natural world. Being all on one side of a single divide, consciousness is regarded as essentially undifferentiated. The mind, with its rational ideas, is seen to animate mechanically the bodily machine.[3]

Notably, the dualistic philosophy, with its unbridgeable divide between the mental and physical, cannot easily accommodate the concept of habit, in the fullest and most meaningful sense, nor recognize its full significance in a complex world. For the dualistic philosophy, action is purposeful, and without purpose there is no human action. The concept of purpose is thus given no gradations or blurred edges. Whatever action is considered it must emanate from some undifferentiated notion of purpose.

For example, when confronted with the possibility of gradations of purposeful action, the Austrian theorists – the high priests of choice and purposefulness – generally react by placing all actions in the same category, that of 'conscious, active, or creative choice' (Buchanan 1982: 15). Hence, von Mises (1949: 13) wrote:

> The vigorous man industrially striving for the improvement of his condition acts neither more nor less than the lethargic man who sluggishly takes things as they come. For to do nothing and to be idle are also action, they too determine the course of events. . . . Action is not only doing but no less omitting what possibly could be done.

Thus immersed in the mire of Cartesian dualism, von Mises implicitly re-defines action as that which 'determines the course of events', in contrast to its earlier spirited definition as 'purposeful behaviour'. In sum, for von Mises, inaction is action, and the title of his book *Human Action* becomes emptied of much of its meaning.

If the abstention from action is to be regarded as purposeful in the manner suggested, then it would imply that we continuously scrutinize not only ourselves but also our entire environment for opportunities to act: a continuous and omniscient monitoring process governing all potential deeds.

Ironically, the reason why such a monitoring process is not feasible derives from the very sort of consideration that the Austrians have quite rightly brought to the fore in a different context: the impossibility of dealing with and processing the vast quantity of information that is involved in the planning of a modern economy (Hayek 1935, 1948). But a similar point applies to the human mind as well. Both our physiology and our environment are so complex that the human mind cannot commit all the sensory data it receives to the same level of conscious deliberation.

An alternative to Cartesianism is to regard the mind as a hierarchical system (Koestler 1967; Simon 1968). Higher levels are concerned with deliberative and strategic decisions, using 'rules of thumb'. Lower down the hierarchy are habits, which do not require full deliberation, but may occasionally be moulded or altered by higher-level decisions. Accordingly, habit is defined as 'a more or less self-actuating disposition or tendency to engage in a previously adopted or acquired form of action' (Camic 1986: 1044). Lower still are relatively permanent reflexes and autonomic actions like breathing.

In such a hierarchical, systems view, as Arthur Koestler (1967: 238) argues, human consciousness 'is not an all-or-nothing affair but a matter of degrees. There is a continuous scale of gradations which extends from the unconscious . . . up to bright, wide-awake states of arousal.'

To some it may appear paradoxical, but to re-assert the importance of the notion of purposeful action it is necessary to establish habitual, unreflexive behaviour, as its real and conceptual opposition. For without such an irreducible hierarchy of levels of consciousness and intent (Koestler 1964, 1967, 1978, 1980) there is the danger that one level or type of consciousness and purposefulness will dissolve conceptually into another.[4]

The re-instatement of the concept of habit is important in a number of respects. By establishing a non-deliberative category of behaviour it is possible, first, to find the basis for some degree of stability and continuity in social life. Second, it enhances the idea of choosing or deliberative behaviour with which it contrasts. Third, as indicated above, it provides a basis for a genuinely evolutionary theory in economic and social science.

Simon's behaviouralist analysis has also emphasized the functional necessity of decision-making rules. An evolutionary approach goes further by considering both the origin of those rules, and the combined effects of individual decisions within the economic system as a whole.

Rules and conventions have to come from somewhere, and at least in a long-run analysis it is important to explain how and why they should change. The central limitation of the behavioural research programme is that it focuses almost exclusively on the decision-making of the given individual agent. Two important aspects are thus neglected.

First, insufficient attention is given to the processes through which the agent's repertoire of rules may be created or changed through time, and the social framing of individual choice through culturally acquired meanings and norms (Lloyd 1972; Douglas 1973). Second, neglected too are the unintended consequences that result from the actions of agents interacting with one another. For these reasons, despite Simon's emphasis on the problems of dealing with information overload and uncertainty, and his adoption of some aspects of systems theory, the behaviouralist approach is inadequate as a theoretical foundation.

CONCLUSION

This paper has highlighted sets of problems involved with the prevailing conception of rationality in orthodox economics. The first is the suggestion that agents are capable of global calculations on a massive scale. The work of Simon undermines this presumption.

If this assumption is dropped, and it is simply assumed that agents act as if they are so capable, some alternative rationale for the assumption of rational, maximizing behaviour must be found. Typically, it has been justified on the grounds that the rational agents will be selected in some evolutionary process through time. However, this justification raises a second and seemingly insurmountable set of alternative problems, of which economists are currently less aware.

In making this critique of the Friedman–Hayek 'evolutionary' argument for rationality, the importance of habits and routines in economic life has been established. Habit in the fullest and most meaningful sense contrasts with the Cartesian dualism involved in the orthodox notion of rationality. It is argued in this paper that a more viable notion of human action involves a bounded and multilevelled process of monitoring and deliberation, with different degrees and levels of consciousness.

By taking a fully procedural and systemic view, involving the multiple feedbacks between individuals, institutions and rules, a more rigorous evolutionary approach may eventually offer a viable alternative to models incorporating global rationality with given individuals. At the very minimum we should recognize that a more acceptable notion of rationality and human action involves tiered and selective processes of cognition, in which both habit and social conditioning are preponderant.

NOTES

1 However, Lamarckian and other types of heterodox evolutionary theory do embody a notion of intentional behaviour.
2 Loasby (1976), Hodgson (1988), Shackle (1969) and others argue that mechanical or deterministic functions cannot represent intentionality or conscious choice. However, O'Sullivan (1987) seems to take a different view.
3 For relevant discussions see Capra (1982), Koestler (1967, 1980) and Hodgson (1988).
4 An illustration of the perils herein is the story of the relegation of the concept of habit in sociology, as related by Charles Camic (1986). After occupying pride of place in the writings of Emile Durkheim and Max Weber, and in sociology generally around the beginning of the twentieth century, the concept of habit was purposefully excised from that discipline. Arguably, a similar process has occurred within economics as well (Waller 1988). In this case it has been aided both by Cartesian dualism, and the growing mathematical formalism of economic theory.

REFERENCES

Alchian, A. A. (1950) 'Uncertainty, evolution and economic theory', *Journal of Political Economy* 58: 211–22.
Buchanan, J. M. (1982) 'The domain of subjective economics: between predictive science and moral philosophy', in I. M. Kirzner (ed.) *Method, Process and Austrian Economics*, Lexington, Mass.: Heath.
Camic, C. (1986) 'The matter of habit', *American Journal of Sociology* 91: 1039–87.
Capra, F. (1982) *The Turning Point: Science, Society and the Rising Culture*, London: Wildwood House.
Dobzhansky, T. *et al.* (1977) *Evolution*, San Francisco: Freeman.
Douglas, M. (ed.) (1973) *Rules and Meanings*, Harmondsworth: Penguin.
Elster, J. (1983) *Explaining Technical Change*, Cambridge: Cambridge University Press.
Friedman, M. (1953) 'The methodology of positive economics', in M. Friedman, *Essays in Positive Economics*, Chicago: University of Chicago Press.
Gould, S. J. (1978) *Ever Since Darwin: Reflections in Natural History*, London: Burnett Books.
—— and Lewontin, R. C. (1979) 'The Spandrels of San Marco and the Panglossian paradigm: a critique of the adaptationist programme', *Proceedings of the Royal Society of London, Series B* 205: 581–98.

Hayek, F. A. (ed.) (1935) *Collective Economic Planning*, London: Routledge & Kegan Paul.
—— (1948) *Individualism and Economic Order*, Chicago: University of Chicago Press.
—— (1982) *Law, Legislation and Liberty* (3 vol. combined edn), London: Routledge & Kegan Paul.
Heiner, R. A. (1983) 'The origin of predictable behavior', *American Economic Review* 73: 560–95.
Hey, J. D. (1979) *Uncertainty in Microeconomics*, Oxford: Martin Robertson.
Hodgson, G. M. (1988) *Economics and Institutions: A Manifesto for a Modern Institutional Economics*, Cambridge: Polity Press.
Kimura, M. (1983) *The Neutral Theory of Molecular Evolution*, Cambridge: Cambridge University Press.
Koestler, A. (1964) *The Act of Creation*, London: Hutchinson.
—— (1967) *The Ghost in the Machine*, London: Hutchinson.
—— (1978) *Janus – A Summing Up*, London: Hutchinson.
—— (1980) *Bricks to Babel*, London: Hutchinson.
Lloyd, B. B. (1972) *Perception and Cognition*, Harmondsworth: Penguin.
Loasby, B. J. (1976) *Choice, Complexity and Ignorance: An Enquiry into Economic Theory and Practice of Decision Making*, Cambridge: Cambridge University Press.
Marshall, A. (1920) *The Principles of Economics* (8th edn), London: Macmillan.
Mayr, E. (1963) *Animal Species and Evolution*, Cambridge, Mass.: Harvard University Press.
Mill, J. S. (1844) *Essays on Some Unsettled Questions of Political Economy*, London: Longman, Green, Reader & Dyer.
Mises, L. von (1949) *Human Action: A Treatise on Economics*, London: William Hodge.
Nelson, R. R. and Winter, S. G. (1982) *An Evolutionary Theory of Economic Change*, Cambridge, Mass.: Harvard University Press.
O'Sullivan, P. J. (1987) *Economic Methodology and Freedom to Choose*, London: Allen & Unwin.
Pollak, R. A. (1970) 'Habit formation and dynamic demand functions', *Journal of Political Economy* 78: 745–63.
Robbins, L. (1935) *An Essay on the Nature and Significance of Economic Science* (2nd edn), London: Macmillan.
Shackle, G. L. S. (1969) *Decision, Order and Time* (2nd edn), Cambridge: Cambridge University Press.
Simon, H. A. (1955) 'A behavioral model of rational choice', *Quarterly Journal of Economics* 69: 99–118.
—— (1957) *Administrative Behaviour* (2nd edn), New York: Free Press.
—— (1959) 'Theories of decision-making in economic and behavioral sciences', *American Economic Review* 49: 253–83.
—— (1962) 'The architecture of complexity', *Proceedings of the American Philosophical Society* 106: 467–82.
—— (1968) *The Sciences of the Artificial*, Cambridge, Mass.: MIT Press.
—— (1976) 'From substantive to procedural rationality', in S. Latsis

(ed.) *Method and Appraisal in Economics*, Cambridge: Cambridge University Press.

—— (1983) *Reason in Human Affairs*, Oxford: Basil Blackwell.

Thaler, R. H. and Shefrin, H. M. (1981) 'An economic theory of self-control', *Journal of Political Economy* 89: 392–406.

Ullmann-Margalit, E. (1978) 'Invisible hand explanations', *Synthese* 39: 282–6.

Waddington, C. H. (1975) *The Evolution of an Evolutionist*, Ithaca: Cornell University Press.

Waller, Jr, W. J. (1988) 'Habit in economic analysis', *Journal of Economic Issues* 22: 113–26.

Wicksteed, P. H. (1910) *The Commonsense of Political Economy*, London: Routledge.

Wiltshire, D. (1978) *The Social and Political Thought of Herbert Spencer*, Oxford: Oxford University Press.

Winston, G. C. (1980) 'Addiction and backsliding: a theory of compulsive consumption', *Journal of Economic Behavior and Organization* 1: 295–324.

Winter, Jr, S. G. (1964) 'Economic "natural selection" and the theory of the firm', *Yale Economic Essays* 4: 225–72.

5

BEYOND THE LOGICAL THEORY OF RATIONAL CHOICE

Bill Gerrard

INTRODUCTION

The axiom of rationality is the cornerstone of modern economics. Economic behaviour is interpreted as the outcome of optimizing choices by rational economic agents. Yet despite its axiomatic status, this choice-theoretic approach remains problematic. For many the assumption of rational economic agents itself represents a methodological choice in which the demands of logical tractability have taken precedence over the needs of empirical realism. It is this fundamental methodological problem in economics to which this paper is addressed.

The main argument of this paper is that it is necessary to recognize both the power and the limitations of the purely logical approach to human behaviour. The empirical relevance of economic analysis can be extended by encompassing the logical theory of rational choice within a more general framework of analysis. In this way it is hoped to avoid the twin dangers of mere dogmatic assertion of the correctness of the logical approach and the nihilistic scepticism that is induced in reaction. Both positions are indicative of a decadent subject field, breeding an atmosphere of destructive intolerance which hinders the continuing search for practical knowledge. The aim must always be not only to deconstruct an existing approach to show its limitations but to go on to reconstruct, retaining the valid elements but encompassed within a more general approach.

THE LOGICAL THEORY OF RATIONAL CHOICE

In economic theory a choice is deemed to be rational if, given some set of alternatives, the agent chooses that alternative which is preferred to all others. This can be written formally as:

$$\text{Max } U(X_1, \ldots, X_n; I_t)$$

where the four components of the rational choice are: Max, the optimization objective; $X_1, \ldots, X_n$, the feasible choice set; $U(\ )$, the preference ordering; and I_t, the available information set.

Each of the components embodies a series of assumptions which define the domain of relevance of the logical theory of rational choice.

The optimization objective

The agent is assumed to be in a choice situation, that is, recognizing that there is a choice to be made. The behaviour of the agent is deliberate. Alternatives are considered and a choice is made of the best alternative available. This excludes non-deliberate behaviour in which no consideration is given to alternative choices. Thus habitual or conventional behaviour maintained without its appropriateness being assessed constitutes non-rational behaviour. The deliberate choice of alternatives known not to be optimal is also excluded.

The feasible choice set

The feasible choice set consists of all the alternatives that are feasible given the constraints on the agent's choice. These constraints are features of the choice situation which are beyond the control of the agent. For example, in the case of the consumer the feasible choice set is the budget set containing those bundles of goods which are affordable given the consumer's budget constraint determined by the consumer's income and the prices of the goods. The feasible choice set is a subset of the set of all possible choices, feasible and non-feasible.

The preference ordering

The preference ordering is a set of pairwise comparisons over the entire choice set. It provides an ordinal ranking with respect to the agent's preferences over the alternative choices. A pairwise comparison between any two alternative choices, x and y, must take one of the following mutually exclusive forms:

(a) xPy, x is strictly preferred to y; or
(b) yPx, y is strictly preferred to x; or
(c) xIy (or yIx), neither x nor y are strictly preferred, that is, the agent is indifferent between the two choices.

The assumed properties of the preference ordering are known as the axioms of choice. There are four axioms of choice:

Axiom 1 (Completeness): Given any two alternative choices, x and y, either xPy or yPx or xIy must hold.

The axiom of completeness ensures that there are no gaps in the agent's preference ordering. Given any two choices, the agent is always able to rank them. But the agent may find it difficult to form a preference ordering over alternatives which differ qualitatively. Alternative choices may be multidimensional in the range of attributes offered. The axiom of completeness implies that the agent can reduce these qualitative differences to a single dimension of quantitative differences over which an ordinal ranking can be made. This excludes choices situations characterized by partial (or even complete) incommensurability between alternatives.

Axiom 2 (Independence): The preference ranking between any two alternative choices is independent of any other alternative choice.

The axiom of independence means that the agent's preference ordering is based on pairwise comparisons which are invariant with respect to all other possible choices. The ranking of two choices, x and y, does not depend on the availability or otherwise of another choice, z. The pairwise comparison is not context-specific. This excludes situations such as strategic voting in which the choice between two alternatives determines the availability of other alternatives.

Axiom 3 (Reflexivity): For any choice x, it must be the case that xIx.

The axiom of reflexivity means that the agent must be indifferent between any choice and itself. This excludes the possibility of choice evaluation being context-specific.

Axiom 4 (Transitivity): If choice x is weakly preferred to choice y (xPy or xIy) and choice y is weakly preferred to choice z (yPz or yIz), then choice x must be weakly preferred to choice z (xPz or xIz).

The axiom of transitivity yields the following implications:

(a) If xPy and yPz (or yIz), then xPz.
(b) If xIy and yPz, then xPz.
(c) If xIy and yIz, then xIz.

The axiom of transitivity requires that pairwise comparisons be consistent with each other. This is a necessary condition for an optimal choice to exist. If the preference ordering is intransitive, then it is possible for the agent to get locked into a preference cycle such as xPy, yPz and zPx. In such a situation the agent always prefers the third choice to the outcome of the current pairwise comparison.

Taken together, the four axioms of choice provide the necessary conditions for a preference ordering to yield an optimal choice. The additional assumptions that preferences are monotonic and strictly convex ensure that the preference ordering is well-behaved. The assumption of monotonic preferences implies that the agent always prefers more rather than less. This rules out the possibility of satiation. Strict convexity is required to ensure the uniqueness of the optimal choice.

The available information set

The available information set contains three types of information: (a) information on the constraints facing the agent; (b) information on the membership of the feasible choice set; and (c) information on the nature of each alternative in the feasible choice set including information on the consequences associated with each choice. The logical theory of rational choice assumes that the agent has a complete information set so as to be able to identify the optimal choice. This excludes the possibility of sub-optimal choices due to the incompleteness of the available information set.

The defining characteristic of the logical theory of rational choice is its formality. It reduces choice to a problem of pure logic, a matter of deducing the best means to attain given ends. Furthermore the theory is structured so as to ensure that the rational choice is conclusive. A well-defined objective function implies the existence of a single optimal choice. The assumption of complete information implies that the optimal choice is identified by the agent. Following Latsis (1976), the logical theory of rational choice can be described as a single-exit model. Given any choice situation there is a unique optimal choice. This is in contrast to multiple-exit models of choice in which there are no a priori conclusive choices. The logical approach is very powerful theoretically because it offers analytical tractability. Choice situations can be analysed in a mathematical framework using the techniques of constrained optimization. Determinate theoretical results can be derived. The logical approach also allows predictions to be derived with respect to the behaviour of agents in any particular situation. In this way the logical theory of rational choice can be moved from the purely theoretical domain into the empirical domain.

The information assumption plays a crucial role both in the use of the logical approach as a theoretical model of choice and in its operationalization as a predictive tool. At the theoretical level it is necessary to assume that the agent has a complete information set, that is, the agent possesses sufficient information on the feasible choice set to be able to identify a single optimal choice. At this degree of generality and in situations involving only a single agent, it is not necessary to assume that the agent's information set contains only information that is true in some objective sense. It is sufficient only that the agent uses information which is believed to be true. This allows for rational mistakes, that is, choices that are optimal given the agent's information set but sub-optimal in the light of information unknown to or not believed by the agent. The rationality of the mistaken choice will depend on the rationality of the mistaken belief. Thus the rational choice is conditional on the subjective information set of the agent. The objectivity or subjectivity of the information set is treated as irrelevant at the purely theoretical level with regard to the problem of the agent identifying an optimal choice. The logical approach assumes only that the agent chooses that alternative which is optimal given the agent's objective function and information set.

The objectivity or subjectivity of the agent's information set is an important issue in respect of the operationalization of the logical theory of rational choice in the empirical domain. If the logical theory of rational choice is interpreted in a subjective manner then the predictions concerning the behaviour of agents in any choice situation are conditional on the precise nature of the information set of each agent. This moves the problem into the realm of multiple-exit models. Changes in the agent's information set will imply changes in the predicted behaviour. Given the practical difficulties in ascertaining the nature of the information set of an individual agent, the subjective approach is clearly at odds with the demand for empirical tractability. It is, therefore, usually assumed that the agent has perfect information, that is, complete and objectively true information on the choice situation. The perfect information assumption provides tractability to the empirical problem of predicting agent behaviour. Predicted behaviour is no longer conditional on the agent's information set. In its strongest form the objective approach has a correspondence notion of knowledge in the sense that the agent is assumed to know the true nature of the world. A weaker form of correspondence is also used in which the agent is assumed to possess information on the model considered to best correspond with the true nature of the world. Whether the correspondence is final or provisional the analytical implication is the same. Predicted behaviour depends only on the 'objective' properties of the choice situation. The necessity of the perfect information assumption in empirical applications of the logical theory of rational choice has led to its almost universal use in theoretical models of choice.

The perfect information assumption can take several forms depending on the nature of the choice situation. The choice situation may be non-stochastic or stochastic. In the case of non-stochastic choice a situation of certainty is assumed. Perfect information represents certain knowledge of the true nature of the world. In the case of stochastic choice a situation of risk is assumed. Perfect information represents complete information on the probability distribution of the possible states of the world. The probability distribution is assumed to be either final or provisional. The 'final' probability distribution constitutes the objectively true probability distribution whereas the provisional probability distribution is based on observed frequencies. In the latter case the underlying stochastic process is assumed to be ergodic (Davidson 1982). An ergodic stochastic process is one in which phase (time-series) and space (cross-sectional) averages converge in the limit as the number of realizations becomes infinite. In other words an ergodic stochastic process is one in which the provisional probability distribution tends towards the final probability distribution. These two ideal types of choice situation, certainty and risk, are often combined to give a mixed risk-certainty case in which agents are assumed to know with certainty the non-stochastic component of a stochastic choice situation. This mixed case is particularly prominent in the rational expectations literature.

The logical theory of rational choice is formulated to yield tractability both theoretically in the form of deterministic models and empirically in the form of testable predictions. This tractability is based on the twin assumptions of a well-defined objective function and perfect information which together ensure that there is a single optimal choice in any choice situation. However, despite its theoretical and empirical tractability the logical theory of rational choice has been the subject of continual criticism throughout the development of economics. The principal criticism levelled at the logical approach is its perceived lack of explanatory power. The patent non-realistic nature of its assumptions, it is argued, means that the logical approach is unable to explain how choices are actually made and without such explanatory power the logical theory of rational choice is inadequate. There are a number of arguments that can be made as a rebuttal of this criticism. Several of these arguments are used by Friedman (1953) in his classical defence of the logical approach. Broadly speaking, defenders of the logical approach invoke a two-stage argument. First, it is denied that there is any need to provide a realistic account of how choices are made. A model is viewed as an 'as if' construct which can be used to predict choice. It is not the function of such a model to describe the actual process of choice. Indeed, such descriptions are deemed to be of little relevance for analytical purposes. From this instrumentalist stance the logical theory of rational choice is a good model if it has predictive power. This instrumentalist defence is usually supplemented with arguments to justify the predictive power of a model based on non-realistic assumptions. Some form of validation process is postulated. The agent is assumed to be operating in an environment which induces convergence towards the optimal choice. For example Friedman argues that profit-maximizing behaviour by firms is validated by competitive market conditions which act as a Darwinian selection process ensuring that only profit-maximizing firms survive. If a validation process exists and is sufficiently strong then the logical theory of rational choice could be said to possess explanatory power despite its non-realistic assumptions.

GENERALIZING THE THEORY OF CHOICE

The logical theory of rational choice is predominant in modern economics. This is hardly surprising given the theoretical and empirical tractability it provides for analyses of economic behaviour. In this respect it will never be surpassed. It will continue to be the starting point for economic theory. But it has its limitations, highlighted by the periodic bouts of criticism over its lack of realistic assumptions as witnessed in the marginalist controversy and the continuing discussions over Friedman's methodological views. The debates over the logical theory of rational choice have tended to produce two entrenched oppositional views. In essence it is a conflict over whether tractability or realism should be the ultimate criterion for determining the usefulness of an economic theory. The conflict is wrong-headed. There is surely room for both views within a more general framework which acknowledges the need for different types of theories in different situations. There is a need to define the domain of relevance for a particular theory, to recognize both its uses and its limitations. By encompassing the logical theory of rational choice within a more general theory of economic behaviour it is possible to transcend the tractability–realism oppositional duality. This encompassing approach offers an alternative both to the belief that the logical theory of rational choice is unlimited in its potential for application within economics as well as to the almost nihilistic line of criticism which argues for the complete abandonment of the logical approach. Neither stance is conducive to progress in economics.

In trying to generalize beyond the logical theory of rational choice the first step is to attempt to define its domain of relevance, particularly its limitations. The logical approach offers theoretical and empirical tractability. However, it is only descriptive of in very simple choice situations. In more complex ations it is clearly unrealistic to assume that the agent a well-defined objective function or perfect information. ued above, the logical approach can retain explanatory power in such situations if there is a sufficiently strong validation process ensuring that the agent is motivated by optimization and converges towards its actualization. It is the existence and strength of this validation process that is the key element in determining the degree of usefulness of the logical theory of rational choice in any specific situation. The crucial questions concern the nature of the agent's learning process and the competitiveness (in a Darwinian sense) of market conditions. It is not enough merely to assert the existence of a strong validation process. The actual paths of dynamic adjustment need to be studied. If the choice situation is complex and there is no strong validation process at work, then the logical theory of rational choice is unlikely to be useful in any profound way. Indeed it may be very misleading in such situations. The tractability of the logical approach and its potential for mathematical sophistication may disguise its lack of relevance. The concern for tractability may blind the researcher to those aspects of the situation which are not amenable to a formal logical approach. This is the target at which the critics should aim. It is not the non-realistic nature of the logical theory of rational choice which is the problem *per se* but rather the failure to give sufficient attention to the conditions required for its validation.

The problem of analysing the behaviour of agents in complex situations devoid of a strong validation process has received little attention in economics. The main contribution to such an analysis is to be found in the work of Herbert Simon on bounded rationality. Simon focuses on one particular aspect of complexity, namely, the limited ability of individuals and organizations to gather and process information. Simon (1976) describes the logical approach as adopting a notion of substantive rationality which he believes is only appropriate in very simple choice situations. Once the choice situations become complex Simon argues that the appropriate notion of rationality is one of procedural rationality. Agents follow rules and standard operating procedures which are used to search out an alternative that satisfies some aspiration level. Agents are satisficers rather than optimizers. The search process comes to an end when a satisfactory alternative is identified. Agents do not continue to seek indefinitely for the best alternative. The complexity of the choice situation renders this a hopeless task as in the case of finding the best chess move, a choice problem which Simon has studied closely.

Simon's analysis of procedural rationality provides one important route for generalizing the theory of economic behaviour. It is also instructive with respect to the methodological implications of moving beyond the logical theory of rational choice. The analysis of complex, non-validating choice situations takes the researcher into the realm of multiple-exit models. In any situation there may be a range of possible decision rules. The actual decision rules used by the agent will be context-specific, the result of the social and historical experience of the agent. History matters. Thus, in trying to construct choice models it is important to use assumptions that are realistic in the context of the situations under analysis. The usefulness of any particular set of assumptions cannot be determined a priori.

Simon's work provides a framework for analysis, a starting point which has been widely quoted but little used. However, it is by no means the definitive point of departure for generalizing the theory of economic behaviour. Simon is concerned with the use of rules in the search process. This is only one particular aspect of complexity, albeit an important one. There are other aspects. In particular there is the question of the presuppositions which agents have about the nature of their information. Simon's repeated reference to the problem of playing chess is indicative of his concern with 'objective' choice situations. In this respect Simon shares common ground with the logical theory of rational choice. Complexity is largely treated by Simon in terms of the quantity of information. For Simon, complexity equals incompleteness of the information set. The status of the agent's information is not seen as problematic. Consideration of the effects of the fallibility of knowledge provides another route for moving beyond the logical theory of rational choice.

Complexity does not only result in the incompleteness of the agent's information set. If agents do not possess perfect information about the choice situation, then an interpretive problem arises. Agents must interpret the available information in the context of some set of presuppositions about the choice situation. Different interpretations are possible. Thus agents face a situation of uncertainty. This is another aspect of complexity. The information set can no longer be treated as certain knowledge in the sense of correspondence with the true nature of the world. Rather an agent's information set contains knowledge in the form of a set of justified partial beliefs about the possible nature of the world. This knowledge is not objective but a matter of interpretation. As such it is fallible. The partial and fallible nature of knowledge is the defining characteristic of a situation of uncertainty.

Uncertainty is a third type of choice situation in addition to those of certainty and risk. The fallibility of an agent's knowledge differentiates uncertainty from certainty. The partial nature of the agent's knowledge in the sense of the agent being unable to construct a complete probability distribution covering all possible outcomes differentiates a situation of uncertainty from that of risk. This distinction is originally due to Knight (1921). This particular feature of the partiality of knowledge was also highlighted by Keynes in *A Treatise on Probability* (1921). Keynes argued that numerical probabilities form only a small subset of all probabilities. For the most part probabilities are non-numerical and often non-comparable.

The economics literature abounds with references to behaviour under uncertainty. However, there is virtually no work on behaviour under uncertainty where uncertainty is defined as the absence of a complete probability distribution. In almost all cases the analysis of behaviour under uncertainty is, in effect, the analysis of behaviour under risk. Situations of risk are tractable. Agents can be assumed to optimize the expected value of their objective function. The notion of rational choice as optimization remains intact under situations of risk. Not so once one moves into situations of uncertainty. There is an assumption that agents act under uncertainty as if they are facing a situation of risk. But this seems to imply myopia on the part of the agents who are assumed to ignore the effects of uncertainty. This is an heroic assumption and one which sits ill with the notion of rationality. Agents who are aware of the fallibility and partiality of their knowledge may adjust their behaviour to cope with this. To treat uncertainty as risk is to ignore a whole range of problems which could constitute a fertile research programme.

It is an urgent task in economics to begin to construct a framework of analysis for behaviour under uncertainty. One possible starting point is Keynes's discussion of economic behaviour under uncertainty in the *General Theory* (1936). The *General Theory* represented in one respect the culmination of Keynes's concern over thirty years or so with the problems of probability and uncertainty. Keynes's early attempts to deal with these issues resulted in *A Treatise on Probability*. In this work Keynes adopted a formal logic approach to the theory of probability. Keynes conceived of probability as the degree of belief it is rational to hold in a non-conclusive argument given the available evidence. Keynes's approach in *A Treatise on Probability* has much in common with the logical theory of rational choice in style and atmosphere. After *A Treatise on Probability* Keynes became more concerned with the other non-logical aspects of behaviour under uncertainty. Using terminology which Keynes himself took from the mathematician Frank Ramsey (1931), it could be said that Keynes moved from the realm of formal logic to that of human logic. The latter is concerned with the 'useful mental habits' which people actually employ. Keynes's discussion in the *General Theory* of the investment decision is an analysis of the application of human logic in the face of an unknowable future.

From Keynes's discussion of the investment decision it is possible to derive some general propositions about behaviour under uncertainty. First, when confronting new unknown situations, agents tend to assume a similarity with other previously experienced situations unless they have specific reasons to believe otherwise. In the absence of knowledge agents tend to fall back on the conventional assumption of the uniformity of nature. Thus, in the case of the investment decision Keynes argued that entrepreneurs will usually assume that the future will be the same as the present unless there is any specific news indicating the contrary. This implies that the past experience of the agent is crucial in determining current behaviour. History matters. Second, under conditions of uncertainty agents are concerned not only with the predicted outcomes of alternative choices but also with the confidence with which these predictions are made. In his discussion of the investment decision Keynes argued that the behaviour of entrepreneurs depends on the state of long-term expectations. The state of long-term expectations is made up of two components: the predicted rate of return of the investment project under consideration (i.e. the marginal efficiency of capital) and the level of business confidence. This reflects the distinction in *A Treatise on Probability* between probability and weight. The probability of an argument is the rational degree of belief given the available evidence. The weight of an argument is an assessment of the amount of relevant evidence on which the probability judgment is based. Increasing the amount of relevant evidence will increase the weight of an argument but the associated probability may increase, decrease or remain constant depending on the nature of the additional evidence. Thus probability and weight are different dimensions in the assessment of a non-conclusive argument. In situations of uncertainty agents may attempt to assess their degree of uncertainty in terms of the confidence of their predictions. Their behaviour may change not only because their predictions change but also if their level of confidence changes.

The distinction between an expectation and the confidence with which it is held leads to a third general proposition about behaviour under uncertainty. As the level of confidence in an expectation falls, agents are likely to become more cautious. This will lead them to try to reduce the degree of irreversible commitment in any decision. This may even result in the decision being postponed. The importance of this precautionary motive is stressed by Keynes throughout the *General Theory*. In economic behaviour the precautionary motive expresses itself as the demand for liquidity. In the investment decision, a fall in business confidence leads to the postponement of investment plans. Entrepreneurs prefer to keep their options open by holding money (or other liquid assets) rather than real assets. Investment in real assets involves a degree of irreversibility. It is costly to change investment decisions at some future date. Money, on the other hand, provides a safe haven. It is perfectly liquid in the sense of allowing agents to alter their behaviour in the future without cost. It is this precautionary reaction to uncertainty which ultimately underlies Keynes's theory of involuntary unemployment.

The conventional assumption of uniformity, the role of confidence and the precautionary motive constitute three possible elements in a framework of analysis for behaviour under uncertainty. A whole range of testable hypotheses can be derived. For example, betting experiments can be used to test whether or not the degree of information which agents have about the choice situation affects their staking behaviour. The precautionary motive implies that the size of the stake proportional to available resources would tend to fall as agents become less confident about the outcome, *ceteris paribus*.

The contributions of Simon and Keynes are, therefore, suggestive of how the logical theory of rational choice could be encompassed within a more general framework able to deal more adequately with behaviour in complex, non-validated choice situations. In such situations it is unlikely that agent behaviour will tend to converge towards some optimum. The dynamic adjustment path is more likely to be one of punctuated equilibrium. The behaviour of agents is likely to be characterized by relatively long periods of stability interspersed by short periods of radical change. Agents will maintain current rules of search until it becomes clear that these rules are outmoded, no longer able to achieve satisfactory outcomes. Likewise agents will maintain their current interpretive frameworks until a sufficient weight of anomalous evidence accumulates to instigate moves towards the adoption of a new framework. This is the sort of process which Kuhn (1962) has described in the context of the behaviour of scientific communities in terms of paradigms and scientific revolutions. It is a general characteristic of behaviour under uncertainty. Agents maintain their established perceptions and behaviour patterns until there is sufficient reason to change.

The process of adjusting behaviour in situations of uncertainty is plagued with difficulties. Agents can always find reasons to maintain established perceptions and behaviour patterns, even in the face of evidence to the contrary. Anomalies can be dismissed through various immunizing stratagems. Under conditions of uncertainty, agents can never know whether change or stability is the best solution. This dilemma is unavoidable. However, the possibility of unsatisfactory solutions may be heightened if agents have excessive confidence in their current modes of behaviour. This can create a problem of bounded vision, a failure to acknowledge sufficiently the fallibility of any particular interpretation of available evidence. It is well-documented that many cases of strategic failure are due to bounded vision (Huxham and Dando 1981). It could be argued that the preoccupation of economists with the logical theory of rational choice is an instance of bounded vision.

SUMMARY AND CONCLUSIONS

This paper has considered the nature and limitations of the standard method for the analysis of economic behaviour. This standard method has been termed the logical theory of rational choice. Economic behaviour is conceptualized in a purely logical manner as the outcome of a process of constrained optimization. The assumptions of the logical theory of rational choice have been outlined. The logical approach provides theoretical and empirical tractability to the study of economic behaviour and hence it has been, and will continue to be the starting point for economic research. However, it has its limitations. It is only likely to be a realistic explanation of behaviour in very simple choice situations. It can only retain explanatory power in more complex situations if there is a strong validation process at work, that is, a dynamic adjustment path converging towards optimizing outcomes. Competition in the form of a Darwinian struggle of the survival of the fittest may act as just such a validation process.

Once the analyst turns to consider the domain of complex, non-validated choice situations, the logical theory of rational choice is of limited use. There is a need to develop a more general theory of economic behaviour which encompasses the theory of rational choice. The contributions of Simon and Keynes can provide useful starting points in this respect. Simon's notion of procedural rationality stresses the role of rules and standard operating procedures in determining agent behaviour. Keynes's analysis of the investment decision in the *General Theory* is suggestive of how agents behave under uncertainty. In particular Keynes's analysis emphasizes the conventional assumption of uniformity, confidence and the precautionary motive. These two contributions could form the basis for a research programme on behaviour under non-validated complexity.

It is important not to underestimate the power of the logical theory of rational choice. But likewise it should not be overestimated. Tractability should blind the researcher to the question of relevance. This is particularly important in considering behaviour under uncertainty. Uncertainty by its very nature is an intractable problem. The methods of analysis must be appropriate to dealing with the essential vagueness of the object of study. In particular, the realism of the assumptions of a model of behaviour under uncertainty becomes a crucial determinant of the usefulness of a model in any specific situation. Professor Wildon Carr's remark (quoted by Rothschild 1947: 328) is very apt in this context: 'It is better to be vaguely right than precisely wrong.'

REFERENCES

Davidson, P. (1982) 'Rational expectations: a fallacious foundation for studying crucial decision making processes', *Journal of Post Keynesian Economics* 5: 182–98.

Friedman, M. (1953) 'The methodology of positive economies', in M. Friedman, *Essays in Positive Economics*, Chicago: University of Chicago Press.

Huxham, C. S. and Dando, M. R. (1981). 'Is bounded vision an adequate explanation of strategic decision-making failures?', *Omega* 9: 371–9.

Keynes, J. M. (1921) *A Treatise on Probability*, London: Macmillan.

—— (1936) *The General Theory of Employment, Interest and Money*, London: Macmillan.

Knight, F. H. (1921) *Risk, Uncertainty and Profit*, Boston: Houghton Mifflin.

Kuhn, T. S. (1962) *The Structure of Scientific Revolutions*, Chicago: University of Chicago Press.

Latsis, S. J. (1976) 'A research programme in economics', in S. J. Latsis (ed.) *Method and Appraisal in Economics*, Cambridge: Cambridge University Press.

Ramsey, F. P. (1931) *The Foundations of Mathematics and Other Logical Essays*, London: Routledge & Kegan Paul.

Rothschild, K. W. (1947) 'Price theory and oligopoly', *Economic Journal* 57: 299–320.

Simon, H. A. (1976) 'From substantive to procedural rationality', in S. J. Latsis (ed.) *Method and Appraisal in Economics*, Cambridge: Cambridge University Press.

6

POST-MODERNITY AND NEW CONCEPTIONS OF RATIONALITY IN ECONOMICS[1]

Shaun Hargreaves Heap

INTRODUCTION

Somewhat surprisingly, the spirit of post-modernity seems to have found its way into economics. I say somewhat surprisingly only because economics is usually regarded as the hard-nosed, nay 'serious' (dismal?) social science, and post-modernity has something of a reputation for the frivolous and faddish. Less surprising is the characteristic irony that has accompanied its arrival in economics. In particular, where I find post-modern ideas most obviously at play is in the growing realization that the dominant, instrumental conception of rationality used in economics is inadequate. And it must surely be one of the supreme ironies that at precisely the time when economists have exported this conception of rationality to the other social sciences with such success, indeed to the point where there are now things like 'rational choice Marxism', economists are actually beginning to have doubts about the adequacy of that instrumental view for their own discipline.

In this chapter, I shall sketch the connections between post-modernity and the developing disquiet over instrumental rationality. I begin in the next section with a brief, scene-setting discussion of post-modern ideas. In particular, I focus on the way that post-modernity treats 'doubt' and 'uncertainty' as something more than the absence of information or an inability to process information. In the following three sections, I suggest that a similar conclusion is increasingly drawn in the rational expectations, game theory and choice under uncertainty literatures in economics. In economics, the 'something more' is felt as a need to expand the notion of human agency to cope with the uncertainty (or underdetermination) of action with respect to the canons of instrumental rationality. The suggested expansions here have only a rough outline (and they are discussed more fully in Hargreaves Heap 1989). However, it is plain from the brief discussion of post-modern ideas on the individual in the next section that they share much in common with them. In a nutshell, they point to an individual who is more clearly socially located and whose actions are more open-ended and creative than the one found in the instrumental model.

SOME BEARINGS

Let me begin with some scene-setting definitions, and then I'll try and make good the claim that economics has been bitten by the post-modernity bug.

First, I should make clear what I mean by instrumental rationality. This is the sort of rationality which associates rational action with the choice of the action which is likely to satisfy best the agent's preferences/objectives. It is rationality set in the means/end framework, whereby we accept the ends and rationality is judged through the choice of the most efficient means towards those ends. I say we accept the ends, that is not strictly true since we require that our ends should be coherent, so that it makes sense to talk of different actions satisfying in different degrees those ends, thereby giving purchase to the notion of efficiency. Accordingly, we require the standard conditions to hold for our preferences so that it is 'as if' we were busily maximizing a well-behaved utility function.

So, instrumental rationality is the assumption we work with when, almost without thinking, we turn every problem into one where agents have objective functions which they attempt to maximize. It's a knee-jerk reaction, it's ubiquitous, it's the dominant rationality assumption, it's the one we have exported to politics in the economics of democracy literature, starting with Downs and running through Buchanan and Tullock and it's the one Becker has applied with such gusto to almost every aspect of social life: marriage, divorce, suicide, crime, punishment, you name it he's done it. Enough said.

Second, I ought to say something about post-modernity. Now, this is a bit trickier and I am liable to get into trouble.

Post-modernity is uncontroversially associated with a variety of ideas. For instance, there is the thought that the individual has become 'de-centred'. There is no essential core which defines an individual because one's sense of self depends in part on what one is not: the self is constituted by the relationship which it has to significant 'others'. However, this need not preclude a sense of individuality. It is just that individuality cannot come through reference to some unchanging essence that one carries through life. Instead, the sense of individuality that post-modernity suggests to us comes from constructing narratives about the self. We should think of weaving fictions through the changing patterns of our life. These fictions give us our identity, but like all fictions they can be re-written tomorrow.

Likewise, there is the activity of 'deconstruction'. This is the practice in literature which denies that any text has an authoritative meaning. To suggest 'the' meaning of a text is to smuggle in, in that immortal phrase, a 'transcendental signifier'. There are no 'metanarratives', that is to say objective foundations for one reading over another, and the activity of deconstruction releases the other meanings which have been suppressed by 'the' dominant interpretation of the text. Since the suggestion that there is such a thing as 'the' meaning excludes other possibilities, it is often regarded as the exercise of power by some group over another and consequently the rediscovery of other meanings is often tinged with a certain democratic popularism. This inversion of traditional hierarchies is found, for instance, in the celebration of popular culture over high culture.

Similarly, there is the celebration of 'play' which comes from combining both these thoughts. For instance, in architecture, we find the playful combination of historical architectural styles. Likewise we have the playful mixing of musical styles, cross-over dressing and the like.

This much on post-modernity will probably pass without comment and I shall pick out some traces of these ideas in economics later. However, there is a more general, controversial question about the epistemological location of post-modernity, which I want to answer in a particular way so as to provide a clear connection with recent developments in economics. I want to argue that post-modernity is an attempt to transcend the traditional opposition between objectivity and relativism.

This is liable to prove controversial because many people find that the only line which connects the hotch-potch of 'play', 'de-centring', 'intertextuality', 'deconstruction', the inversion of cultural hierarchies, etc. is a retreat into relativism. Indeed, this seems a fair assessment, say when you read Baudrillard who seems positively to ooze nihilism. But equally, if you take the protestations of other high-priests like Rorty, Lyotard and Derrida seriously, then there is something funny about this label because they want to deny that they are simply dishing up relativism in some more fashionable form for the late twentieth century. Of course, we could treat these protestations as no more than bad faith, or grant them a bit of post-modernity on their own account and treat the denials as just another rhetorical jest. However, I am inclined to do otherwise and I think there is enough in what they and other critics of modernity have written to warrant a closer look.

So, what do I get from a closer look? Well, first it does seem difficult to slot them into either end of the opposition between objectivity and relativism. There is little doubt that they have rejected the sense of objectivity which goes with the mainstream Enlightenment project, the sense that there are potentially objective foundations for beliefs about ourselves and the world which in principle are accessible to all rational people, across all times and space. They do not subscribe to the view which makes knowledge gradually dissolve the gap between the subjective beliefs which we entertain on these matters and their objective counterparts. Equally, there is no doubt that they are extremely taken by arguments which draw attention to our inability to stand outside time and place, that the criteria of truth or the criteria for accepting belief belong to the language we use to describe the world and not the world itself. So much puts them firmly on the road to relativism. However, it is also clear that they recognize that there is a world which exists independently of our beliefs about it, they are realists in that sense. Furthermore, they plainly place great store on diversity, on pluralism. And it is not obvious, if they have bought the full relativist package, why they should regard either observation worth making. Why should it matter if beliefs owe everything to time and place that there is something which exists independently of those beliefs and why should it matter whether there was a diversity of belief or not, at a moment in time and in a particular piece of space?

Second, it is possible to construe a position which is in

neither camp as something more than a middle position or a muddle. There are several ways in which this argument might be developed. I shall do it by arguing that 'posties' make 'doubt' and 'uncertainty' count for something more substantial than either objectivity or relativism allows.

The point here is really that neither side of the opposition takes doubt very seriously. With relativists it has no special status, it would be no more than an optional extra, something you can build into your beliefs, on a par, say, with whether your language distinguished between a river and stream. And with Enlightenment objectivity, doubt is something to be dispelled, it's like a piece of grit in the system, it forces a wedge between subjective and objective beliefs, and fortunately as knowledge increases so doubt and uncertainty recede: doubt and uncertainty are no more than an absence of knowledge.

Yet, there is, of course, another way of understanding doubt and it seems to capture what the posties are after. Anthony Blunt expresses it well in a play by Alan Bennett when he explains to the Queen, with marvellous resonance for his own life, 'ma'am just because something is not what it is said to be, it does not mean it's a fake . . . it's an enigma'. Likewise, John Berger reminds us that it is the source of our fascination with photographs. Photographs appear to tell us more about the subject at the same time as we seem to know even less about them. At first glance, photographs appear as quintessential instruments of the Enlightenment project, faithfully reporting on the subject by giving us more detail, more information about the physical appearance of the individual, or whatever, than we had before. Yet we all know what this knowledge does to us: it tantalizes. It raises new questions about the subject. Photographs fascinate in this way precisely because they are enigmatic. In short, they suggest a different relationship between knowledge and uncertainty than the one envisaged in the Enlightenment project. In some instances, competition gives way to synergy because the more you know, the more you realize how complicated things are, how much more there is to know; in other words, how little it is that you know.

One reason for making this treatment of doubt the distinguishing feature of post-modernity is that it helps to fix post-modernity in our own times. This happens in two ways. First, the theme of taking 'doubt' and 'uncertainty' somehow more seriously is shared by a number of contemporary authors who do not otherwise self-consciously proclaim post-modernity (for example, the recent books by Macintyre and Hampshire[2]). And this is useful because post-modernity then plausibly begins to look like a genuine *Zeitgeist* rather than some clever sales technique employed by some authors. Second, it clarifies the sense in which 'post-modernity' is separate from 'modernity'. The point here is that it is often complained that many of the so-called ideas of post-modernity have already been set out by writers who clearly belonged to the project of modernity (witness, for instance, the contribution of Nietzsche). So, in what sense is it correct to talk about them as post-modern? The point is well made and it would perhaps be better to talk of post-modernity as a way of describing the recent rise of a tradition which had always been present within modernity but which had hitherto occupied a subordinate position in relation to mainstream Enlightenment thinking. However, it is also possible to argue that one of the distinctive features of contemporary writing in this tradition is that it has made 'doubt' and 'uncertainty' enter into the domain of the individual in a much more penetrating and decisive manner than the earlier writing in this tradition by making it apply to the very concept of an individual. So, again, 'doubt' becomes a useful hallmark because it offers a dimension along which contemporary writers in this tradition can be distinguished.

The second reason for distinguishing post-modernity in this way is that it facilitates the connections between post-modernity and recent developments in economics. In particular, I shall argue that there is a growing recognition in economics as well that 'doubt' and 'uncertainty' are something more than grit in the system (or an optional feature of a set of beliefs on par with whether we distinguish between a river and stream in our vocabulary); and that this appreciation has led to the exploration of new ideas with respect to rationality which incorporate many of the specific post-modern ideas about the individual.

This proposed passage to the economics literature might look suspiciously easy. So, to head-off the suspicion that my identification of post-modernity with an expanded sense of doubt is contrived for the purpose of making that connection, I will conclude this section with a quote from a discussion by W. Januzsczack, art critic of the *Guardian*, of what Art is about in the post-modern world: 'Art today is largely in the business of supplying frisson, little niblets of existential uncertainty, ways of not knowing, mysteries, small after hours pleasures for over-worked urban minds.' Well, I don't know about the urban minds bit, but plainly making doubt and uncertainty central cannot be completely off-the-wall if Januzsczack has scented some of what is going on with post-modernity!

ECONOMIC RESONANCES I: RATIONAL EXPECTATIONS

My first illustration in economics of where 'doubt' and 'uncertainty' are being taken more seriously, where they have become more substantial in a symptomatic post-modern way, is taken from the rational expectations literature.

It will be recalled that the dawning of the rational expectations revolution was bound up with a concern over the arbitrary nature of expectations assumptions, like adaptive expectations. The famous formulation by Muth (1961) was in terms of closing the gap between subjective and objective probability distributions. And the language of the criticism levelled at non-rational expectations schemes was precisely of the same order as an objectivist might make of any relativist position, any position which allowed *ad hoc* subjective expectations schemes to rule the roost when there were objective expectations which could be entertained. Indeed, in those early days of the rational expectations revolution, the sense of doubt and uncertainty which was entertained was precisely the pieces of grit in the system sort I have associated with mainstream Enlightenment thinking. On average you get things right, you do not make any systematic errors, so that abstracting from any complication which might arise from risk aversion, you behave exactly as you would if you were perfectly informed but for random white noise errors.

Furthermore, it will also be recalled that the rational expectations argument was interestingly tied in with instrumental rationality. Again putting the argument loosely, if your expectations-generating procedure yielded systematic errors, then you ought to be able to learn about the causes of the systematic component and thereby remove them. And – and this is the important point as far as the connection with instrumental rationality is concerned – the instrumentally rational agent has every incentive to do so because he or she will profit from the removal of the systematic source of error. It is the old maximizer's eye for the main chance which, together with thought that there is the opportunity for it to go to work when there are systematic errors, yields the rational expectations conclusion.

Put in this way, we have a relatively uncomplicated view which linked instrumental rationality to a kind of objectivist argument against arbitrary expectations schemes. In short, the long march of Enlightenment thinking seemed able to claim another victory in economics with the rational expectations revolution!

However, we now realize that matters are rather more complicated than this objectivist reading allows. There are a variety of complications, but the principal one has arisen because there seem to be rather a lot of settings where there are multiple rational expectations equilibria. For instance, overlapping generations models have been a rich source of multiplicity (see Azoariadis 1981, for path-breaking work and Hargreaves Heap 1991, for a survey). They arise here because of the recursive structure of these models. What you can rationally expect today depends on what will happen tomorrow, and what happens tomorrow will depend on what the next generation thinks will happen the day after, and so on. There is nothing in this chain to fix expectations: today's expectation is supported by tomorrow's and so on; and there are typically any number of sets of expectations which can be linked in this way. For similar reasons we have models of speculative bubbles for asset prices which yield multiple rational expectations equilibria (see Blanchard and Watson 1982). And then there are models with multiple equilibria which do not rely on this recursive structure – see, for instance, Diamond's (1982) trading game where how much you decide to produce depends on what you expect others will produce because this affects the opportunities you have to trade.

The difficulty with multiple rational expectations equilibria is simply not knowing which to choose to entertain when considerations of instrumental rationality are all that you have to go on. All of the rational expectations equilibria are consistent with instrumentally rational behaviour on the part of all individuals, with the result that the instrumentally rational agent appears to suffer from a sort of ineliminable uncertainty. No amount of knowledge about the preferences of other agents and no amount of additional computing power will enable the selection of one expectation to entertain. The problem of expectation formation here has nothing to do with there being grit in the system. Indeed, a little bit of grit might be more of a help than a hindrance here because it might give a reason for fixing on one expectation rather than another. Hence the echo of the enigmatic quality of doubt which is associated with the post-modern recognition that uncertainty arises from something more substantial than grit in the system.

Formally, the problem of selecting a rational expectation is akin to the solution of a co-ordination game because any of the potential rational expectations will become 'the' rational expectation to entertain, so long as it is the one which is chosen by other agents in the economy. Before I explore what might be at stake in the solution to such co-ordination games, I will turn explicitly to game theory to note that similar problems have been surfacing there.

ECONOMIC RESONANCES II: GAME THEORY

Game theory is concerned, of course, with rational action in cases of interdependent decision-making. Since rational action for one player in an interdependent setting will depend on what he or she expects the other player(s) to undertake, this theory promises at one and the same time to provide a theory of rational action and rational belief to entertain with respect to the actions of the other player(s). It is now well-known that game theorists have proposed, by assuming that agents are instrumentally rational and that they have common knowledge of the game and each other's rationality, the Nash equilibrium concept (or the related perfect equilibrium concept for games with a dynamic structure) as the solution to the question of rational action/belief. The Nash equilibrium strategies recommend themselves to players because they are the best action available to the player which is consistent with his or her knowledge that the other players are acting instrumentally rational in the same knowledge that other players are instrumentally rational. In effect, it embodies the condition of rational expectations as no agent is allowed to entertain an expectation which he or she knows will be falsified by the instrumentally rational actions of the other player(s).

This looks extremely promising as a theory of action and belief formation in these settings, but it has run into several serious difficulties recently. First, there is an unresolved problem of equilibrium selection when there are multiple Nash or perfect equilibria. The problem is exactly the same as the one which has surfaced with respect to multiple rational expectations equilibria and it raises the same issue of how co-ordination games are solved. An individual's choice is underdetermined when there are several Nash or perfect equilibria because any of the Nash/perfect equilibria will satisfy the conditions of instrumental rationality and knowledge provided it is selected by others.

This problem has assumed large proportions recently with the proof of several Folk theorems for repeated games. These theorems demonstrate that there are an infinite number of perfect equilibria in these 'super games'. The theorems were first proved for infinitely repeated games and it is not hard to understand how they arise because one can imagine ever more complicated conditional/punishment strategies being developed when there is an infinite horizon. The same intuition holds when the game always has some chance of being repeated again, but one might suppose that it would not be consistent with finitely repeated games. After all, a punishment strategy must be consistent with rational end-play and punishments which are costly will not be undertaken in the last play of the game when there is no future which they can affect. And if punishments will not be played at the end, then backward induction seems likely to rule them out in earlier plays. However, and notwithstanding these thoughts, there is also a Folk Theorem for finitely repeated games, albeit one with controversial features (see Fudenberg and Maskin 1986).

So again, we have been drawn in the recent literature to the problem of solving co-ordination games. Instrumental rationality seems to need a general solution to co-ordination games if it is to escape from both the indeterminacy of multiple rational expectations equilibria and multiple Nash/perfect equilibria. Does it get any help from game theory itself? No, not unsurprisingly game theory offers no help here. If it could help, it would already have come to the rescue in cases of multiple Nash/perfect equilibria. Instead, game theory simply recognizes that co-ordination games have multiple Nash equilibria.

In these circumstances, it seems only appropriate to recognize that a problem of ineliminable doubt has surfaced for instrumentally rational agents.[3] After all, players in game theory have complete knowledge of each other's preferences and they each know that each is instrumentally rational and they still cannot decide what to do. In short, the problem cannot be construed as grit in the system in game theory because there is simply no grit there.

It is worth pausing to notice the significance of the indeterminacy in co-ordination games. To appreciate this, what has to be recognized is that bargaining games are ubiquitous and they are all forms of co-ordination games (there are any number of ways of dividing the pie between two people and each person only has to co-ordinate their claim with that of the other so as to avoid claims which exceed the size of the pie for it to be a solution). What is interesting about making this connection is that the same conclusion regarding the inadequacy of instrumental rationality has also been emerging explicitly in the bargaining literature.

For instance, Nash offered a unique solution to the bargaining game through an axiomatic approach: only one solution satisfies several apparently plausible axioms. The well-recognized difficulty with this approach is that a couple of the axioms (symmetry and independence of irrelevant alternatives) do not seem to have any foundation in instrumental rationality and so it is not obvious why instrumentally rational bargainers would be influenced by them when seeking a solution. Likewise, several attempts have been made to explain how the Nash solution might be generated by actual bargaining processes (see Harsanyi 1977 and Rubinstein 1982). However, careful examination of these attempts are typically finding that 'something', which cannot be traced to instrumental rationality, has been smuggled into the analysis to single out the Nash solution (see Sugden 1990 and Varoufakis 1991).

So, to summarize, several strands in the recent economics literature are confronting a problem of ineliminable uncertainty in the form of equilibrium selection in co-ordination games. This echoes the post-modern concerns with uncertainty and doubt and to pursue this connection, I shall turn to what might be involved in providing an account of equilibrium selection.

Hahn (1987) has talked about the need to add 'history', but I think that may miss the point unless it is understood that 'history' here denotes something more than the history of playing the game between instrumentally rational agents, because no amount of knowledge of play in the past between instrumentally rational people will give you a fix on what you do now. Since it will only be some non-instrumental component which fixed play in the past, and for that non-instrumental component to have any relevance today, it must be because it is a part of our decision-making apparatus today.[4]

In other words there has to be something non-instrumental at work in our decision-making, and it has to be shared with others if it is to do the task of co-ordinating. My own preferred way of describing what is involved here is to refer to people as procedural rational. That is to say that individuals rely upon shared procedures, shared rules of thumb in response to this 'substantial' species of doubt they encounter when relying on instrumental rationality alone.[5] I like this because it has obvious affinities with the underlying linguistic philosophy of the posties. It is the shared rules of a particular language which help to fix meanings for them, just as I would have it that it is the shared rules of thumb or conventions which solve the co-ordination problem.

However, the choice of terms has its disadvantages. In particular, it has a familiar ring to it from Simon's work, and this is a misleading reference because Simon's rules of thumb are purely personal affairs. It does not matter whether they are shared or not. They are short-cut devices which economize on a scarce resource, our brain time. Simon's procedural rationality is an ersatz form of instrumental rationality: given enough computing power the behaviour of Simon's procedurally rational agent would increasingly approximate the instrumentally rational agent. In fact, Simon's procedurally rational agent is really modelled on the analogy of uncertainty as grit. Whereas, the whole point about the difficulty with selecting a rational expectation or a Nash/perfect equilibrium is that no amount of information and computing power would enable the instrumentally rational agent to make a decision, instead it is precisely the shared aspect of a procedure that enables the co-ordination which is crucial to equilibrium selection. The procedure is a necessary addition rather than symptomatic of some subtraction from ideal-type human agency.

To see from another angle that there is something significantly different at work in the part played by procedures, it is worth exploring the mental contortions of the instrumentally rational agent who uses procedures purely instrumentally. Consider how such an agent might explain why it is rational to follow a particular procedure. It is rational because others follow that procedure and it thereby co-ordinates action from which I benefit. But why do others follow that procedure? Like me, they follow that procedure because they believe that others will follow that procedure and given those beliefs it serves them well to abide by the procedure. But why do they hold those beliefs? Only because other agents hold those beliefs and so on. The procedure which is used hangs by its bootstrap: it is not used because it, rather than some other, meshes with each agent's instrumental rationality. It is its own warrant: it is there because it is there and it only becomes instrumentally rational to use once it is there. However, that thought cannot be allowed too much space, otherwise it will become corrosive. It will be tempting to find no reason to follow that procedure rather than another since it has no origin in instrumental rationality and once agents succumb to this temptation, the procedure then fails to co-ordinate. In other words, the instrumentally rational agent is forced to complicate his or her own psychology, to allow for a non-instrumental source of action, if only to further his or her own instrumental rationality!

The suggested paradox is real enough because the complication must be genuine. One cannot believe in a procedure because it is instrumental to do so, because there is no instrumental reason for believing in one procedure rather than another. The device unravels the moment it is recognized as a device. Instead, the belief in one procedure rather than another has to come from another source which is relevant to the agent's rationality. There are direct echoes of this motivational change in the post-modern literature. For instance, Rorty (1986) quotes approvingly a similar paradox from Schumpeter 'to realise the relative validity of one's convictions and yet stand for them unflinchingly is what distinguishes a civilised man from a barbarian'. It is not exactly the same but it bears a familial resemblance which can be made even stronger. For instance, it is sometimes argued that Hume's account of ethics turns on this problem of convention selection. Ethics provide reasons for following one procedure rather than another. From this perspective any ethics will do so long as they single out one procedure to follow, and hence 'one's convictions are only relative', and yet they must also be believed in absolutely otherwise they fail to provide a reason for using the co-ordinating convention.

Another aspect of the similarity comes from noticing that what creates the paradox is the sort of self-reflexivity which is at the heart of post-modern thinking. The person steps back and sees that on instrumental grounds, he or she must also be rational (or act) for non-instrumental reasons. The same self-reflexivity was at work with rational expectations. It is the move which says 'hold on we can't just have any old set of expectations generating schemes because we can see that expectations affect the very outcomes which we are entertaining expectations about, and recognizing that this is what is going on we must form our expectations in a different way'.

Actually, with post-modernity, the self-reflexive turn often also cashes in as a distinctive type of 'knowingness'; and this is worth noting because it takes us neatly to the next stage of the argument. It is the knowingness that says 'look you and I both know this is a game, we can stand back from the proceedings and enjoy knowing that it's a game, we can "play" and have a laugh'. It is the way, for instance, those Benson and Hedges advertisements work on us: the advert isn't saying anything like you smoke B and H and you'll become an electric plug, or a pyramid, or a parrot, or whatever. It does not naturalize the object the way many adverts do. It does not place the object on a desert island, so that we elide using the product with being on a desert island. Nor is it like the Chanel no. 5 advert which just has a picture of Catherine Deneuve, thus telling us very economically that Chanel no. 5 imparts Frenchness, the qualities of glamour, beauty, sophistication and so on. Instead, the B and H adverts play on the strangeness of their locations. They work first and foremost by acknowledging that adverts are a game and they invite us to share in that complicity and laugh with them and admire with them their ingenuity as they change the rules (see Williamson 1985). They are miniature works of art because they play on the strangeness in exactly the manner we associate with modern and now self-consciously with post-modern art (just as the earlier Januzsczack quote suggests).

The Gold Blend coffee advert is another good example as it arrests our attention by mixing a soap with an advertisement. It also embodies the joking that goes with this knowingness as the characters seem to be joking about the fact that they are advertising coffee, in turn encouraging us to believe that maybe the advert is a vehicle for their romance and not the sale of coffee. Indeed in an exemplary fashion, the advertisement 'deconstructs' itself.

Now, that may seem like a bit of a digression but it is designed to convey that post-modernity is not just about recognizing that there are shared conventions, but also that they are in some measure arbitrary and can be played with, broken and joked about. In other words, we do not just have to add in procedural rationality, we also have to make space for a kind of creative decision-making; this is a theme in the economics literature that I turn to in the next section. I might add parenthetically that if the excursion into the world of advertising was not very convincing on this point, then Rorty (1986) is a more substantial source because he identifies the small acts of creativity which come with telling new stories about oneself as the crucial aspect of turning oneself into an individual.

Before I take this cue to discuss creative decision-making in economics, there is a final illustration of my general argument from game theory which is worth bringing out. It relies on Binmore's (1987) critique of the perfect equilibrium concept.

Let me remind you of his argument. He is concerned with dynamic games, like the centipede game which I have reproduced in Fig. 6.1. You have two players, I and II, making a series of sequential moves of down or across: down ends the game with payoffs given in parenthesis and across shifts the game to the next decision node, except at the last one where the game also ends.

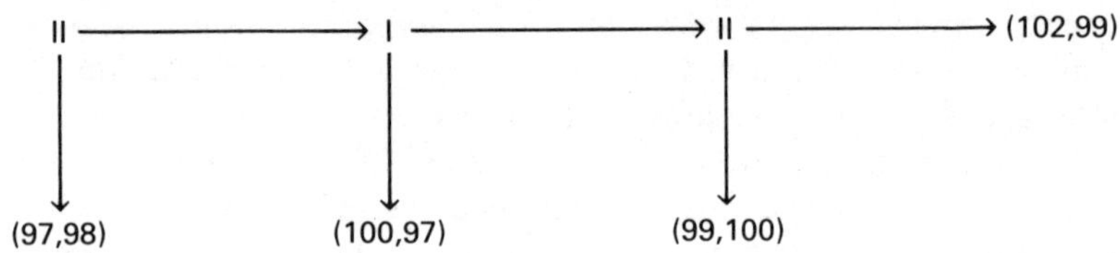

Figure 6.1 The centipede game

The background to the concern is that for dynamic games of this kind, the perfect equilibrium concept is usually regarded as the appropriate solution concept: it is a development of the Nash equilibrium concept and it relies on an assumption of common rationality.

The perfect equilibrium has player II playing down at the first decision node. The logic works backwards from the last decision node. If this was reached then player II plays down since $100 > 99$ and this would yield a worse outcome for player I (99) than if player I had chosen to play down at the second node. So, if the second decision node was reached player I will play down. But as down at the second node yields a worse payoff to player II than playing down at the first node ($97 < 98$), it follows player II will play down at the first node. And there we have our perfect equilibrium.

In other words, the equilibrium strategy of playing down at the first node emerges from a consideration of what would happen should agents not follow this strategy and find themselves at the second and third decision nodes. The issue, then, for Binmore is the inconsistency between the supposition of rationality that has player II playing down and the counterfactual which supports this behaviour which involves agents playing across. To put this slightly differently, is there a way of explaining how agents might reach later decision nodes that does not undermine the assumption of common rationality which has agents not proceeding beyond the first node? Or let me put it like this, what would you do if you were playing the game and the second decision node was reached? Couldn't you think, or wouldn't it be tempting to think, well, player II has played across once when that is not what I would have predicted, maybe, she or he will do the same at the third node, so I'll play across now because 102 is better than 100? If you find this line of reasoning at all attractive then you have departed from a presumption of common rationality and you have stepped outside the perfect equilibrium solution concept.

Of course, the device first employed by Selten was a trembling hand. He avoided the apparent inconsistency between playing down and a consideration of playing across by allowing for errors in the execution of a strategy. So people might play across as a result of an error. But this is hardly convincing as a general device. Binmore argues that what we have to do is loosen up our conception of rational action so that there are a variety of behaviours which might be consistent with this looser sense of rationality, or that there are, if you like, a variety of rationalities.

This meshes quite nicely with the earlier thought that instrumental rationality leads to underdetermination and must be supplemented by an understanding of how procedures guide action because the procedures are unlikely to be universal and are likely to owe much to time and place. Thus a variety of behaviours are consistent with rationality in the abstract and precise behaviour will depend on the specifics of time and place. Indeed, the connection with post-modernity can be made even plainer if one returns to the ineliminable character of uncertainty. From a post-modern perspective, the only certain thing is the existence of uncertainty. So from this perspective, the assumption of common rationality in orthodox game theory looks flawed from the beginning because it imposes a false certainty on the character of players in the game. No event like the rationality of your opponent should enjoy a prior probability of one. Instead uncertainty demands that all beliefs have a prior probability between one and zero and once this condition is satisfied playing across ceases to be a zero probability event; it is only when it is a zero probability event that we run into the Binmore-type difficulties of inconsistency.

That is a good point to end because it serves to reinforce the twist that I take to be distinctive of post-modernity, the bringing of doubt and uncertainty into the soul of the individual and it is one that is reinforced as I turn now to creative decision-making.

ECONOMIC RESONANCES III: CREATIVE CHOICE UNDER UNCERTAINTY

The obvious example of creative decision-making under uncertainty in economics is entrepreneurship, but it is not the only one. Let me first draw out some post-modern parallels in both the traditional and more recent discussions of entrepreneurship and then I will turn to the experimental literature in economics on decision-making under uncertainty.

What I find fascinating about the seminal works on entrepreneurship, like those of Hayek, is how they emphasize that the central skill or activity of the entrepreneur is arbitrage: that is, the action of noticing hitherto unrecognized opportunities for buying low and selling high. I must confess that I've always thought that this emphasis was a bit off-beam because it seems to make the central entrepreneurial skill too prosaic. And yet, I've become quite taken by it because there is a parallel to be found in post-modern conceptions of creativity.

First, there is a parallel with deconstructionist literary criticism when it brings out the repressed meaning and interpretations of texts. Thus, in exactly the same way that the entrepreneur reveals opportunities for trade which had hitherto been overlooked, the deconstructionist critique recovers meanings which have been repressed. Incidentally, Mary Douglas (1975) offers a rather similar analysis of how the joker makes us laugh. He or she exploits the gaps and anomalies in the social order to provide glimpses of how things might be alternatively organized, thus suggesting the rather appealing association of the joker with the entrepreneur.

The second interesting parallel holds with the prosaic shadow which is cast over entrepreneurship by the traditional description. This has a distinctly post-modern feel to it because it democratizes creativity much as Rorty (1986) does when he reminds us that there is a bit of creativity in even the most *bien-pensant* conformist. This 'democratization' is even clearer in the modern discussions of entrepreneurship. Consider, for instance, the best-selling management potboiler by Peters and Waterman (1982) which attempts to explain how to generate entrepreneurship within a corporation. They have reworked ideas of the human relations school in industrial relations (which, to put it baldly, says treat people as people, treat them nicely, enable them to have self-respect and they will respond creatively and productively) by arguing that successful corporations are successful because they have tapped the creative talents of the ordinary people in the corporation. This plainly has an immediate democratic air about it, but Peters and Waterman give the argument a further post-modern twist. They locate the problem of self-respect in a conundrum which everyone faces: 'he needs to be part of something and stick out' or, to be more precise, 'We desperately need meaning in our lives and will sacrifice a great deal to institutions that will provide meaning for us. We simultaneously need independence, to feel as though we are in charge of our destinies, and to have an ability to stick out' (1982: 56).

Peters and Waterman understand this as an unbreachable contradictory set of impulses, a dualism as they call it, which successful corporations help their workers to negotiate with greater dexterity than the unsuccessful ones (whether it has to be is another matter which we can safely ignore for the purposes of this argument). The negotiation is never completely successful and so you always have to be on your toes (for which, you might cynically read, employ consultants like Peters and Waterman but that too is another matter). What is interesting is that the contradiction cannot ever be finally resolved, there are only ever temporary accommodations. The contradiction is a real one because there can never be a coherent sense of the self. Instead individuals always have a capacity to form contradictory projects. They are beset by what Elster (1978) refers to as contradictory desires, the kind of Groucho Marx syndrome of not wanting to belong to a club that would have me as a member, or which post-modernists would refer to as symptomatic of the decentring of the subject. There is no real, stationary person, there is only a succession of temporary accommodations of contradictory desires.

The same picture of the individual plausibly emerges from the recent experimental literature on choice under uncertainty. It will be recalled that much of the experimental literature confounds the predictions of expected utility theory (the extension of instrumental rationality to decision settings characterized by risk). There have been several attempts to generate explanations of choice which fit the experimental evidence better and one of the more successful ones is regret theory (see Loomes and Sugden 1982). I am giving a liberal gloss over regret theory here, but it is not so implausible to cast it as a theory of individuals grappling with contradictory desires. To be specific, I suggest the interpretation that the regular utility function in this theory as the Promethean self and the additional consideration of rejoice/regret which modifies this function as the Epimethean self, meaning after thought. You will recall that Classical mythology provides equal support for the Epimethean self as for the Promethean one because Prometheus had a brother called Epimetheus who came to regret his acceptance of the gift of Pandora from Zeus. In this way, we would understand choice under uncertainty in terms of a particular accommodation between two otherwise inconsistent selves: the Promethean and the Epimethean selves.[6]

SUMMARY AND CONCLUSION

I have argued that the post-modern concern with making doubt and uncertainty more substantial than 'grit' or an arbitrary feature of a particular language has been matched by a recent and similar concern with uncertainty in economics. Whether it be game theory, rational expectations, entrepreneurship or the experimental literature on choice under uncertainty, the depiction of individuals as instrumentally rational has been found lacking; and the source of the failure is, in each case, bound up with an appreciation of uncertainty.

To fill the gaps left by instrumental rationality, economics has been groping more or less explicitly towards expanded notions of rational actions. In particular, the expansion seems to be occurring along at least two dimensions, both of which echo post-modern themes. One locates the individual in a web of socially irreducible procedures/rules/norms; and the other endows the agent with a creative capacity to rearrange and interpret the shared procedures and the internal inconsistencies which she or he feels. The individual *qua* individual becomes less secure with both these moves and this is one of the central messages of post-modernity. He or she is enmeshed in a set of social relations and his or her identity changes over time. At first sight this may seem rather frightening, but I am inclined to welcome the change. After all, the algorithmic view of instrumental rationality was never very flattering to us and the more open-ended picture of agency which emerges with procedural and creative decision-making looks promising because it allows rational action sensibly to depend on time and place much more than does instrumental rationality.

It would be foolish, however, to claim that fully formed additional senses of rationality have emerged in economics or to claim that there is no role for instrumental rationality. Nevertheless, it would be equally foolish to ignore the seeds of these alternative visions in the literature. Yet I fear the pressures to ignore these signs will be strong and I will conclude with a comment on this because it is connected to the post-modern theme.

The point here is that post-modernity has been born of arguments in epistemology and so is bound to carry with it methodological implications. My fear follows from this because arguments which entail methodological change are never easily appreciated by the orthodoxy in a discipline when it subscribes to a rival methodology. There is a long and a short story to tell about this and there is only time for the short one now. In consequence it is a bit rough at the edges!

The popular methodology of economics is an ersatz form of empiricism which most economists think (falsely) derives some authority because it is taken from the natural sciences. Instrumental rationality fits with this methodological position very well. Of course, it does not have to, but there is an undeniable smugness there; and this is what worries me. It arises because instrumental rationality does not really make us as humans significantly different from the way we think about animals in the natural world. Just as animals might be described as having instincts, or urges, which they act to satisfy, so we have 'desires' or preferences which we act upon. The only difference is that we are endowed with rationality, that is, a calculating capacity to work out how best to do this.

Post-modernity threatens this picture of the individual by making the individual more open-ended and in so doing it threatens to break the perceived tie with 'the' method of the natural sciences. To put it baldly, theory in the social world, by affecting what we think, helps to make the world it studies and there is no equivalent to this in the natural sciences. And once we allow for this difference, it will be difficult to sustain some of the popular methodological principles in economics. In particular, the simple positive/normative distinction and the near exclusive reliance on a form of statistical empirical testing both rely on the kind of independence between theory and the object of that theory which, on this reading, only begins to make sense in the natural world.

So there is much more at stake than just a picture of individual agency. That picture is part of the cement that holds together a methodological approach. To foresake one is to begin to entertain doubts about the other and, quite simply, I have my doubts whether economics is ready to let slip the simple distinction between positive and normative economics and whether it is willing to take case study empirical work more seriously.

NOTES

1 This paper was first presented at the University of East Anglia Seminar on Post-Modernity and it has been completed with the help of the ESRC grant R 000 23 2269 to the project on the Foundations of Rational Choice at the University of East Anglia.

2 There is a rather striking similarity between Macintyre's argument that traditions which are in good working order have to be open to amendment and Hampshire's argument that disputes between conflicting views of the good cannot be resolved by reference to a conception of the good and Lyotard's argument that phrase regimes should not contain the means of their own validation if they are to avoid paradoxes of self-reference. The theme which runs through all is that we should avoid making claims to certainty because they are bound to be false.

3 For further discussion of the problems posed by co-ordination games, see Hollis and Starmer (1991).

4 Some game theorists refer to the need to specify 'out-of-equilibrium' beliefs. So we cannot specify what is that rational action until we have specified what are the irrational actions/beliefs. This echoes rather splendidly the post-modern that no concept like reason can be defined without specifying its other – what it is not.

5 In the game theory and rational expectations literature, a similar move is made when selection occurs through agents basing their expectations on shared 'extraneous' sources of information. The fact that it is 'extraneous' means that it does not have anything to do with the instrumental concerns which are defined within the game and it must be shared otherwise it will not serve to co-ordinate.

6 Another example of the recent discussion of multiple selves in economics is in the literature on self-command, see Schelling (1984) and Hargreaves Heap (1989).

REFERENCES

Azariadis, C. (1981) 'Self fulfilling prophecies', *Journal of Economic Theory* 25: 380–96.

Binmore, K. (1987) 'Modelling rational players: part 1', *Economics and Philosophy* 3: 179–214.

Blanchard, O. and Watson, M. (1982) 'Bubbles and rational expectations and financial markets', in P. Wachtel (ed.) *Crises in the Economic and Financial Structure*, Lexington, Mass: Lexington Books.

Diamond, P. (1982) 'Aggregate demand management in search equilibrium', *Journal of Political Economy*, 90: 881–94.

Douglas, M. (1975) *Implicit Meanings*, London: Routledge & Kegan Paul.

Elster, J. (1978) *Logic and Society*, Chichester: Wiley.

Fudenberg, D. and Maskin, E. (1986) 'The Folk theorem in repeated games with discounting or with incomplete information', *Econometrica* 54: 533–54.

Hahn, F. (1987) 'Information, dynamics and equilibrium', *Scottish Journal of Political Economy* 34: 321–34.

Hargreaves Heap, S. (1989) *Rationality in Economics*, Oxford: Basil Blackwell.

—— (1991) *The New Keynesian Macroeconomics: Time, Belief and Social Interdependence*, Aldershot: Edward Elgar.

Harsanyi, J. (1977) *Rational Behaviour and Bargaining Equilibrium in Games and Social Institutions*, Cambridge: Cambridge University Press.

Hollis, M. and Starmer, C. (1991) 'Offering sight to the blind', unpublished mimeo.

Loomes, G. and Sugden, R. (1982) 'Regret theory: an alternative theory of rational choice under uncertainty', *Economic Journal* 92: 805–24.

Muth, J. (1961) 'Rational expectations and the theory of price movements', *Econometrica* 29: 315–35.

Peters, T. and Waterman, R. (1982) *In Search of Excellence*, London: Routledge & Kegan Paul.

Rorty, R. (1986) 'Contingency of language', 'Contingency of selfhood', 'Contingency of community', in *London Review of Books*, 17 April, 8 May and 24 July.

Rubinstein, A. (1982) 'Perfect equilibrium in a bargaining model', *Econometrica* 50: 97–109.
Schelling, T. (1984) 'Self command in practice, in policy and a theory of rational choice', *American Economic Review* 74: 1–11.
Sugden, R. (1990) 'Convention, creativity and conflict', in Y. Varoufakis and D. Young (eds) *Conflict in Economics*, Hemel Hempstead: Harvester Wheatsheaf.
Varoufakis, Y. (1991) *Rational Conflict*, Oxford: Basil Blackwell.
Williamson, J. (1985) *Consuming Passions: The Dynamics of Popular Culture*, London: Boyar Books.

7

KEYNES ON RATIONALITY

Ted Winslow

Interpretations of Keynes's economics frequently provide excellent illustrations of the misunderstanding that results from the failure to read texts hermeneutically. Following Gadamer, I take the essence of hermeneutic reading to be the willingness to have one's fundamental presuppositions put 'in question' by the text and this in two senses. First, the reader must always remain open to the possibility that the author's fundamental premises differ from her own. Second, she must also remain open to the possibility that the author's premises are better than her own. According to Gadamer (1989: 298–9), the two senses are related. A reader who is unable to put his or her fundamental premises in question in the second sense will not be able to do so in the first sense either. The reader enters into a dialogue with the author about the subject matter; a dialogue in which the author must be allowed to make claims upon the reader.

Keynes himself was well aware of the need to read in this way.[1] He was frequently critical of his own readers for failing to do so. For example, at the end of his copy of F. A. von Hayek's review of *A Treatise on Money* he wrote:

> Hayek has not read my book with that measure of 'good will' which an author is entitled to expect of a reader. Until he has done so, he will not see what I mean or know whether I am right. He evidently has a passion which leads him to pick on me, but I am left wondering what this passion is.
>
> (Keynes 1973c: 243)

Reading the *General Theory* with understanding required a 'struggle of escape from habitual modes of thought and expression'. Understanding was impeded not by the new ideas, which were simple and should have been obvious, but by the strength of the attachment to 'old ones, which ramify, for those brought up as most of us have been, into every corner of our minds' (1973a: xxiii).

Most readers[2] of Keynes's economics come to their reading committed to the 'rational' choice axioms which form the foundation of contemporary orthodoxy, and they read in a way that denies Keynes the opportunity to bring this foundation into question. This is as true of many Keynesians as of the critics of Keynes, of some exponents of the 'economics of Keynes' as of the exponents of Keynesian economics.[3] Indeed, so strong is the dogmatic attachment to orthodox premises, it does not even occur to most economist readers that Keynes's premises might differ from their own.[4] This paper points to evidence suggesting that, in fact, Keynes's premises differ radically from those currently dominant in economics. To begin with, his conception of rationality differs from the dominant conception. Second, he attributes significant irrationality to belief and behaviour.

The paper is divided into two parts. The first examines Keynes's view of the nature of rational belief. The second attempts to show that the premise of agent irrationality plays an important role in his economics.

KEYNES ON THE NATURE OF RATIONAL BELIEF

From the beginning, Keynes maintained that an individual's belief is rational where that individual can support it with good reasons. He also consistently maintained that the source of good reasons is direct acquaintance. He was, in this sense, always a foundationalist, though his view of the foundations altered over time. This section begins with an examination of the evolution of Keynes's beliefs about direct acquaintance. It then examines the evolution of his view of the other beliefs which direct acquaintance can ground.

Direct acquaintance: Keynes's early beliefs

At the beginning of *A Treatise on Probability* Keynes distinguishes between rational and irrational degrees of belief. There are, he claims, grounds independent of our opinion which determine the degree of belief it is rational to hold in given circumstances. Probability is not

> subject to human caprice. A proposition is not probable because we think it so. When once the facts are given which determine our knowledge, what is probable or improbable in these circumstances has been fixed objectively, and is independent of our opinion. The theory of probability is logical, therefore, because it is concerned with the degree of belief which it is *rational* to entertain in given conditions, and not merely with the actual beliefs of particular individuals, which may or may not be rational.
>
> (Keynes 1973b: 4)

At the beginning of chapter 2, this distinction is reiterated.

> There is, first of all, the distinction between that part of our belief which is rational and that part which is not. If a man believes something for a reason which is preposterous or for no reason at all, and what he believes turns out to be true for some reason not known to him, he cannot be said to believe it *rationally*, although he believes it and it is in fact true.
>
> (Keynes 1973b: 10)

Rational beliefs are those for which we have good, as opposed to preposterous or no reasons. What then are good reasons?

The ultimate basis of rational belief is what Keynes (1973b: 12) calls 'direct acquaintance'. He claims there are three forms of direct acquaintance: experience, understanding and perception. The objects of each form are: sensations (experience), ideas or meanings (understanding), and facts or characteristics or relations of sense-data or meanings (perception). All knowledge is ultimately the result of contemplating the objects of direct acquaintance. Such contemplation grounds direct knowledge which, in turn, because it includes perception of logical probability relations, grounds indirect knowledge by argument 'about' and possibly 'of' other propositions ('of' when it grounds a degree of belief of certainty).

Because individuals differ in their direct knowledge, what is rational for one individual to believe is not necessarily rational for another. It follows that much of what might be regarded as irrational belief is perfectly rational. Individuals can rationally invest propositions which are false with some degree of belief so long as their direct knowledge justifies the degree. Keynes claims that ignorance of this point is partly responsible for the 'excessive ridicule' that has been 'visited on the supposed irrationality of barbarous and primitive peoples' (1973b: 273–5). Irrational beliefs are those which are incompatible with our direct knowledge.

Keynes's recognition of the existence and importance of irrationality pre-dates the *Treatise*. Lawson (1990: 39, n.12) points to his distinction, in an as yet unpublished 1906 Apostles paper, 'Egoism', between a 'rational motive as a ground for action' and a 'psychological motive as an efficient cause of action'. This distinction also informs his discussion of investor expectations in a 1910 paper, 'Great Britain's foreign investments', a discussion which, as we shall see, anticipates his treatment of these expectations in his later economics. He claims the investor

> will be affected, as is obvious, not by the net income which he will actually receive from his investment in the long run, but by his expectations. These will often depend upon fashion, upon advertisement, or upon purely irrational waves of optimism or depression. Similarly by risk we must mean, not the real risk as measured by the actual average of the class of investment over the period of years to which the expectation refers, but the risk as it is estimated, wisely or foolishly, by the investor.
>
> (Keynes 1971e: 46)

In the *Treatise* (1973b: 106) Keynes claims that 'it must be admitted that there are many instances in which variation of belief is occasioned by purely psychological causes'.[5] He describes the *Treatise* as concerned, in contrast, 'with the general theory of arguments from premisses leading to conclusions which are reasonable but not certain'. The *Treatise* (1973b: 15) also points to a particular psychological cause of irrational beliefs and behaviour – 'pure instinct or irrational associations of ideas (acquired or inherited)' (1973b: 15). Beliefs which have this as their source 'cannot fairly be called knowledge'. This is the same source pointed to by psychoanalysis. It renders the beliefs it anchors immune to rational critique. As we shall see, Keynes gives an important role in his economics to ideas arising in this way.

Keynes also points in the *Treatise* to specific examples of irrational beliefs. For example, while recognition of the nature of rational belief will, he claims, show that the beliefs of 'barbarous and primitive peoples' have been the object of excessive ridicule, nevertheless 'savages often greatly overestimate the value of their crude inductions, and are to this extent irrational' (1973b: 275). In addition, we ourselves 'while we depreciate the former probability of beliefs which we no longer hold . . . tend . . . to exaggerate the present degree of certainty of what we still believe' (1973b: 275). In illustration, he claims that beliefs which we all hold to be well-established may require for their justification just appreciable a priori degrees of probable belief in other propositions that most of us would dismiss out of hand, beliefs which we ridicule when we find them in others. He claims, for example, that 'our belief in the real existence of other people, which we all hold to be well established, may require for its justification the combination of experience with a just appreciable a priori possibility for animism generally' (1973b: 274–5).

Even in the *Treatise*, Keynes is aware that he cannot construct a fully adequate theory of rational belief on these foundations. He admits to being unable to justify induction (1973b: 293–4). The problem is that his premises about direct acquaintance prevent it from providing an adequate foundation for belief in the assumptions required for rational induction. The assumptions which cannot be grounded are the uniformity of nature, the law of causation and what he calls the inductive hypothesis. The problem is traceable to the conception of direct acquaintance Keynes adopts, specifically to his atomic conception of experience and understanding. By atomic in this context, I mean his adoption of the view that the elements of meaning and the elements of experience have essences which are independent of their relations. Consequently, our direct knowledge about empirical entities cannot go beyond 'a mere expression of our understanding or sensation of them'. Keynes attempts to get round this by simply asserting that 'we are capable of direct knowledge about empirical entities which goes beyond a mere expression of our understanding or sensation of them' (1973b: 293). All he does in defence is to point out that there are cases, such as belief in the uniformity of nature and in the law of causation, where such knowledge is commonly assumed (1973b: 294).

He admits, however, that he is unable to enunciate the valid principle which would justify the inductive method and points to the imperfect understanding of the theory of knowledge as the source of the difficulty.

> I do not believe that any conclusive or perfectly satisfactory answer to this question can be given, so long as our knowledge of the subject of epistemology is in so disordered and undeveloped a condition as it is in at present. No proper answer has yet been given to the enquiry – of what sorts of things are we *capable* of direct knowledge?
>
> (Keynes 1973b: 291)

Keynes also points to the undeveloped condition of epistemology as a source of difficulties in other contexts (1973b: 333). A. N. Whitehead subsequently offered a solution to the problem of grounding the inductive hypothesis based on a different view of the nature of direct acquaintance. As I shall now attempt to show, Keynes made changes in his own views very similar to the changes proposed by Whitehead.

Direct acquaintance: Keynes's mature beliefs

At some point after 1921, Keynes made significant changes in his beliefs about direct acquaintance. I have attempted elsewhere (Winslow 1986a: 425–7) to give a detailed account of these changes. They are recorded in his criticisms, in 'My early beliefs' (Keynes 1972b: ch. 39), of his early beliefs about experience – criticisms which, as we shall see, are very like Whitehead's criticisms of these same beliefs.

Keynes claims his early beliefs combined 'a dogmatic treatment as to the nature of experience with a method of handling it which was extravagantly scholastic' (1972b: 438). He follows Ramsey in defining 'excessive scholasticism' as 'the treatment of what is vague as if it were precise and trying to fit it into an exact logical category' (Ramsey, as cited by Keynes 1972b: 343). Keynes here appears to be recognizing a source in experience of 'vague knowledge', a source additional to the sensations with which he had identified experience in *A Treatise on Probability* (see Winslow 1989a). As will be established below, this brings his mature view of direct acquaintance in contact with the view of A. N. Whitehead.

Ramsey used the phrase 'excessive scholasticism' critically to describe G. E. Moore's approach to ordinary language. Moore held that fundamental issues in philosophy could be resolved by means of an analysis of the precise meaning of ordinary language.

In opposition to this, Ramsey argued that meaning was vague rather than precise and that philosophy could change meaning (Ramsey 1965: 116, 117 and 136–7; see also Whitehead 1929a: 12, 1933: 234).

In 'My early beliefs', Keynes makes the same criticism of this aspect of 'Moore's method'. According to this method, he claims

> you could hope to make essentially vague notions clear by using precise language about them and asking exact questions. It was the method of discovery by the instrument of impeccable grammar and an unambiguous dictionary. 'What *exactly* do you mean?' was the phrase most frequently on our lips. If it appeared under cross-examination that you did not mean *exactly* anything, you lay under a strong suspicion of meaning nothing whatever. It was a stringent education in dialectic but in practice it was a kind of combat in which strength of character was really much more valuable than subtlety of mind.
>
> (Keynes 1972b: 440)

Notice that some notions are described as '*essentially* vague'. I take this to mean that Keynes holds them to be vague on account of the nature of the experience to which they refer rather than on account of some failure of insight or definition.

In a 1931 review of a posthumously published set of Ramsey's papers, *The Foundations of Mathematics*, Keynes (1972b: 338–9) adopts Ramsey's view that what Ramsey calls 'human logic' may be able to provide adequate foundations for degrees of belief, induction and ontological premises. In agreeing with Ramsey that the analysis of degrees of belief belongs to human logic, he abandons his *Treatise* view that logical probability relations provide the foundation for rational degrees of belief. While accepting Ramsey's separation of this field of study from descriptive psychology and formal logic, he rejects Ramsey's claim that pragmatism can ground the mental habits which are its subject matter. As I shall now attempt to show, A. N. Whitehead argued that the changed view of experience which Keynes appears to have adopted enabled 'direct intuitive observation' to provide the method which Keynes claimed pragmatism could not provide.

Whitehead makes essentially the same criticisms of conventional philosophic methods as Ramsey and Keynes.[6] He claims (1938: 74) they involve 'dogmatic' attachment to 'the presupposition that all knowledge starts from the consciousness of spatio-temporal patterns of sensa'. This presupposition imports a false sense of 'clarity' into our conception of our experience (1938: 111–12). While accepting 'direct intuitive observation' as the ultimate foundation for all knowledge, Whitehead rejects the traditional 'empiricist' account of experience. 'All knowledge is derived from and verified by, direct intuitive observation. I accept this axiom of empiricism as stated in this general form' (1933: 177; see also 1929a: 39, 1938: 112). He also claims, however, that exponents of the '*a priori* doctrine of sensationalism' have 'arrogated to themselves the title of empiricists' (Whitehead 1929a: 145). In opposition to the view that experience is made up entirely of sensations, Whitehead claimed that 'the study of human knowledge should start with a survey of the vague variety, discernible in the transitions of human experience' (1938: 75).

Whitehead also makes the same criticism as Keynes and Ramsey of the conventional approach to meaning and language. He calls 'the belief that [philosophy's] working hypotheses are clear, obvious, and irreformable' the 'Dogmatic Fallacy' (1933: 144). The belief ignores that 'except perhaps for the simpler notions of arithmetic, even our more familiar ideas, seemingly obvious, are infected with this incurable vagueness' (1933: 145). He calls the belief that philosophy can reveal but cannot change the meanings implicit in ordinary language 'The Fallacy of the Perfect Dictionary'.

> There is an insistent presupposition continually sterilizing philosophic thought. It is the belief, the very natural belief, that mankind has consciously entertained all the fundamental ideas which are applicable to its experience. Further it is held that human language, in single words or in phrases, explicitly expresses these ideas. I will term this presupposition, 'The Fallacy of the Perfect Dictionary'.
>
> (Whitehead 1938: 173)

He claims both these fallacies are instances of what Keynes and Ramsey call excessive scholasticism (1938: 173).

What is required in place of these methods is what Keynes and Ramsey call human logic ('logic in the broadest sense of that term – the logic of discovery', Whitehead 1929b: 67–71). 'Our task is to understand how in fact the human mind can successfully set to work for the gradual definition of its habitual ideas' (1933: 145;

see also 1929c: 106). Human logic involves appeal to 'direct insight' rather than deduction or 'verbal analysis within the limits of the dictionary' (1938: 173). It is possible, by means of such an appeal, to change meaning and thereby 'enlarge the dictionary' (1938: 173). In fact, 'the great difficulty of philosophy is the failure of language. . . . Language halts behind intuition. The difficulty of philosophy is the expression of what is self-evident. Our understanding outruns the ordinary usages of words' (1938: 49).

These changes in Keynes's beliefs about direct acquaintance left important aspects of his view of rational belief unchanged. Rational beliefs are still those which are justified by the individual's direct knowledge which is in turn based on direct acquaintance. As the mature Keynes appears to conceive it, however, direct acquaintance can ground rational belief in an organicist view of degrees of belief, the uniformity of nature and the law of causation. Since it remains the case that individuals differ in their direct knowledge, beliefs which are rational for one individual may not be rational for others. Irrational beliefs continue to be those which are incompatible with our direct knowledge and which have their source in 'pure instinct or irrational associations of ideas'.

Keynes's discussions after 1921 of the nature of direct acquaintance indicate only the direction in which he thought a solution to the problems posed in *A Treatise on Probability* might eventually be found. A much fuller discussion is available in Whitehead. Whitehead's discussion, in turn, is similar in fundamental respects to Husserl's phenomenology.[7] Moreover, the phenomenological Marxists, particularly Karel Kosik (1976) and Enzo Paci (1972), have developed phenomenology in a way which links it directly to economics.[8] Consequently, those interested in further exploration of Keynes's notion of human logic and its application to economics do not need to begin where Keynes left off. A great deal of work in this field has already been done.

Changes in Keynes's ontological beliefs

In association with this change in his view of the nature of direct acquaintance, Keynes changed his ontological beliefs. I have written at length elsewhere (Winslow 1986a, 1989a) about one aspect of this, the change in his conception of the nature and implications of organic interdependence. This was associated with fundamental changes in his view of induction and probability, changes which altered his view of the origin of uncertainty and provided a ground for his claim that expectations of future yield from capital assets are normally fundamentally uncertain.

There were other changes in Keynes's ontological beliefs. The particular ones I wish to consider here are those found in his mature view of objective values and motivation. In differentiating, in his discussion of Tinbergen's early work in econometrics (Keynes 1973d: 285–320), the ontological premises appropriate in the moral from those appropriate in the physical sciences, Keynes emphasizes, in addition to organic interdependence, the role of values, motives and psychological factors. 'Economics is essentially a moral science and not a natural science. That is to say, it employs introspection and judgments of value' (1973d: 297). This point is reiterated in another letter to Harrod on the same subject.

> I also want to emphasise strongly the point about economics being a moral science. I mentioned before that it deals with introspection and with values. I might have added that it deals with motives, expectations, psychological uncertainties. One has to be constantly on guard against treating the material as constant and homogeneous. It is as though the fall of the apple to the ground depended on the apple's motives, on whether it is worth while falling to the ground, and whether the ground wanted the apple to fall, and on mistaken calculations on the part of the apple as to how far it was from the centre of the earth.
>
> (Keynes 1973d: 300)

Keynes is claiming the moral sciences must take account of final causation. His premises about final causation are very different, however, from the utilitarian premises of orthodox economics. To begin with, he assumes values are objective. This assumption is part of both his early and his mature beliefs. Over time, however, his view of the content of objective values changed. At the same time, he came to believe that only a tiny minority were or could be motivated by rational and/or true value beliefs. The motives of the overwhelming majority embodied irrational and false beliefs about value. The irrational and false beliefs to which particular attention is paid in his economics are those which lead to the dominance in motivation of the love of money, money-making and power, a motivation which Keynes misleadingly associates with Benthamism in 'My early beliefs'. This approach assumes that direct acquaintance can ground beliefs about value and that conventional value beliefs are not grounded and are, therefore, irrational. As we shall see, Keynes assumes they are irrationally rooted in 'pure instinct or irrational associations of ideas'.

Early and late Keynes assumed that values are objective. His early understanding of this was dominated by Moore's *Principia Ethica*. The mature Keynes continued to believe in important aspects of Moore's doctrine. In particular, he continued to believe that goodness was an attribute of certain states of consciousness achieved by contemplating appropriate objects and that among the most valuable states were 'the pleasures of human intercourse and the enjoyment of beautiful objects' (Moore 1903: 188). The continuity was not complete, however. Some changes resulted from the switch to an organic view of interdependence; others from a change in his psychological views.

As I pointed out above, in abandoning atomism Keynes appears to have abandoned the *Treatise on Probability*'s logical theory of probability. There are hints in his writing that he may have become much more favourably disposed towards a frequency theory of probability.[9] Whitehead, it happens, had developed such a theory on the foundation of his philosophy of organism.[10] Whitehead's theory does not identify probability with the number of times something occurs in repeated trials; rather, the frequency with which probability is identified is the truth frequency of a proposition in a particular class of propositions. In normal circumstances, the class is given by what Whitehead calls real potentiality. Real potentiality is in turn defined in terms of an organicist ontology. The result is that real potentiality is constantly changing as the present becomes past and alters the conditions from which present real potentiality emerges. Though stability of truth frequencies is not ruled out, there is no presumption (as there is in the conventional frequency theory) that the frequencies will be stable. Since ethics, on Keynes's theory, is concerned with consequences, it is closely linked to probability.

As Bateman (1988: 1101–2) points out, Keynes's initial critical reconstruction of Moore was based on the rejection of Moore's implicit theory of probability in favour of a logical theory. Moore (1903: 162–3) argued that strict obedience to generally useful moral rules was required because, although there were cases where obedience would not produce the best results, the probability of us knowing rightly when such a case was before us was always less than the probability that obedience would produce the best result. This argument appears to be based on the conventional frequency theory of probability; it implicitly assumes that the probability that obedience will produce the best result is a constant given presumably by the frequency with which it has in fact given the best result. In contrast, the probabilities associated with Keynes's logical theory are not constant; they vary with variations in direct knowledge. Keynes's initial rejection of this aspect of Moore's argument had the result, therefore, that rules were overturned in favour of examining each set of circumstances on its merits. This followed from the fact that the probabilities could be expected to change with changes in the circumstances. Whitehead's organicist frequency theory leads to the same conclusion. In this theory, as in Keynes's logical theory, the probabilities change with changes in circumstances.

The adoption of an organic view of interdependence did alter Keynes's ethical beliefs in other ways, however. In particular it led him to abandon an atomic for an organic individualism. Though he continued to believe that 'nothing really exists or feels but *individuals*' (William Paley, as cited by Keynes 1972b: 449), he altered his conception of the relation between the individual and the whole, an alteration which affected his ethical views by, for example, making it possible to justify actions likely to produce self-sacrifice. In some circumstances such actions might produce the best possible state of mind.[11]

Paradoxically, given his continued adherence to a theory of probability that justified 'nonconformity with the right and duty of fearless individual judgment', Keynes came to believe on other grounds (namely, his changed psychological beliefs[12]) in the importance of uncritical obedience to rules. He argued that habits of uncritical obedience must be inculcated in most people because most do not possess even the rudiments of what is required for rational judgment. They lack 'the wisdom, experience and self-control' necessary successfully to 'judge every individual case on its merits' (1972b: 446). In consequence, 'immoralism' was not, as he claimed early Bloomsbury had believed, an appropriate ethical stance for everyone. The belief that it was had been 'flimsily based . . . on an *a priori* view of what human nature is like, both other people's and our own, which was disastrously mistaken . . . the view that human nature is reasonable' (1972b: 447). Though Russell had failed fully to realize its implications, his view that 'in fact, human affairs are carried on after a most irrational fashion' (1972b: 449) was correct.

This change in Keynes's psychological beliefs led to further changes in his ethical beliefs. He added 'spontaneous, irrational outbursts of human nature' to the list of good states of mind (1972b: 448) and 'the order and pattern of life amongst communities and the emotions which they can inspire' to 'the objects of valuable contemplation and communion' (1972b: 449). Civilization, he now claimed, was 'a thin and precarious crust erected by the personality and will of a very few, and only maintained by rules and conventions skillfully put across and guilefully preserved' (1972b: 447).[13]

As I shall now attempt to show, the premise that 'human affairs are carried on after a most irrational fashion' also plays an important role in his economics.

IRRATIONALITY AND ECONOMIC MOTIVATION

As we have just seen, 'My early beliefs' records Keynes's rejection of the belief that human nature is reasonable. This belief ignored the 'deeper and blinder passions', the 'vulgar passions' (1972b: 449–50). It overlooked the 'insane and irrational springs of wickedness in most men' (1972b: 447).

Though Keynes, consistent with his organic view of social interdependence, allows the form taken by irrationality to vary with the circumstances in which individuals develop and live, he assumes the ultimate source of irrationality is largely innate.[14] He once said of Marxism, for example:

> How can I adopt a creed which, preferring the mud to the fish, exalts the boorish proletariat above the bourgeois and the intelligentsia who, with whatever faults, are the quality of life and surely carry the seeds of all human advancement.
> (Keynes 1972a: 258)

In a 1925 address to the Liberal Summer School, he advocated autocratic party structures as a means of minimizing the influence of the 'mass of ill-understanding voters' in matters of party economic policy. The right solution to such matters involves 'intellectual and scientific elements which must be above the heads of the vast mass of more or less illiterate voters' (1972a: 295–6). Of participants in stock markets he says that

> the vast majority of those who are concerned with the buying and selling of securities know almost nothing whatever about what they are doing. They do not possess even the rudiments of what is required for a valid judgment, and are the prey of hopes and fears easily aroused by transient events and as easily dispelled. This is one of the odd characteristics of the Capitalist System under which we live, which, when we are dealing with the real world, is not to be overlooked.
>
> (Keynes 1971d: 323)

Keynes also remained a supporter of eugenics to the end of his life. In some 1946 remarks to the Eugenics Society introducing the Society's gold medal winner for that year, Alexander Carr-Saunders, Keynes describes eugenics as 'the most important, significant and, I would add, *genuine* branch of sociology which exists' (1946: 40).[15] My own view is that Keynes's treatment of irrationality as largely innate is an old atomist skin.[16]

As Bateman (1988: 1105) points out, the attribution of utilitarian motivational premises to Keynes is a serious misinterpretation. On the other hand, Keynes did not believe that most people were or could be motivated by rational pursuit of the good. Although he claims that he and his friends were saved by Moore from Benthamism, he also claims they were 'perhaps alone' in their generation in being so saved (1972b: 445). The 'popular Ideal' continued to be dominated by the Benthamite tradition; the 'economic criterion and the economic motive' remained dominant in the lives of most people (1972b: 445–6). This does not mean, however, that Keynes believed that the utilitarian motivational premises of neoclassical economics are sufficiently realistic as a description of actual motivation to provide an adequate psychological foundation for economic analysis. The motives Keynes associates with the Benthamite tradition are very different from the motives which neoclassical orthodoxy assumes underpin economic behaviour.

In *A Treatise on Probability*, as we have seen, Keynes points to 'pure instinct or irrational associations of ideas' as a source of irrational motives. In 'The end of laissez-faire', he explicitly points to instinct as the source of the motives dominant in capitalism. He claims 'the essential characteristic of capitalism' is 'the dependence upon an intense appeal to the money-making and money-loving instincts of individuals as the main motive force of the economic machine' (1972a: 293). He also explicitly claims these motives are irrational. In 'Economic possibilities for our grandchildren' he looks forward to a time when

> we shall be able to afford to dare to assess the money-motive at its true value. The love of money as a possession – as distinguished from the love of money as a means to the enjoyments and realities of life – will be recognized for what it is, a somewhat disgusting morbidity, one of those semi-criminal, semi-pathological propensities which one hands over with a shudder to the specialists in mental disease.
>
> (Keynes 1972a: 329)

Irrationality plays an important role in each of the 'three fundamental psychological factors' (1973a: 246–7) underpinning the *General Theory*.

The psychological propensity to consume

Keynes points to the money-making and money-loving instincts in his account of the motivation behind saving and consumption. In 'A short view of Russia' he associates capitalism with 'the social appeal to the hoarding instinct as the foundation of the necessary provision for the family and the future' (1972a: 269). In *The Economic Consequences of the Peace* he claims that in the nineteenth century saving and accumulating became the focus for 'all those instincts of puritanism which in other ages has withdrawn itself from the world and has neglected the arts of production as well as those of enjoyment' (1971a: 11–12).[17] In his biographical sketch of Jevons, he points again to the hoarding instinct, an instinct Jevons is said to share with many others, as the irrational source of Jevons's mistaken belief that economic growth would be brought to an end by limited supplies of coal. He claims this belief was rooted in 'a psychological trait, unusually strong in him, which many other people share, a certain hoarding instinct, a readiness to be alarmed and excited by the idea of the exhaustion of resources' (1972b: 117).

At least two of the subjective factors to which Keynes points in his *General Theory* account (1973a: 188) of the motivation behind saving involve these instincts.[18] These factors are: (1) 'To enjoy a gradually increasing expenditure, since it gratifies a common instinct to look forward to a gradually improving standard of life rather than the contrary, even though the capacity for enjoyment may be diminishing'; and (2) 'To satisfy pure miserliness, i.e. unreasonable but insistent inhibitions against acts of expenditure as such'.[19] In both *A Treatise on Money* (1971d: 176–7) and the *General Theory* (1973a: 319) Keynes points to an irrational feeling which he calls '"psychological" poverty' as an important influence on the consumption of the wealthy.

The psychological attitude to liquidity

Keynes's account of liquidity preference also points to important irrational elements. I pointed above to the role given to 'the money-making and money-loving instincts' in his account of the dominant motives in capitalism. In his discussion of the relation between uncertainty and liquidity preference in the 1937 *Quarterly Journal of Economics* summary of the *General Theory* (1973d: 116), he claims that the capacity of 'our desire to hold money as a store of wealth' to act as 'a barometer of the degree of our distrust of our own calculations and conventions concerning the future' is based 'partly on reasonable and partly on instinctive grounds'. He also claims this 'feeling about money' is 'itself conventional or instinctive'.[20] In the *Tract on Monetary Reform* (1971b: 55) he points to 'the deep instincts by which the love of money protects itself' as the source of an irrational 'violent prejudice' on the part of investors against capital levies.

The psychological expectation of future yield from capital assets

We come finally to the third of Keynes's fundamental psychological factors – 'the psychological expectation of future yield from capital assets'. Most of the discussion of the role of irrationality in Keynes's economics has centred on his treatment of this factor. Shackle claims 'Keynes's whole theory of unemployment is ultimately the simple statement that, rational expectation being unattainable, we substitute for it . . . irrational expectation' (Shackle, as cited in O'Donnell 1989: 248). Many others (e.g. Meeks 1981; Lawson 1985, 1987, 1988, 1990; Kregel 1987; Meltzer 1988: 280–5; O'Donnell 1989: ch. 12) reject this interpretation. In what follows, I will attempt to show that Keynes does claim that expectations of future yield are usually irrational. I will begin with a brief discussion of his notion of uncertainty.

Already in *A Treatise on Probability* Keynes points to the senses in which expectations can be uncertain. They are uncertain where they are (1) based on low weight (a relatively small amount of relevant evidence), or (2) based on non-numerical probabilities. They may also be (3) fundamentally uncertain, meaning by this expectations for which it is not possible to determine whether they are '*more* likely than not, or *less* likely than not, or *as* likely as not' (1973b: 32). Though Keynes retained these concepts of uncertainty, his understanding of them altered as a result of the changes in his ontological premises and the linked changes in his view of the nature of probability.[21]

Elsewhere (Winslow 1989a), I have attempted to show that Keynes believes expectations of future yield from capital assets are normally (though by no means always – on this see O'Donnell 1989: 256–7) fundamentally uncertain in the sense just defined. This belief is connected to his move to an organic view of interdependence. Contrary to what Shackle appears to argue, however, and as has been pointed out by Meeks, Lawson and O'Donnell, the existence of fundamental uncertainty is not in itself sufficient to produce irrational beliefs and behaviour. As pointed out above, where fundamental uncertainty exists and where in addition we have good reason for doing something rather than nothing (for example, to avoid the fate of Buridan's ass; Keynes 1979: 294), 'it will be rational to allow caprice to determine us and to waste no time on the debate' (1973b: 32). Note, however, that rational behaviour involves consciousness of the fact that our knowledge is insufficient to enable us to rank alternative courses of action and the conscious decision in the light of this to allow caprice to determine us. As Keynes describes them, the practices individuals employ in forming their expectations of the prospective yields of capital assets do not meet these requirements for rationality.

In the *General Theory*, Keynes claims that because

> it is reasonable . . . to be guided to a considerable degree by the facts about which we feel somewhat confident, even though they may be less decisively relevant to the issue than other facts about which our knowledge is vague and scanty, . . . the facts of the existing situation enter, in a sense

> disproportionately, into the formation of our long-term expectations; our usual practice being to take the existing situation and project it into the future, modified only to the extent that we have more or less definite reasons for expecting a change.
>
> (Keynes 1973a: 148)

Lawson (1990: 24) and others read this passage as claiming that our usual practice in the formation of our long-term expectations of future yield from capital assets is rational. Shortly after this passage, however, Keynes (1973a: 152) explicitly claims that the practices employed in reaching the expectations that 'exercise a decisive influence on the rate of current investment' are not rational. He is discussing the formation of the expectations which determine share valuations in the stock market. These expectations govern 'certain classes of investment' and thus 'exert a decisive influence on the rate of current investment' (1973a: 151). According to Keynes, the participants in stock markets make 'these highly significant daily, even hourly, revaluations of existing investments' by 'tacitly' agreeing

> as a rule, to fall back on what is, in truth, a *convention*. The essence of this convention – though it does not, of course, work out quite so simply – lies in assuming that the existing state of affairs will continue indefinitely, except in so far as we have specific reasons to expect a change.
>
> (Keynes 1973a: 152)

Keynes claims this conventional practice cannot be philosophically justified. To begin with, 'we know from extensive experience' that 'it is most unlikely that the existing state of affairs will continue indefinitely. The actual results of an investment over a long term of years very seldom agree with the initial expectation.' We cannot, therefore, rationalize our behaviour by arguing that we have no reason to expect change.[22] Nor, he claims, can we rationalize our behaviour by arguing that because we are completely ignorant about the specific kind of change which will take place we are justified in assigning equal probabilities to change in either direction and so justifying the projection of the present. As is shown in *A Treatise on Probability*, 'the assumption of arithmetically equal probabilities based on a state of ignorance leads to absurdities'. Finally, he claims explicitly that the convention is philosophically untenable.

> We are assuming, in effect, that the existing market valuation, however arrived at, is uniquely *correct* in relation to our existing knowledge, and that it will only change in proportion to changes in this knowledge; though, philosophically speaking, it cannot be uniquely correct, since our existing knowledge does not provide a sufficient basis for a calculated mathematical expectation. In point of fact, all sorts of considerations enter into the market valuation which are in no way relevant to the prospective yield.[23]

In illustration of this, he points to the fact that

> day-to-day fluctuations in the profits of existing investments, which are obviously of an ephemeral and non-significant character, tend to have an altogether excessive, and even an absurd, influence on the market. It is said, for example, that the shares of American companies which manufacture ice tend to sell at a higher price in summer when their profits are seasonally high than in winter when no one wants ice. The recurrence of a bank-holiday may raise the market valuation of the British railway system by several million pounds.
>
> (Keynes 1973a: 153)

In *A Treatise on Money* (1971d: 322–4) this characteristic of the mass psychology which dominates stock markets is described as a 'psychological phenomenon', an exaggeration of the tendency of 'even the best informed' to be 'sensitive – over-sensitive if you like – to the near future, about which we may think that we know a little . . . because, in truth, we know almost nothing about the more remote future'. This leads 'the wisest' to become speculators (in the sense given this term in the *General Theory* (1973a: 158)) who 'anticipate mob psychology' and 'ape unreason proleptically'.

This position is reiterated in the 1937 *Quarterly Journal of Economics* article and in the 1937 *Eugenics Review* article, 'Some economic consequences of a declining population'. In the former, Keynes claims (1973d: 114) that, in employing conventions in the formation of our expectations, we 'overlook this awkward fact' that 'we simply do not know'. In particular, in projecting the existing situation into the future 'we assume that the present is a much more serviceable guide to the future than a candid examination of past experience would show it to have been hitherto'. It is not reasonable to proceed by ignoring awkward facts and by making premises which are contradicted by experience. Conventional behaviour 'saves our faces as rational, economic men' but the behaviour only appears rational; it is 'pseudo-rationalistic'.

Keynes (1973d: 124) begins the *Eugenics Review* article by repeating this argument. 'The future never resembles the past – as we well know. But, generally speaking, our imagination and our knowledge are too weak to tell us what particular changes to expect.' In response to this 'we tend . . . to substitute for the knowledge which is unattainable certain conventions, the chief of which is to assume, contrary to all likelihood, that the future will resemble the past'. We do this, he claims, for psychological rather than rational reasons, because 'peace and comfort of mind require that we should hide from ourselves how little we foresee'. This is true 'generally speaking'.[24] In forecasting population, however, our conventional behaviour is doubly irrational. Here, in contrast to the general case, our knowledge is sufficient 'to tell us what particular changes to expect'. So strong is our attachment to the 'convention by which we assume the future to be much more like the past than is reasonable', however, that 'it continues to influence our minds even in those cases [such as population forecasting] where we do have good reason to expect a definite change'. 'The idea of the future being different from the present is so repugnant to our conventional modes of thought and behaviour that we, most of us, offer a great resistance to acting on it in practice.'

Consistent with all this, students in Keynes's lectures in the early 1930s (as cited in Rymes 1989: 116–20) frequently record him as claiming quite explicitly that the 'chief convention' is an irrational way of forming expectations of future yield.

> In fact investment is carried on by people who kid themselves as to their powers of prophecy. Investors follow a 'social convention' of throwing [forward] present facts and make very exact forecasts into the far future which are very influenced by the present situation. Bryce has it that England has kept up this pretence to some degree while in the U.S.A. it has been pushed to a *reductio ad absurdum*.
>
> (Rymes 1989: 116)

> In Bryce, the valuation [of a capital asset] is influenced by the earlier Q's to an irrational extent. People don't like to guess,

> they just usually assume that the later Q's are like the earlier ones, and hence there are great fluctuations in investment.
>
> (Rymes 1989: 119)

> Fallgatter reports extensively that it is hard to see how any rational man can ever invest, the difficulty of making these estimates is so great. Fortunately, it is the habit of human beings to make guesses on very inadequate evidence. People go right on making these guesses, even though there is no recorded instance of one of them ever being right. Actually, the realized Q's vary widely, and it is the early Q's in the series which exert a wholly irrational influence on investors, especially in the United States, where it has gone so far that railway property is valued on the basis of last week's receipts. The English do not go to this extreme, but they really don't see very far along the series. . . . It is good to get investors to be as far-sighted as possible. If a man buys a capital asset not actually to hold it for its full life and collect the Q's but to sell it to someone else before even perhaps one Q had materialised, then he will estimate not so much its real value but its value according to the convention of valuation. Then you must estimate not what the security is intrinsically worth but what a prospective buyer is likely to take it to be worth according to the convention of valuation which the complex and irrational psychology of speculation induces.
>
> (Rymes 1989: 119–20)

Though irrational, conventional behaviour, as this last note suggests, can be sufficiently orderly to be predictable. If it is, then those investors who possess the reasoning abilities 'required for a valid judgment' (according to Keynes 1971d: 323, 1973a: 150, such individuals constitute a small minority of the participants in stock markets) can engage in rational speculation – meaning by speculation 'the activity of forecasting the psychology of the market' (1973a: 158) – because they can base their investing on understanding 'the complex and irrational psychology' underpinning 'the conventions of valuation' and 'aping unreason proleptically'[25] rather than on 'forecasting the prospective yield of assets over their whole life'. Keynes's discussion (1973a: 152–5) of the continuity and stability of conventional behaviour and of the possibility this creates for rational investment is, therefore, not inconsistent with the premise that conventional behaviour is irrational.[26]

This interpretation of Keynes's treatment of 'the psychological expectation of future yield from capital assets' is also consistent with his discussion of the philosophy of forecasting in his 1938 correspondence with Townshend. He claims there that we very frequently face fundamental uncertainty when attempting to make rational choices 'concerning conduct where consequences enter into the rational calculation'. There are, he claims, 'millions of cases . . . where one cannot even arrange an order of preference. When all is said and done, there is an arbitrary element in the situation' (1979: 289).[27] This point is reiterated in a second letter. (Notice that the motives on which Keynes claims we fall back are said to be decided by, among other things, 'instinct'.[28])

> Generally speaking, in making a decision we have before us a large number of alternatives, none of which is demonstrably more 'rational' than the others, in the sense that we can arrange in order of merit the sum aggregate of the benefits obtainable from the complete consequences of each. To avoid being in the position of Buridan's ass, we fall back, therefore, and necessarily do so, on motives of another kind, which are not 'rational' in the sense of being concerned with the evaluation of consequences, but are decided by habit, instinct, preference, desire, will, etc.
>
> (Keynes 1979: 294)

The frequency theory of probability associated with Whitehead's philosophy of organism explains why knowledge of the probabilities of short-term yields of investments is not relevant to estimating the probabilities of what Keynes calls 'prospective yields' – the yields of investments over their whole life. In this theory, as pointed out above, the statistical basis of probabilities is provided by the truth frequencies characteristic of what Whitehead calls 'real potentiality'. These frequencies will be stable if the factors determining them are stable. Whitehead himself claims, in his discussion of business forecasting (1933: ch. 6) that change has become so ubiquitous and so rapid that this condition is frequently not met.[29] In the case of long-term investment, Keynes claims, as we have seen, that we know from experience that the relevant factors are not stable. For this reason, we know that knowledge of the truth frequencies relevant to estimating the probabilities of short-term yields is not relevant to estimating the probabilities of prospective yields.

Though the conventions do not provide a rational basis for belief and behaviour, Keynes does claim, as we have seen, that their use is necessary. 'The necessity for action and for decision compels us as practical men to overlook this awkward fact' (1973d: 114). 'As living and moving beings, we are forced to act. Peace and comfort of mind require that we should hide from ourselves how little we foresee' (1973d: 124). Just as a conventional or instinctive feeling about money enables the actual possession of money to allay anxiety in some circumstances (namely when the forecasting conventions have weakened), employment of the forecasting conventions also 'lulls our disquietude'. The use of conventions enables individuals to avoid disabling anxiety. Here again, however, as is suggested by the correspondence with Townshend, we are in the realm of belief and behaviour based on 'pure instinct or irrational associations of ideas'.

This is the source of the connection between consciousness of fundamental uncertainty and disabling anxiety. Anxiety is not a rational feeling. In fact, it usually acts as an obstacle to rational belief and behaviour. It has an irrational source. So also do the conventions whose use enables the individual to avoid disabling anxiety (see Winslow 1989b). In the particular case of anxiety about the possibility of losing money, its source is an irrational association between the idea of losing money and a deeper, blinder, more vulgar idea.

SUMMARY AND CONCLUSION

Keynes's view of rationality is rooted in an epistemology. He was a foundationalist who believed that direct acquaintance could provide rational and objective foundations for belief. His beginning view of direct acquaintance was 'empiricist'. Empiricism in this context refers to a particular interpretation of experience rather than to the general claim that experience provides the ultimate grounds for belief. Keynes subsequently abandoned this interpretation of experience for an interpretation which links him to Whitehead and to modern Husserlian phenomenology. Experience interpreted in this new way can provide grounds for adopting an organicist social ontology. This ontology incorporates the notions of internal relations, abstraction, freedom and objective values. It provides a foundation for a changed view of probability, induction and ethics.

Keynes also made significant changes in his psychological beliefs. He came to believe that 'human affairs are carried on after a most irrational fashion'. The irrationality took a particular form in an entrepreneur economy – a form which emphasized 'the money-making and money-loving instincts' – because of the nature of the organic interdependence governing the development of the 'animal spirits' in such an economy. Keynes gives an important role to this irrationality in his accounts of saving, liquidity preference and long-term expectations – the *General Theory*'s 'three fundamental psychological factors'.

NOTES

1 This is not surprising given that Keynes's mature philosophical views have much in common with Husserlian phenomenology, the philosophical tradition from which important aspects of hermeneutics, at least in the form it takes in Gadamer, derive.

2 There have always been important exceptions. George Shackle (1967, 1974) very early on recognized that something was at work in Keynes's economics that could not be handled in standard choice theoretic terms. There is also a growing body of contemporary literature which recognizes that Keynes's economics is not grounded in orthodox premises. Contributors to this literature include: Lawson (1985, 1987, 1988, 1990); O'Donnell (1989); Bensusan-Butt (1978, 1980); Dow (1985); Rotheim (1988); Bateman (1987, 1988); Carabelli (1988); Fitzgibbons (1988); Brown-Collier (1985a, b); Brown-Collier and Bausor (1988); and Mini (1974). Several non-economist readers have also noticed that Keynes employs unorthodox premises: Brown (1985) and Goodman (1969).

3 Leijonhufvud, for example, attempts to rescue Keynes's conclusions from inconsistency with the axiomatic foundations of orthodoxy by supplementing the core of those foundations with auxiliary hypotheses. He adopts this interpretive strategy while admitting that there are passages in which Keynes explicitly claims that the behaviour being analysed is irrational (Leijonhufvud 1968: 193–6, 233).

4 Hahn and Hollis (1979: 3), for example, make the following claim:

> In macro- no less than in micro-economics pure theory rests on propositions about individual action. To generalize, it needs to take the individual agent as typical or representative of others. Generality is achieved by conceiving the individual as a rational economic man and asserting that mankind at large is as rational as he. For instance the analysis of investment, savings and liquidity preference which occupies most of Keynes's *General Theory* takes just this form.

5 These two instances are representative of Keynes's general tendency to use the word 'psychological' to mean 'irrational'. Other examples

are: his claim in *A Treatise on Money* (1971d: 328) that a contractually determined relation between bank rate and the rate clearing banks pay on fixed deposits 'reacts – psychologically, perhaps, rather than rationally – on the rates at which the banks are disposed to lend'; his description (1973a: 58) of the dividing line between supplementary cost and windfall losses as 'partly a conventional or psychological one' and (1973a: 57) of the effect of supplementary cost on consumption as a 'psychological effect', a 'psychological influence' (he claims the cost is typically overestimated because of the capitalist's 'ingrained habits of "prudence" and of preferring the possibility of future benefits to the certainty of present ones' (1981, pt 2: 690; see also 1973a: 100)) and his use (1972a: 353–4) of the term 'psychological reasons' to describe the cause (the mistaken though widespread belief that the interest rate is directly affected by loan-expenditure) which may force governments to reduce loan-expenditure as a 'necessary prelude to a lower long-term rate of interest', a curtailment which, since 'the whole object of the policy is to promote loan-expenditure, we must obviously be careful not to continue . . . a day longer than we need'.

6 Whitehead's relation to Keynes and the similarity of Keynes's mature philosophical views to Whitehead's are examined in greater detail in Winslow (1986a, 1989a).

7 For an account of phenomenology and its results similar in fundamental respects to Whitehead's account of speculative philosophy see Husserl (1970).

8 Paci and others associated with him have themselves pointed to the close correspondence between Whitehead's account of the methods and results of speculative philosophy and Husserl's account of the methods and results of phenomenology. See, for example, Paci (1964).

9 For a more detailed treatment of this see Winslow (1989a).

10 Keynes knew of Whitehead's version. As is well known, *A Treatise on Probability* is based on Keynes's fellowship dissertation for King's College. Whitehead, who with W. E. Johnson had been designated an examiner of the dissertation when it was first presented in December 1907, was critical of, among other things, Keynes's treatment of the frequency theory. Among the amendments incorporated in the second version of the dissertation, the first having failed to win Keynes's election, is an extended discussion of a frequency theory like Whitehead's, a discussion based, according to Keynes (1973b: 110, n. 1), on 'some suggestions in favour of the frequency theory communicated to me by Dr Whitehead'. This discussion was retained in *A Treatise on Probability* (1973b: 109–20). The discussion does not, however, connect Whitehead's version to organicist ontological premises. This connection is made clear in Whitehead's own writings on the topic (1923: 100–11, 1925: ch. 10, 1928, 1929a: 89–90, 199–206), writings designed in part as a response to Keynes's *Treatise* (see Whitehead 1923: 111, 1929a: 206).

11 This is made clear in his obituary for Julian Bell (1972b: 358–60). He locates Bell's motive for participation on the republican side in the Spanish Civil War in a judgment about good states of mind, a

judgment internally connecting an individual state of mind with the state of mind of others. The threat of a fascist victory meant that for Bell the future held no peace 'whenever his imagination had to pass from the specious present to consider it'. His openness to this feeling enabled him to see that there 'might be things which deserved and required a sacrifice', an insight not shared by the early Bloomsbury. For this reason Keynes (contradicting his own early beliefs) claims

> there was no inconsistency, but rather a deep inner consistency, between the inbred nonconformity with the right and duty of fearless individual judgment [the position with which Keynes identified himself early and late] which led him to his first sympathies [beauty (poetry) and love – the sole goods of early Bloomsbury] and that which impelled him past all dissuasions to an ultimate sacrifice *which did not take him by surprise* [my emphasis].

– a sacrifice justified by reasonable 'care about the human race and what happens to it'. Bell was killed by a bomb from an insurgent aeroplane whilst driving his ambulance on the Brunete Front on 18 July 1937.

12 As pointed out above, there is evidence that 'My early beliefs' exaggerates the difference between Keynes's early and mature beliefs. The premise that there is an important element of irrationality in human affairs appears very early in his writing.

13 For a more detailed account of the impact of the change in Keynes's psychological beliefs on his ethical and political beliefs, see Winslow (1990: 804–17).

14 In particular, and contrary to what I claimed in Winslow (1986b), the existence of fundamental uncertainty does not necessitate irrational behaviour. Where no rational basis exists for ranking alternative courses of action, it is rational, according to Keynes, to choose capriciously. I am indebted to Meeks (1981), Lawson (1985) and O'Donnell (1989) for this point.

15 I owe this reference to Fishburn (1983) as cited in O'Donnell (1989: 341).

16 On old skins in Keynes's writing, see 1971c: xviii.

17 Notes taken by students in Keynes's lectures in the early 1930s (Rymes 1989: 173–4) have him associating the miserly attitude of the state to public expenditures with puritanism and a 'pecuniary psychology'. He claimed one of the important factors preventing England from reaching full employment was the

> still strong Puritan thinking towards grandiose expenditures. There have been historical forms of extravagance but in England, given Gladstonian finance, they have lost their virtue. [Investment in] the great civic buildings of antiquity represented a high proportion of income. The readiness of the Egyptians to build pyramids, and so forth, was a great help to maintaining employment. We have cut off some grand possibilities with our pecuniary psychology. In some modern states, this Puritanism is disappearing: witness the grandiosity of Russia, Germany and Italy.

> Before we shall escape from our Puritanism we shall have to have a new economic theory.

In the original galleys (1973c: 238) of his reply to Dennis Robertson's 1931 review of *A Treatise on Money*, Keynes called the policy of using high interest rates to bring a boom to a premature end 'sadistic puritanism' and claimed that to understand it we would have to have recourse to psycho- rather than economic analysis (see also 1973a: 326–9). In the *Treatise* (1971c: 246) he appears to locate the motivation behind the policy in an unconscious need for punishment arising out of 'suppressed reactions against the distastefulness of capitalism'. This would explain the 'gloomy satisfaction' those responsible for the policy ('puritans of finance – sometimes extreme individualists') get from its painful consequences.

18 Motivation, as Keynes represents it, involves a mix of rational and irrational elements. The *General Theory* account of the subjective factors behind saving and consumption, for example, points to rational as well as irrational factors.

19 In student lecture notes from the Michaelmas Term 1934 the second motive listed here is described as 'to satisfy instinct of pure miserliness – avarice' (Rymes 1989: 147).

20 The nature of this irrationality is more fully discussed in Winslow (1986b: 571–6).

21 On this see Winslow (1989a).

22 This contrasts with the context of short-term expectation formation. Here 'the circumstances usually continue substantially unchanged from one day to the next. Accordingly it is sensible for producers to base their expectations on the assumption that the most recently realised results will continue, except in so far as there are definite reasons for expecting a change' (1973a: 51; see also 1971c: 144–5). Meltzer (1989: 13–14, 68), in attempting to use this account of short-term expectations as part of the foundation for his claim that Keynes holds expectations in general to be rational, overlooks both this contrast between short- and long-term expectations and Keynes's claim in the *Treatise on Money* that

> in fact [short-term] forecasting is certain to be imperfect, and likely, moreover, in the present state of ignorance, to have a bias in one direction. For, with the existing mentality of entrepreneurs, to-day's spot price for finished goods, which is certain, has far more influence in determining entrepreneurs' decisions as to the rate of new input into the machine of process than the prospective price at the end of the production-time, which is to them quite uncertain; whereas it is wholly the latter price and not at all the former which ought to influence them.
>
> (Keynes 1971c: 363–4)

23 Meltzer (1988: 145) cites part of this passage in support of his claim that Keynes regards expectations as rational. 'Keynes anticipates the rational expectationists in his discussion of changes in short- but not

long-term values. He remarks that "the existing market valuation, however arrived at, is uniquely *correct* in relation to our existing knowledge of the facts".' What Keynes actually says, of course, is that people *mistakenly assume* that 'the existing market valuation . . . '.

24 Lawson (1990: 23) claims the statements made use of here 'refer to the convention in question only in the context of forecasting population change'. In fact, the discussion in which the statements are found is a discussion of forecasting in general, a discussion which reiterates the claims made in the *General Theory* and in the *Quarterly Journal of Economics* article. Population forecasting is marked off from forecasting in general by the fact that whereas 'generally speaking our imagination and our knowledge are too weak to tell us what particular changes to expect' in the case of population forecasting 'we do have good reason to expect a definite change'. In both cases: 'we assume, contrary to all likelihood, that the future will resemble the past'; 'we assume the future to be much more like the past than is reasonable'.

25 'The professional investor is forced to concern himself with the anticipation of impending changes, in the news or in the atmosphere, of the kind by which experience shows the mass psychology of the market is most influenced' (1973a: 155).

26 It is sometimes argued that Keynes's claim in the *General Theory* that 'we must not conclude from this [the role of animal spirits] that everything depends on waves of irrational psychology' demonstrates that he did not assume the existence of 'permanently unreasoning psychological forces' (Meeks 1981: 16; Meltzer 1988: 282; O'Donnell 1989: 261). Keynes's precise claim, however, is that everything does not depend on '*waves* of irrational psychology' [my emphasis]. Expectations can be *stable* even though they depend on permanently unreasoning psychological forces. In fact, on a psychoanalytic interpretation it is a characteristic of the irrational psychology Keynes attributes to business men that sharp cyclical swings, 'waves', of irrational optimism and pessimism will be separated by long periods of stable, even though irrational, expectations. The anal-sadistic origin of this psychology combined with the impact of the formation and break down of psychological groups imparts to business mass psychology elements of manic-depression. This connection is developed in the work of Karl Abraham (1927), a psychoanalyst with close connections to the members of Bloomsbury. Many of the psychological characteristics which Keynes associates with the boom, collapse and depression phases of the trade cycle correspond to the psychological characteristics of the cycle of mania and depression that characterizes manic-depressive illness (see Winslow 1989b). For example, Abraham (1927: 148) provides an explanation of what Keynes calls 'psychological' poverty in these terms. In the illness as in the economy such cycles are interrupted by fairly long 'free intervals'.

27 This repeats the language of *A Treatise on Probability* respecting situations of fundamental uncertainty.

Is our expectation of rain, when we start out for a walk, always *more* likely than not, or *less* likely than not, or *as* likely as not? I am prepared to argue that on some occasions *none* of these alternatives hold, and that it will be an arbitrary matter to decide for or against the umbrella.

(Keynes 1973b: 32)

28 In claiming that the 'motives of another kind' on which we fall back in the face of fundamental uncertainty 'are not "rational" in the sense of being concerned with the evaluation of consequences', Keynes is not excluding rational motives. In this situation rationality consists of allowing 'caprice to determine us'. The conventions, however, have the individual ignore the awkward fact of fundamental uncertainty, i.e. the conventions assume it is possible to reach decisions by means of an evaluation of consequences.

29 Our sociological theories, our political philosophy, our practical maxims of business, our political economy, and our doctrines of education, are derived from an unbroken tradition of great thinkers and of practical examples, from the age of Plato in the fifth century before Christ to the end of the last century. The whole of this tradition is warped by the vicious assumption that each generation will substantially live amid the conditions governing the lives of its fathers and will transmit those conditions to mould with equal force the lives of its children. We are living in the first period of human history for which this assumption is false. . . . Our traditional doctrines of sociology, of political philosophy, of the practical conduct of large business, and of political economy are largely warped and vitiated by the implicit assumption of a stable unchanging social system. . . . In the present age, the element of novelty which life affords is too prominent to be omitted from our calculations. A deeper knowledge of the varieties of human nature is required to determine the reaction, in its character and strength, to those elements of novelty which each decade of years introduces into social life. . . . We are faced with a fluid, shifting situation in the immediate future. Rigid maxims, a rule-of-thumb routine, and caste-iron particular doctrines will spell ruin. The business of the future must be controlled by a somewhat different type of men to that of previous centuries.

(Whitehead 1933: 92–7)

REFERENCES

Abraham, K. (1927) *Selected Papers on Psychoanalysis*, London: Hogarth Press.

Bateman, B. W. (1987) 'Keynes's changing conception of probability', *Economics and Philosophy* 3: 97–119.

—— (1988) 'G. E. Moore and J. M. Keynes: a missing chapter in the history of the expected utility model', *American Economic Review* 78: 1098–106.

Bensusan-Butt, D. M. (1978) *On Economic Man*, Canberra: Australian National University Press.

—— (1980) *On Economic Knowledge*, Canberra: Australian National University Press.

Brown, N. O. (1985) *Life Against Death: The Psychoanalytic Meaning of History*, Middletown, Conn.: Wesleyan University Press.

Brown-Collier, E. K. (1985a) 'Keynes' view of an organic universe: the implications', *Review of Social Economy* 43: 14–23.

—— (1985b) 'Methodology and the practice of economics: a critique of Patinkin's interpretation of Keynes', *Eastern Economic Journal* 11: 373–83.

Brown-Collier, E. K. and Bausor, R. (1988) 'The epistemological foundations of *The General Theory*', *Scottish Journal of Political Economy* 35: 227–41.

Carabelli, A. M. (1988) *On Keynes' Method*, London: Macmillan.

Dow, S. (1985) *Macroeconomic Thought, A Methodological Approach*, Oxford: Basil Blackwell.

Fishburn, G. (1983) 'Keynes and the age of eugenics', *The Age Monthly Review* 3.

Fitzgibbons, A. (1988) *Keynes's Vision: A New Political Economy*, Oxford: Clarendon Press.

Gadamer, H. G. (1989) *Truth and Method* (2nd edn), New York: Crossroad.

Goodman, G. J. W. (1969) *The Money Game*, New York: Dell.

Hahn, F. H. and Hollis, M. (1979) *Philosophy and Economic Theory*, Oxford: Oxford University Press.

Husserl, E. (1970) *The Crisis of the European Sciences and Transcendental Phenomenology*, Evanston: Northwestern University Press.

Keynes, J. M. (1946) 'Open remarks: the Galton lecture, 1946', *The Eugenics Review* 38: 39–40.

—— (1971a) *The Collected Writings of John Maynard Keynes*, Donald Moggridge (ed.), vol. 1, *The Economic Consequences of the Peace*, London: Macmillan for the Royal Economic Society.

—— (1971b) *Collected Writings*, vol. IV, *A Tract on Monetary Reform*, London: Macmillan.

—— (1971c) *Collected Writings*, vol. V, *A Treatise on Money: The Pure Theory of Money*, London: Macmillan.

—— (1971d) *Collected Writings*, vol. VI, *A Treatise on Money: The Applied Theory of Money*, London: Macmillan.

—— (1971e) *Collected Writings*, vol. XV, *Activities 1906–1914: India and Cambridge*, London: Macmillan.

—— (1972a) *Collected Writings*, vol. IX, *Essays in Persuasion*, London: Macmillan.

—— (1972b) *Collected Writings*, vol. X, *Essays in Biography*, London: Macmillan.

—— (1973a) *Collected Writings*, vol. VII, *The General Theory of Employment, Interest and Money*, London: Macmillan.

—— (1973b) *Collected Writings*, vol. VIII, *A Treatise on Probability*, London: Macmillan.

—— (1973c) *Collected Writings*, vol. XIII, *The General Theory and After: Preparation*, London: Macmillan.

—— (1973d) *Collected Writings*, vol. XIV, *The General Theory and After: Defence and Development*, London: Macmillan.
—— (1979) *Collected Writings*, vol. XXIX, *The General Theory and After: A Supplement*, London: Macmillan.
—— (1981) *Collected Writings*, vol. XIX, *Activities 1922–9: 2 Vols, The Return to Gold and Industrial Policy, I and II*, London: Macmillan.
Kosik, K. (1976) *Dialects of the Concrete*, Holland: Reidel.
Kregel, J. A. (1987) 'Rational spirits and the post Keynesian macrotheory of microeconomics', *De Economist* 135: 520–32.
Lawson, T. (1985) 'Uncertainty and economic analysis', *Economic Journal* 95: 909–27.
—— (1987) 'The relative/absolute nature of knowledge and economic analysis', *Economic Journal* 97: 951–70.
—— (1988) 'Probability and uncertainty in economic analysis', *Journal of Post-Keynesian Economics* 11: 38–65.
—— (1990) 'Keynes and the analysis of rational behaviour', paper presented at the Ninth Keynes Seminar at the University of Kent, Canterbury.
Leijonhufvud, A. (1968) *On Keynesian Economics and the Economics of Keynes, A Study in Monetary Theory*, Oxford: Oxford University Press.
McCloskey, D. (1985) *The Rhetoric of Economics*, Madison: University of Wisconsin Press.
Meeks, J. G. (1981) 'Keynes on the rationality of the investment decision under uncertainty', unpublished mimeo.
Meltzer, A. H. (1988) *Keynes's Monetary Theory: A Different Interpretation*, Cambridge: Cambridge University Press.
Mini, P. V. (1974) *Philosophy and Economics*, Florida: University Press of Florida.
Moore, G. E. (1903) *Principia Ethica*, Cambridge: Cambridge University Press.
O'Donnell, R. M. (1989) *Keynes: Philosophy, Economics and Politics*, London: Macmillan.
Paci, E. (1964) 'Whitehead e Husserl', *Aut Aut* 7–18.
—— (1972) *The Function of the Sciences and the Meaning of Man*, Evanston: Northwestern University Press.
Ramsey, F. P. (1965) *The Foundations of Mathematics*, Totowa, New Jersey: Littlefield, Adams & Co.
Rotheim, R. (1988) 'Keynes and the language of probability and uncertainty', *Journal of Post-Keynesian Economics* 11: 82–9.
Rymes, T. K. (1989) *Keynes Lectures, 1932–35: Notes of a Representative Student*, Ann Arbor: University of Michigan Press.
Shackle, G. L. S. (1967) *The Years of High Theory*, Cambridge: Cambridge University Press.
—— (1974) *Keynesian Kaleidics*, Edinburgh: Edinburgh University Press.
Whitehead, A. N. (1923) 'Uniformity and contingency', in *Essays in Science and Philosophy*, New York: Philosophical Library, 1948.
—— (1925) *Science and the Modern World*, New York: Free Press, 1967.
—— (1928) *Symbolism: Its Meaning and Effect*, Cambridge: Cambridge University Press.

—— (1929a) *Process and Reality*, New York: Free Press, 1978.
—— (1929b) *The Function of Reason*, Boston: Beacon Press, 1958.
—— (1929c) *The Aims of Education*, New York: Free Press, 1967.
—— (1933) *Adventures of Ideas*, New York: Free Press, 1967.
—— (1938) *Modes of Thought*, New York: Free Press, 1968.
Winslow, E. G. (1986a) '"Human logic" and Keynes's economics', *Eastern Economic Journal* 12: 413–30.
—— (1986b) 'Keynes and Freud: psychoanalysis and Keynes's account of the animal spirits of capitalism', *Social Research* 53: 549–78.
—— (1989a) 'Organic interdependence, uncertainty and economic analysis', *Economic Journal* 99: 1173–82.
—— (1989b) 'Psychoanalysis and Keynes's account of the psychological characteristics of the trade cycle', unpublished mimeo.
—— (1990) 'Bloomsbury, Freud, and the vulgar passions', *Social Research* 57: 785–819.

8

PUBLIC CHOICE, STABILITY AND SOCIAL RATIONALITY

David Mayston

INTRODUCTION

The discussion of rationality at the level of individual behaviour is the subject matter of most of this volume. However, in the real world many decisions and choices are made at a more collective level, involving choices by committees, electorates, parliaments, government departments and public authorities. How important is the concept of rationality in this wider context, and how can we ensure properties of rationality in such public decision-making, if indeed it is desirable to achieve these properties? It is these two questions which will be the subject of the present chapter.

RATIONALITY IN PUBLIC CHOICE

A key reason for being concerned with the issue of rationality at the social level is that its existence is by no means guaranteed, even if we assume rational behaviour by all individuals in the society. The interpretation of rationality here is by reference to whether there exists a well-behaved preference ordering for the society for the alternatives between which it may have to choose. Since our analysis is quite general, we will denote these alternatives as simply x, y, z, etc., although in practice x, y and z may be Presidential candidates, allocations of government resources, or any other alternatives between which the society may have to choose.

We may define a preference ordering over a set S of alternatives as the satisfaction of the following three properties for the binary preference relation R, where xRy denotes that 'x is considered at least as good as y'.

a. *Completeness*: For every pair x, y of alternatives in S (for $x \neq y$), either xRy or yRx or both.

This axiom requires that the decision-maker can make up his or her mind about the nature of his or her preference between any given pair of alternatives in S. The permitted case of both xRy and yRx can be interpreted as indifference between x and y (denoted xIy), rather than a failure to formulate a preference relationship between the two. The case of xRy and not yRx implies that x is strictly preferred to y, which we will denote as xPy.

b. *Reflexivity*: For every alternative x in S, xRx.

This axiom simply requires that each alternative is considered at least as good as itself.

c. *Transitivity*: For all x, y, z in S, xRy and yRz implies xRz.

This axiom, in conjunction with the two earlier axioms, implies that the binary preference relations form a ladder-like ranking or 'ordering', where the possibility of indifference between two or more alternatives implies that they may be given the same ranking or rung on the ladder.

However, we may readily show that non-transitive preferences are indeed quite possible once we have preferences and choices being formulated by groups of individuals operating under some form of constitution, such as that of majority rule. In the following example of collective choices, there are three individuals, I, II and III, each with their own 'rational' individual preference ordering.

Table 8.1 Non-transitivity in collective choice

		Individual		
		I	II	III
Preference ranking	1st	x	y	z
	2nd	y	z	x
	3rd	z	x	y

Under piecewise majority voting, individuals I and III strictly prefer x to y, and outvote individual II to give a social preference of xPy. Similarly individuals I and II strictly prefer y to z, and outvote individual III to give a social preference of yPz. However, individuals II and III strictly prefer z to x, and outvote individual I to give a social preference of zPx. The resulting preferences xPy,

yPz and zPx are then intransitive and 'irrational', even though each individual in the society has a 'rational' individual preference ordering and has acted rationally, under the well-defined and much-used social decision rule, of majority voting.

THE SIGNIFICANCE OF SOCIAL IRRATIONALITY

We can identify a number of problems that arise if the above 'rationality' properties of social preferences are not achieved. The first of these is that there may be no clear social choice from amongst the set of alternatives S being considered that can defeat all others in the set. If we extend the notion of 'defeat' here to include that of social indifference, this is equivalent to the 'social choice set', $C(S)$, being empty. $C(S)$ is defined here as the set of socially most preferred alternatives in S, i.e.

$$C(S) = \{x: x \text{ is in } S \text{ and } xRy \text{ for all } y \text{ in } S\} \tag{1}$$

If $C(S)$ contains a single alternative, it is the uniquely 'best' alternative that is socially strictly preferred to all other alternatives in S. If $C(S)$ contains more than one alternative, they are socially indifferent to each other, and socially strictly preferred to all other alternatives in S, so that there are several socially 'best' alternatives from which to choose.

However, if $C(S)$ is empty, as it is in Table 8.1, there is no clear set of 'best' alternatives, and the process of social choice has not been clearly resolved. Thus in Table 8.1, there exists no majority winner, i.e. an alternative which is capable of defeating all other alternatives in the set of policies being considered. As we note below, each of the policy alternatives x, y and z is capable of being defeated by a majority vote in favour of some other of the remaining two alternatives. The voting process may then be searching for something that does not exist, potentially undermining the electorate's faith in the voting process, but also failing to yield a clear social winner.

A second problem that arises is that of possible instability in the choices made by the society, once we can no longer assume the above properties of social rationality (or close analogues to them, such as the 'quasi-transitivity' property that is equivalent to the transitivity condition c, but with the strict preference relation P replacing the weak preference relation R). Rather than having just three individuals, we may, for example, have three political parties (or other interest groups) with preferences as in the above example. An initial government coalition between parties I and II might then support policy *y*. However any such initial coalition in power would be open to defection by party I breaking away to form a new coalition with party III to pursue policy *x* rather than the policy *y*, since parties I and III both prefer policy *x* to policy *y*.

Yet once in power, party III is open to approaches by party II, since both parties II and III would prefer policy *z* to policy *x*, making the earlier coalition unstable and the new coalition attractive to both parties II and III. Once in power, this coalition can similarly be defeated, by a defection of party II joining with party I to support their more preferred policy *y* rather than *z*. As we have already seen, the coalition of parties I and II pursuing policy *y* is itself in turn open to defeat and instability.

Instability of coalition governments is indeed something we observe quite regularly in countries such as Italy. Aside from the problem of there being no clear socially best alternative, an inability to generate a stable government may have associated with it several substantial side costs. The first of these occurs if there are costs of policy implementation and of changing direction with each change of coalition. Thus a shift in government policy over time under different coalitions of voter support, from a policy of nationalization to one of de-nationalization to one of partial re-nationalization to one of privatization, may incur significant transaction costs and transitional costs of dislocation during managerial reorganizations.

The second form of side cost occurs if the process of social choice is itself not costless. Thus, in other examples, the coalition between the interest groups I and III may only succeed in defeating the interest group II through a war or civil strife, if the option of a democratic simple majority decision at the ballot box or in a parliament is not available. Majority winners here may then relate more to the weight of military power than the counting of votes in a formal election, with the coalition between groups I and III jointly able to exert sufficient combined military power or influence to defeat group II. Again, potential instability, through the shifting of coalitions, and the threat or actuality of war, has indeed been an important feature of the real world, and the international relations scene, for many decades.

A further important feature of international politics and political history is the prevalence over many years, and in many different countries, of dictatorship, either by a single autocratic individual or by a totalitarian single party. The attractions of the imposition of dictatorship, through a military coup or other means of overthrowing or preventing majority rule, can be seen from the position of individual (or interest group) III in the above example. III is initially in coalition with II to implement policy *z*, which is III's most preferred alternative. The threat of defection under majority rule voting of II to join with I would lead to policy *y*, which is III's least preferred outcome. If III has friends in the military, there is a clear temptation to overthrow majority rule to ensure the persistence of III's (and possibly the military's) most cherished policy *z* rather than the policy *y* which III and the military may abhor. Similarly, the threat of instability by the failure to find a stable social choice by more democratic means may itself encourage dictatorship.

A fourth problem which may result from the lack of achievement of the properties of social 'rationality' is that of path dependence of any choice which is made. Thus committees may use various procedural rules which mean that once an alternative has been considered and rejected, it cannot subsequently be reconsidered. This makes the final choice dependent upon the sequence in which the alternatives are considered. Suppose in Table 8.1 that the committee first considers alternatives *x* and *y*. It will choose alternative *x* and reject *y* if the committee either formally uses a majority vote on the issue, or decides according to the weight of the majority support in the discussion of the two policies. Both individuals II and III then have an incentive to raise the possibility of policy *z* and vote in favour of policy *z* rather than policy *x*, making this the final committee choice following the discussion of all three of the possible policies.

However, if the initial discussion had been of the relative merits of policies *x* and *z*, *x* would have been eliminated initially from the discussion because of the majority preferences of individuals II and III for *z* rather than *x*. Individuals I and II then have an incentive to raise and vote for policy *y* rather than policy *z*, making policy *y* the final choice. Conversely if the initial choice had been between *y* and *z*, *z* would have been eliminated and then *y* would have been compared unfavourably with *x*, making *x* thc final choice.

Thus any one of the three alternatives *x*, *y* and *z* could have ended up as the final choice depending on the sequence in which the three alternatives were considered. This then introduces the additional related problem of the possibility of manipulation of the agenda, and the associated sequence in which the alternatives are to be considered, to ensure that the manipulator's own policy preference is chosen.

A sixth problem associated with the possible non-existence of a social preference ordering is that, if such an ordering does not exist, there is no well-behaved objective function for public policy-makers to maximize in their attempts at policy optimization. We could not then bring to bear on policy problems the host of useful operational research and other mathematical tools that now exist for optimization of well-defined objective functions under specified constraints.

Optimal tax policy, as in Diamond and Mirrlees (1971), would then appear to make no sense without some well-defined criterion by which to judge whether society prefers one set of tax policies to another. In general we would still, though, expect policy-makers to search for Paretian efficient policy solutions. By definition, these are ones such that it is impossible to make any one individual in the society better off without making another individual in the society worse off. From Kuhn and Tucker's (1950) Theorems 4 and 5, we can represent the search for such Paretian efficient policies as being equivalent to the constrained maximization of the function

$$\sum_{i} v^i u^i \qquad (2)$$

where the u^i represent ordinal individual utility functions, and the v^i are some set of constant weights on these functions. However, there is no guarantee that we could then integrate the whole series of Paretian efficient policy solutions that are mapped out by varying the v^i weights in equation (2) into a set of non-intersecting indifference maps for society that would enable us to choose between all of these Paretian efficient policy solutions in a consistent way.

A seventh problem associated with the lack of any guarantee of social rationality is that demand estimation becomes more difficult. In the estimation and forecasting of consumer demand, the usefulness of prediction is typically in the context of being able to predict demand for different commodities by large groups of individuals, such as those in a town or whole country. However, the theory of consumer behaviour (see, for example, Deaton and Muellbauer 1980) analyses predominantly consumer demand at the level of a single individual. The standard predictions of consumer theory depend upon the existence of transitive preferences, with well-behaved indifference curves. Without such transitive preferences, the associated 'integrability' conditions for the existence of well-behaved indifference curves will not be satisfied. Without such integrability, the standard result of the symmetry of the matrix of compensated (Slutsky) demand derivatives will not hold. This requires that for all commodities k and j:

$$\frac{\partial x_k^i}{\partial p_j} + x_j^i \frac{\partial x_k^i}{\partial M^i} = \frac{\partial x_j^i}{\partial p_k} + x_k^i \frac{\partial x_j^i}{\partial M^i} \tag{3}$$

where x_k^i is individual i's demand for good k, p_k is commodity k's price and M^i is the individual's income. Such a symmetry yields an important set of restrictions on the consumer's demand equations that significantly reduces the number of parameters to be estimated (see, for example, Court 1967). Thus in the case of the linear expenditure system (see, for example, Deaton and Muellbauer 1980) this restriction enables the number of parameters to be estimated to be reduced from $n(n+1) - 1$ to $2n - 1$, where n is the number of commodities. In the case of simply 20 commodities, this involves a very large reduction from 419 parameters to 39.

Without special restrictions on individual preferences, such as homotheticity and resultant linear Engel curves, the existence of transitive community indifference curves and the associated symmetry of the Slutsky matrix for aggregate demand behaviour will not be guaranteed. We then have no a priori justification for making the above major reduction in the number of parameters facing the econometrician in the empirical estimation of market demand, thereby substantially increasing the difficulties of empirical estimation.

THE PARETO PRINCIPLE

Even aside from problems related to intransitivity of social preferences, there arises the question of whether society is 'rational' enough to choose an alternative x rather than alternative y, when all individuals in the society would prefer x to y. If not, then we might infer that society is not even rational enough to make a choice that is in the best interest of all its members.

In line with both traditional welfare economics and the ethics of democracy, we can define the Pareto principle as being that a unanimous preference in favour of x rather than y by all members of the society (i.e. xP^iy for all i, where P^i denotes individual strict preference) implies that the society prefers x rather than y, that is,

Condition P: If for any pair (x, y) of alternatives in S, xP^iy for all individuals i in the society, then xPy.

In some circumstances, condition P might be regarded of dubious desirability. Thus, if all members of the society are addicted to an activity, such as smoking or taking heroin, that is not conducive to their welfare, it might be considered desirable socially to disregard their preferences. A further possible objection to the Pareto principle occurs under conditions of uncertainty, where the alternatives x and y are risky prospects. It could be argued that many real world choices do indeed involve risky prospects. Choices at political elections are typically not between binding contracts specifying all that will follow from electing one candidate or party rather than another. Instead they are often between incompletely specified promises of uncertain validity about an uncertain future world. As in state preference theory (Hirschleifer 1966), individual preferences then embody within them subjective probabilities as to the different outcomes that each risky prospect, x, might involve. If there were good reasons for believing that all the individuals in society were misinformed about these prospects, there might be a case for overriding these subjective probabilities, and hence not making these individual preferences sovereign in the way the Paretian principle implies.

However, in cases where individuals are regarded as being sufficiently rational and well-informed to be the best judges of their own welfare, we may regard the imposition of the Paretian condition as being desirable. It should be noted here, though, that the Pareto condition is by no means equivalent to the requirement that society should prefer x to y if it is possible for the gainers from the move from y to x to compensate the losers, through a redistribution of income starting at x, as under the Kaldorian compensation test (Kaldor 1939). So long as compensation is not actually paid, the potential Pareto improvement will remain only a potential improvement and distinct from an actual Pareto improvement, such as is required for condition P to apply.

Condition P can itself be regarded as a fairly weak expression of social rationality. If society fails to choose alternative *x* rather than *y* when all its members prefer *x* to *y*, and both alternatives are feasible, then the society itself appears as irrational. However, 'choosing' *x* rather than *y* is itself a rather stronger notion than 'preferring' *x* to *y*, with scope for many a slip between the two. Organizational inefficiency may be one source of such a divergence. Techniques then exist, as in Mayston and Jesson (1988), to show the extent of the feasible across the board Pareto improvement on all relevant desired dimensions of achievement, such as pupil examination results.

An important second source of divergence between social preference and social choice arises if there is no mechanism to enforce the Pareto preference. Again the stability of the social choice is an important consideration. In the classic prisoner's dilemma case each individual player has an incentive to attempt to depart from the alternative *x* that is Pareto preferred to the alternative *y*, such as by engaging in a socially damaging activity that brings them a short-term individual reward. In the example of Table 8.2, the two players are fishing fleets who each have a choice between overfishing the sea to which they both have access, or restricting their level of fishing. The coordinates of the alternative outcomes denote the catch in tons of fleets 1 and 2 respectively.

Table 8.2 The prisoner's dilemma: the case of overfishing

Fleet 2 / Fleet 1	Overfishing	Restricted fishing
Overfishing	$y = (3, 3)$	$z = (5, 1)$
Restricted fishing	$w = (1, 5)$	$x = (4, 4)$

In the absence of enforceable contracts or similar arrangements, each fleet acting alone has an incentive to overfish, since whatever the choice made by the other fleet it achieves a greater catch by overfishing rather than by restricting its fishing activity. The outcome *y* where both overfish, however, is Pareto inferior to alternative *x*, where both sides restrict their fishing. Under alternative *x*, the fish are allowed time to breed, here with a resultant population increase of one-third, permitting a higher long-term sustainable catch.

The achievement of social rationality, in the form of the avoidance of long-term damage to the environment that makes all individuals in the society worse off, then requires more than reliance on individual rationality, if such individual rationality is defined in terms of immediate personal advantage, disregarding the attractions of cooperative behaviour. Rather, social rationality then needs mechanisms of public choice, such as enforceable agreements or a Law of the Sea, that can overcome the instability that otherwise threatens a departure from a Pareto preferred outcome.

THE POSSIBILITY OF RATIONAL SOCIAL CHOICE

Whilst the above problems associated with a lack of social rationality are potentially troublesome, we need to know how widespread they are. Rather than concentrating on the problems of particular social choice mechanisms, such as majority rule, we can now examine the more general notion of a social choice rule. This is defined in the following way:

> A social choice rule is defined as a functional relationship f that determines one and only one social preference relation R when faced with a given set $R^1, \ldots, R^n$ of individual preference orderings.

If we are to avoid the earlier problems associated with intransitivities in the social preferences, we may impose the following condition on our social choice rule:

> *Condition O*: The social choice rule f generates a social ordering over S, i.e. a complete, reflexive and transitive set of binary social preference relations R over S.

If we are to have a social choice rule that can handle any set of individual preferences it may face, we require also the following condition to hold:

> *Condition UD*: The domain of the social choice rule $R = f(R^1, \ldots, R^n)$ shall include all logically possible combinations of individual preference orderings.

A further such condition is that no individual is a dictator, in the sense of being able to pre-empt the social preference as being identical to his or her own, irrespective of the preference of other individuals in society, i.e.

> *Condition ND*: There exists no individual j in society such that for all pairs x, y in S, xP^jy implies xPy.

In addition to the Pareto condition P discussed above, Arrow (1951) also imposed the following condition which he labelled 'independence of irrelevant alternatives':

> *Condition IIA*: The social preference between any pair of alternatives x, y in any subset T of S shall be not change if there is no change in individual preferences between any pair of alternatives in T.

This leads to the following impossibility theorem due to Arrow (1951) which shows that the problem of achieving the properties of social 'rationality' inherent in Condition O is significantly wider than the particular case involved in Fig. 8.1:

> Impossibility theorem: There exists no social choice rule that satisfies Conditions O, UD, P, ND, and IIA.

An important corollary of the theorem is that any social choice rule that satisfies the 'rationality' Condition O, with its guarantee of transitivity and stability, must be dictatorial if we impose also Conditions UD, P and IIA. Is the human race then doomed to a choice between dictatorship and instability, both of which have exacted a very heavy toll on its previous history? How can we escape from this dire conflict?

POLITICS, DICTATORSHIP AND STABILITY

One partial way out of the problem is to relax Condition UD by assuming that individual preferences come from a restricted domain of possible individual preference orderings. One particular case of interest here is that of single-peaked preferences, as in Fig. 8.1. There is a single (quantitative or qualitative) dimension, such as a left-wing to right-wing political spectrum, along which individuals array themselves in terms of their most preferred (or 'individual optimum') policy stance. Single-peakedness requires that the further one moves away from the individual optimum on any one side of the optimum, the less the individual prefers that policy stance. With an odd number of voters, majority voting can

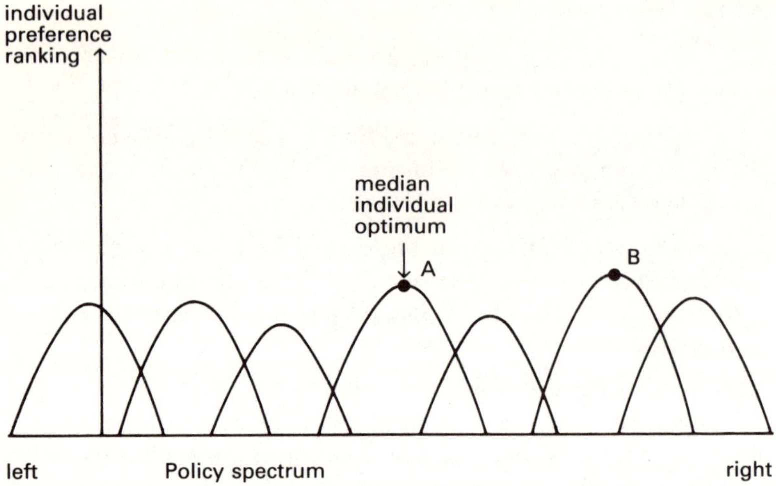

Figure 8.1 Single-peaked preferences

here be shown to lead to a stable outcome, that of the optimum policy stance of the median individual, i.e. the individual who has an equal number of other individuals' optima to either side.

Similarly, under two-party competition for voters' support there is pressure on each party to shift its policy stance to the centre ground defined by the median individual's optimum. So long as at least one party is sufficiently 'spatially mobile' to capture the centre ground in this way, it can secure at least as many votes as its opponent party. Thus if Party I locates at point A, corresponding to the median individual optimum, and Party II locates elsewhere at B, Party I will be the most preferred choice of all four individuals either to the left of, or at, the median individual optimum. Party II will be the most preferred choice of the remaining three individual voters, but will lose the election. A party which fails to appeal to the centre ground risks being usurped in favour of a party with this appeal.

When we turn to the more general case where individual preferences may be over alternatives in a multidimensional policy space, the necessary and sufficient condition for a set of individual preferences to generate a ('rational') social ordering under majority rule voting is that every triple of alternatives must satisfy the following property:

Extremal restrictedness: If xP^iy and yP^iz for some individual i, we require zP^jy and yP^jx whenever zP^jx for any individual j in the society, where (x,y,z) is any ordered triple obtainable from the triple of alternatives.

The definition of necessary here, as in Sen (1970), is that any violation of the condition yields a list of individual orderings such that some assignment of these orderings to the individuals in the society results in a failure to obtain a social ordering under majority rule.

Extremal restrictedness can readily be broken, as can be seen from the following example. Consider a society in which there are two groups of individuals. Group I consists of *centralists*, and Group II consists of *secessionists* who prefer greater freedom from central control. The society faces three key alternatives:

1 Alternative x involves centralized control over the society by the centralists, high prosperity for those in Group I, and medium prosperity for, and no oppression of, those in Group II.
2 Alternative y involves centralized control over those in Group II through oppression by those in Group I, medium prosperity for those in Group I, and low prosperity for those in Group II.
3 Alternative z involves decentralization together with greater prosperity for, and no oppression of, those in Group II, but loss of status and prosperity for those in Group I.

It is quite reasonable to expect that for all individuals in Groups I and II respectively:

$$xP^{I}yP^{I}z \text{ and } zP^{II}xP^{II}y \qquad (4)$$

The preferences involved in (4), however, breach the extremal restrictedness condition. From our above discussion it follows that there is some assignment of individuals in the society to these two groups that makes majority rule fail to achieve a social welfare function with its guarantee of the 'rational' transitivity condition and its associated stability properties.

It is important to note here also, however, that this conclusion has some force even without formal majority rule being embodied in the constitution of the society. If we count individuals not in their natural units but rather according to how much political power each has, whether by formal voting power in key power forums, or through more informal pressure, then by definition the group with the largest political power will win the contest. A similar conclusion follows by substituting the word 'military' for 'political' if it comes down to an armed conflict. The preferences involved in (4) involve both Groups I and II gaining from moving away from the heavy-handed oppressive centralism of alternative y, and towards the 'reformist' alternative x. Over time, the political and economic oppressiveness of the solution y may then give way to the more reformist solution x, as both Groups I and II come to see it in their interest to make this Pareto improvement.

However, the society faces a major conflict between whether or not then to move on to the alternative z involving the break up of the centralist regime. Alternative z is clearly the most preferred alternative of the secessionists of Group II, but the worst outcome for those in Group I. The greater political power of Group II under the less oppressive reforms involved in the move from alternative y to alternative x may cause the social preference zPx to become gradually more likely. In the event of this social choice in favour of alternative z, rather than the new status quo x, being made, or becoming a serious possibility, those in Group I have a strong incentive to seek to revert to alternative y.

If those in Group II are in the numerical majority, or can achieve secession more directly if unchallenged, either majority rule or inaction by those in Group I will lead to Group I's worst outcome z being chosen. In order to avoid this outcome, Group I may seek to impose dictatorship and the enforced imposition of alternative y. The Prague Spring associated with the earlier choice of alternative x would then be short-lived, as the centralist forces of the political society reassert themselves. Only after the elapse of some years may the reformist pressures towards the Pareto-superior alternative x regain force, and the process begin again, either recycling or moving towards alternative z. Over time, however, new empires and centralizing power bases may prove attractive to those in Group I, and a new variant of alternative y be brought to reign by Group I winning ground over those in Group II.

That extremal restrictedness is a strong condition can be seen in Fig. 8.2, in which there is a society of just two individuals, with intersecting indifference curves in the policy space. The condition is satisfied for the triple x,y,z, but not for the triple x,y',z. It can be seen that only weak restrictions on the individual indifference maps will lead to triples such as x,y',z occurring that

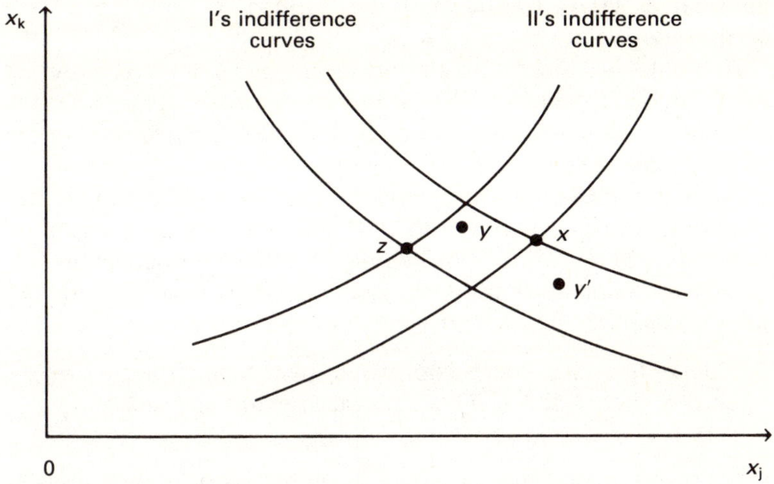

Figure 8.2 Extremal restrictedness

breach the extremal restrictedness condition (see Kramer 1973). Cases will then occur where majority rule fails to generate a ('rational') social ordering.

That individual indifference curves may cross in the space of policy variables is indeed quite likely. As we have seen, single-peakedness guarantees stability of the outcome under majority rule so long as there are two competing parties without ideological constraints that inhibit their spatial mobility across the one-dimensional policy spectrum. However, once there is more than one policy dimension, and individuals differ in their marginal trade-offs between these different dimensions, preferences are no longer single-peaked and the required extremal restrictedness condition, that guarantees stability under majority rule, will be broken.

THE RATIONALITY OF ARROW'S IIA CONDITION

Relaxing the unrestricted domain condition, therefore, does not provide a particularly attractive escape route under majority rule once one moves to a multidimensional policy space. If one wishes to maintain the unrestricted domain condition, together with the Pareto and non-dictatorship conditions, a corollary of Arrow's theorem is that one must relax the independence of irrelevant alternatives (IIA) condition if the 'rationality' properties of a social ordering are to be achieved.

It should be noted that the achievement of a social ordering itself implies a form of 'independence of irrelevant alternatives condition', which can be defined by two conditions involving the social choice set $C(S)$.

As noted above, in the 'irrational' case of socially intransitive preferences resulting from Table 8.1, $C(S)$ may be empty with no 'majority winner' capable of beating all other alternatives in $S = \{x,y,z\}$ under majority rule. We then have the following conditions for $C(.)$ itself to behave 'rationally':

> *Condition I*: The social choice rule over S generates a non-empty choice set $C(T)$ when faced with any non-empty subset T of S.

Condition I thus excludes cases of cyclical preferences, such as may occur under majority rule. In order for the social choice rule to satisfy Condition I when faced with individual transitive preferences it would thus have to be a rule other than that of majority voting.

> *Condition II*: We require that if any given alternative x is in the set T, and T is itself a subset of X, and X is a subset of S, then if x is in the choice set of X, it must also be in the choice set of T.

Condition II implies that if x can beat other alternatives in a choice involving all alternatives in the larger subset X of S, it can also beat the smaller number of alternatives that are in any strict subset T of X. The inclusion of additional 'irrelevant' alternatives that are in the set $X–T$ but not in T does not then cause the alternative x in T to be able to beat, or equal, all other alternatives in T, if it cannot beat, or equal, all of them in a straight fight between alternatives simply in T, with alternatives in $X–T$ excluded.

> *Condition III*: We require that if any two given alternatives x and y are both in $C(T)$ and T is a subset of X, and X is a subset of S, then x is in $C(X)$ if and only if y is in $C(X)$.

This condition requires that the implied indifference between x and y when they are both in $C(T)$ is preserved if either one of them is in the choice set of a larger set X that contains T. Including 'irrelevant' additional alternatives in the set $X–T$ does not then change the implied social indifference that arises if they are both in the choice set over the smaller subset T.

We then have the following result derivable from Sen (1969):

Proposition: A social choice rule satisfies Conditions I, II and III if and only if it satisfies Condition O.

In other words, our additional conditions for the 'rational' behaviour of the social choice set $C(S)$ are automatically satisfied if we do achieve a social ordering over S, and indeed together require that we achieve a social ordering over S. Since Conditions II and III already involve a form of 'independence of irrelevant alternatives' condition, we can see that it is not at all obvious why we should impose Arrow's additional Condition IIA. The above proposition implies that if all we require is Conditions I, II and III, a social ordering over S will be sufficient, without any further requirement for Condition IIA to be imposed as well. Indeed as Arrow's impossibility theorem implies, the additional imposition of Arrow's Condition IIA may actually prevent the attainment of the 'rational' social ordering condition.

One justification for Condition IIA that has been used is that it excludes 'interpersonal comparisons'. This is on the grounds that Condition IIA excludes consideration of individual preference information, other than knowledge of individual preference orderings over S, in order to derive social preferences over S. However, a crucial point here is the source of the interpersonal comparison. Clearly Condition IIA does exclude any 'essentialist' notion that individual preferences are inherently measurable, such as on a classical utilitarian cardinal scale of the degree of pleasure or pain involved. Such a cardinal hedonistic calculus would go beyond the notion of simply an ordinal utility function as simply a numerical representation of the assumed individual preference ordering over S.

However, it is important to note that Condition IIA does not exclude 'interpersonal comparisons' of the form 'one man, one vote'. Majority rule, which incorporates this maxim, does indeed satisfy Condition IIA. It is, moreover, perfectly compatible with Condition IIA to apply the rule of giving Mr Smith one vote, Mr Jones three votes, and Mrs Brown two votes. Condition IIA is not at all the same thing as the anonymity condition described by May (1952) which would require the same number of votes for each person.

Furthermore, Condition IIA does not imply any requirement that any given individual has the same number of votes irrespective of which alternatives are involved in the choice of the particular subset T of S that is being considered. To do so would involve the quite distinct condition of neutrality (May 1952.) It is thus perfectly compatible with Condition IIA to allow Mr Smith one vote, Mr Jones three votes and Mrs Brown two votes, in the choice between x and y, and yet allow Mr Smith four votes, Mr Jones one vote and Mrs Brown two votes, in the choice between x and z. So long as this assignment of votes does not depend on individual preferences beyond their immediate directions of preference between x and y and between x and z respectively, Condition IIA will be satisfied, whether or not the above weighting system is derived from any 'interpersonal comparison' or social view of the relative worth of the three individuals when faced with these different alternatives.

What then is the crucial feature of Condition IIA that causes it to be so destructive of achieving the social 'rationality' properties of Conditions I, II and III, and hence of a social preference ordering? We shall argue that this critical feature of Condition IIA is that it contains a 'virus' associated with a disease that has afflicted large parts of welfare economics, as well as social choice theory, and which was diagnosed in Mayston (1979) as being that of 'quasi-ordinalism'. This involves the neglect of relevant, purely ordinal, features of individual preference orderings. Such a neglect has its origins not only in the work of Arrow (1951) but also in Hicks's (1946) over-reaction in *Value and Capital* to the earlier tradition of utilitarianism, as discussed in Mayston (1974, 1976).

The strength of IIA in excluding even ordinal information about individual preferences can be seen from Fig. 8.3. In a social choice between alternatives x and y, Arrow's IIA condition prevents individual preference information involving the 'irrelevant' alternative z from being taken into account. Yet knowledge of individual preferences involving alternatives such as z is needed to know the individuals' marginal rates of substitution, or 'willingness to pay', for an increase in the policy variable x_k at x compared to a variation in the individual's consumption, x_1^i, of a numeraire good one, both of which change in the move from x to y. Clearly the marginal rate of substitution is a piece of purely ordinal individual preference information, which would be excluded here by imposition of Arrow's IIA condition.

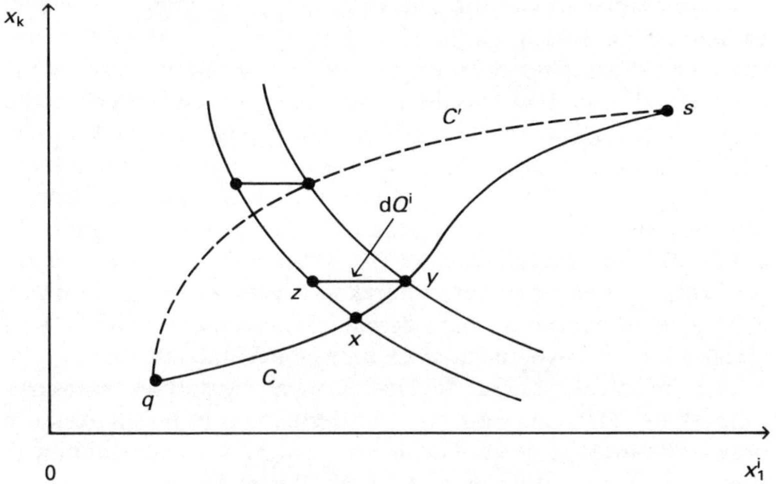

Figure 8.3 Path dependency

However, even if we take into account individual marginal rates of substitution in the social choice, as consumers' surplus measures do, we are still not in general guaranteed a transitive social ordering. The consumers' surplus criterion for determining the social preference between a pair of alternatives, such as s and q, involves

$$sRq \text{ whenever } \triangle CS = \sum_i \triangle CS^i \geqslant 0 \qquad (5)$$

where

$$\triangle CS^i = \int_C dQ^i \text{ where } dQ^i = \sum_k MRS_k^i(x)\, dx_k \qquad (6)$$

where C is a path of integration from s to q, and $MRS_k^i(x)$ is individual i's marginal rate of substitution between the policy variable k and individual i's consumption of a numeraire good one at a typical point x along this path of integration. In geometric terms, as in Fig. 8.3, dQ^i involves the horizontal distance in the direction of the numeraire commodity between point $y = x + dx$ and the point z that differs from y only in the level of this numeraire commodity and is on the same indifference curve for individual i as the point x.

In general the magnitude of dQ^i, and hence of $\triangle CS^i$ will, however, vary according to the precise path of integration C from q to s. A different path of integration, such as path C' in Fig. 8.3, will in general lead to a different value of dQ^i, and hence of $\triangle CS^i$, for a movement between the same pair of individual indifference curves as those passing through x and y. When we have some gainers and some losers in the move from q to s, (5) involves the sum of positive and negative values to the individual $\triangle CS^i$ terms, whose individual magnitudes now vary with the path of integration taken by q and s. The overall sign of the social gain $\triangle CS$ from q to s may also then vary according to which path of integration is taken. The social preference in (5) will then be dependent upon the arbitrary path of integration taken between q and s, in a way analogous to our earlier path dependency problems, with lack of integrability of a well-defined social welfare function.

This problem affects not just consumer surplus measures (Silberberg 1972) but also any social choice rule that makes use only of knowledge of individual marginal rates of substitution in the social choice between points such as x and $x + dx$ along any path of integration C between alternatives such as q and s (Inada 1964). In addition, related impossibility theorems (Kemp and Ng 1976; Parks 1976), using conditions similar to Arrow's IIA condition, can be established for the wider concept of a Bergson–Samuelson social welfare function, $W(x)$, where:

$$sRq \text{ iff } W(s) \geq W(q) \text{ with } W(.) = F[u^1(.),\ldots, u^n(.)] \qquad (7)$$

where u^i denotes individual i's ordinal utility function, i.e. a numerical representation of individual i's preference ordering such that:

$$u^i(x) \geq u^i(y) \text{ iff } xR^iy \text{ for all } x, y \text{ in } S \qquad (8)$$

where S is the set of alternatives that might be considered, and R^i denotes weak individual preference for individual i.

THE MARGINAL RATE OF EQUIVALENCE

One of the main symptoms of the disease we have described above as 'quasi-ordinalism' is a belief which Hicks (1946) helped to promote in *Value and Capital*. This is that the only ratios of marginal utilities which are measurable under ordinal individual preferences are those evaluated at the same point, i.e. marginal rates of substitution between different commodities or between different policy variables.

However, such a belief can readily be shown to be misguided,

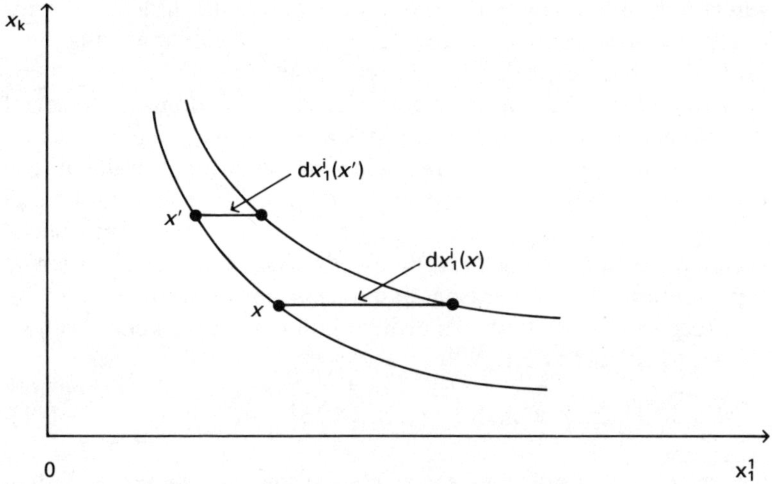

Figure 8.4 Ordinal individual preferences

as demonstrated in Mayston (1976). Rather the existence of ordinal individual preferences that are representable by a (differentiable) ordinal utility function implies an ability to compare the marginal utilities to the individual of any two policy variables *at any two points on the same individual indifference surface*. In particular, the following ratio, of the marginal utilities u^i_1 of individual i's consumption of a numeraire commodity one, evaluated at any two points x and x', on the same individual indifference surface is a purely ordinal, measurable feature of the individual's ordinal preferences:

$$\frac{u^i_1(x)}{u^i_1(x')} = \frac{dx^i_1(x')}{dx^i_1(x)} = \text{MRE}^i(x,x') \tag{9}$$

where the marginal rate of equivalence, MRE^i, between the indifferent points x and x' is defined as the value of the increase in the numeraire commodity one at point x' that makes individual i just as well off as does a small unit increase in the numeraire commodity at point x, as in Fig. 8.4.

We may readily show that

$$\text{MRE}^i(x,x') = \exp\left[\int_{C''} \sum_k \frac{\partial \text{MRS}^i_k . dx^k}{\partial x^i_1} \right] \tag{10}$$

where C'' is any path of integration along the individual's indifference surface from x to x', with (10) again involving only ordinal individual preference information.

Ordinality of individual preferences gives freedom to the social choice mechanism to place any positive relative weight, such as w^i, on each individual i receiving an additional unit of the numeraire commodity along any one path Z^i across individual indifference surfaces. However, once having made this initial social weighting, the achievement of a 'rational' social ordering representable by a Bergson–Samuelson social welfare function that respects the individual's ordinal individual preferences can be shown to require that:

$$sRq \text{ iff } \int_C \sum_i \sum_k w^i.\mathrm{MRE}^i(x,x').\ \mathrm{MRS}^i_k.\ \mathrm{d}x_k \quad (11)$$

where x' lies along the path Z^i and on the same individual indifference surface as x, and C is any path of integration from q to s. Expression (11) can also be shown to be sufficient for the generation of a Bergson–Samuelson welfare function of the form (7), as in Mayston (1982). Using equation (10), the necessary and sufficient integrability conditions for (10) to be independent of the path of integration C can be shown to be equivalent to the requirement that for all policy variables k and j:

$$\left[\frac{\partial \mathrm{MRS}^i_k}{\partial x_j} - \mathrm{MRS}^i_j.\frac{\partial \mathrm{MRS}^i_k}{\partial x^i_1}\right] \quad (12)$$

is symmetric in k and j. Symmetry of these compensated individual derivatives of marginal rates of substitution is itself guaranteed by the assumption of 'rational' individual preference ordering, representable by individual ordinal utility functions u^i.

In other words, *individual rationality guarantees social rationality so long as we take into account not only individual marginal rates of substitution in (11) but also individual marginal rates of equivalence.*

Imposition of Arrow's IIA condition would prevent us from taking into account this additional relevant ordinal individual preference information, since $\mathrm{MRE}^i(x,x')$ in (11) involves individual preference information not just about alternatives x and $x +$ dx along the path of integration C between q and s. Rather it also involves individual preference information involving x' along a path Z^i across the individual's indifference map, about which social choices have already been made, through the specification of the relative social weights w^i.

The problem of social irrationality under voting and other social choice mechanisms satisfying Arrow's IIA condition then results here from permitting too many independent social choices, in contradiction of one another. Once we have already made a social choice between an alternative, such as x and z in Fig. 8.2, involving crossing the individual curves between which the third alternative y' lies, we are not free then to determine the social choice between z and y' in a way that fails to take into account both this earlier social choice and individual preference involving these earlier 'irrelevant' alternatives x and z, if we want to achieve a well-behaved social ordering. To make independent social choices in this way involves a lack of a 'memory' in the social choice rule. Lack of an effective memory directly contributes to unstable and related forms of 'irrational' behaviour in the choices being made.

In contrast, if we are to achieve a 'rational' social welfare function satisfying conditions P and ND, an initial social preference such as zIx must then predetermine our social preferences between z and alternatives such as y' in Fig. 8.2. Alternative y' lies here between the individual indifference curves through x and z for individual II, with xPy' under the Pareto principle. We can then distinguish, as in Mayston (1977), between an initial 'basic' set of social choices which we are free to determine, and those social choices which must depend upon this initial basic set. Our initial 'basic' social choices must involve choices between alternatives in successive individual indifference classes, as in Mayston (1977), and satisfying the above extremal restrictedness condition. In equation (11), this is equivalent to the initial determination of the relative weights w^i on each individual's preferences across a path Z^i across each individual's indifference surfaces.

Once this basic set of social choices has been determined, all other social choices must depend upon those social preferences that are in the basic set and upon 'relevant' individual preference information involving both the new alternatives being considered and those that are involved in the basic set. This is indeed achieved in equation (11) through use of the same set of relative social weights, w^i in social choices involving x, $x + dx$, q and s outside the basic set, as were previously used in the social choices for alternatives along the paths Z^i across individual indifference surfaces. In addition, it is achieved through the use of the now relevant concept of the marginal rate of equivalence involving individual preferences, between alternatives such as x', that are in the basic set.

To refuse to make use of this additional relevant ordinal individual preference information, as Arrow's IIA condition would have us do, is again to succumb to the disease of 'quasi-ordinalism' that acts like a virus destroying the memory of the social choice mechanism. Senile, 'irrational' and unstable behaviour then results from the social choice mechanism, leaving it open to a dictator to take the patient into care under an enforced regime of his own making.

CONCLUSION

We have identified above a large number of reasons why failing to achieve the rationality properties of a social ordering can cause significant difficulties in social decision-making. We have also noted an important inter-relationship between rationality, stability and the threat of dictatorship in the social choices. So long as one makes use of a social decision rule, like majority rule, that satisfies Arrow's IIA condition, such problems will arise whenever one departs from the world of single-peaked individual preferences over a unidimensional policy variable and instead encounters individual indifference curves that cross in multidimensional policy space.

Rational non-dictatorial social choices are then possible in this more realistic multidimensional world, but only if we turn our backs on Arrow's IIA condition by recognizing the real requirements for rational social choices that respect individual ordinal preferences. These are first that we abandon the view that we can make social choices between all pairs of alternatives independently of each other. Instead we must restrict our independent formulations of social preferences to a 'basic set' involving pairs of alternatives lying on *successive individual indifference surfaces in this multidimensional policy space*. Social preferences between all other pairs of alternatives must in general then depend on this basic set of social preferences, and upon additional relevant ordinal individual preference information, such as that involved in our above concept of the marginal rate of equivalence.

The fact that many real world voting processes fail to achieve these requirements for social rationality is a reflection upon political decision-making as a means of formulating social preferences. It is not an argument for allowing the same virus of 'quasi-ordinalism' to infect welfare economics in the way it has done since the original contributions of Hicks (1946) and Arrow (1951). As noted in Mayston (1974), Hicks's *Value and Capital* starts with a quotation from Milton's *Paradise Lost*: 'Reason also is choice.' The issue of social and individual rationality, however, hinges on the opposite question: 'Is choice also reason?' The fall from Paradise of welfare economics, with its sick ward of infected analytical constructs, such as compensation tests and consumer surplus, stems directly from neglect of those variations in the marginal utility of income of a numeraire commodity that we are able to measure under ordinal individual preferences, i.e. those embodied in our above concept of the marginal rate of equivalence. The path back to social rationality then requires a full recognition of the properties which individual rationality, and the existence of an integrable individual ordinal utility function, imply. This is that of the existence of a suitable integrating factor for individual preferences, such as is provided by the marginal rate of equivalence. Social and individual rationality then go hand in hand, but only if we restore the hand which a previous generation of economic theorists has, in effect, been busy attempting to amputate.

REFERENCES

Arrow, K. J. (1951) *Social Choice and Individual Values*, New York: John Wiley & Sons.

Court, R. (1967) 'Utility maximisation and the demand for New Zealand meats', *Econometrica* 35: 424–46.

Deaton, A. and Muellbauer, J. (1980) *Economics and Consumer Behaviour*, Cambridge: Cambridge University Press.

Diamond, P. A. and Mirrlees, J. A. (1971) 'Optimal taxation and public production I: production efficiency; II: tax rules', *American Economic Review* 61: 8–27, 261–78.

Hicks, J. R. (1946) *Value and Capital* (2nd edn), Oxford: Clarendon Press.

Hirschleifer, J. (1966) 'Investment decision under uncertainty: applications of the state preference approach', *Quarterly Journal of Economics* 80: 252–77.

Inada, K. (1964) 'On the economic welfare function', *Econometrica* 22: 316–38.

Kaldor, N. (1939) 'Welfare propositions in economics', *Economic Journal* 49: 549–52.

Kemp, M. and Ng, K. (1976) 'On the existence of social welfare functions, social orderings and social decision functions', *Economica* 43: 59–66.

Kramer, G. H. (1973) 'On a class of equilibrium conditions for majority rule', *Econometrica* 41: 285–97.

Kuhn, H. W. and Tucker, A. W. (1950) 'Non-linear programming', in J. Neyman (ed.) *Proceedings of the Second Berkeley Symposium on Mathematical Statistics and Probability*, Berkeley: University of California Press.

May, K. O. (1952) 'A set of independent, necessary and sufficient conditions for simple majority decision', *Econometrica* 20: 680–4.

Mayston, D. J. (1974) *The Idea of Social Choice*, London: Macmillan.

—— (1976) 'On the nature of marginal utility – a neo-Marshallian theory of demand', *Economic Journal* 86: 493–507.

—— (1977) 'On achieving consistent social choices', *University of Western Ontario Research Report*, 76–22.

—— (1979) 'Where did prescriptive welfare economics go wrong?', in D. Currie and W. Peters (eds) *Essays in Economic Analysis*, London: Croom Helm.

—— (1982) 'The generation of a social welfare function under ordinal preferences', *Mathematical Social Sciences* 3: 109–29.

Mayston, D. J. and Jesson, D. (1988) 'Developing models of educational accountability', *Oxford Review of Education* 14: 321–40.

Parks, R. P. (1976) 'An impossibility theorem for fixed preferences', *Review of Economic Studies* 43: 447–50.

Sen, A. K. (1969) 'Quasi-transitivity, rational choice and collective decisions', *Review of Economic Studies* 36: 381–94.

—— (1970) *Collective Choice and Social Welfare*, San Francisco: Holden-Day.

Silberberg, E. (1972) 'Duality and the many consumer's surpluses', *American Economic Review* 62: 942–52.

9

DISPARITIES BETWEEN HEALTH STATE MEASURES[1]

Is there a rational explanation?

Graham Loomes

INTRODUCTION

The focus of this paper is upon three methods which have been used to elicit health state utilities for the purpose of incorporating them into economic appraisals of health care programmes. Torrance (1986: 18–24) provides a detailed description of each method, which will be summarized only briefly here.

Category rating/visual analogue scales are variants on the idea of taking a straight line to represent some spectrum of health, with one end representing the worst outcome under consideration (often, but not necessarily, death) while the other end represents the best outcome (usually 'normal good health'). These end-points may be assigned convenient numbers, e.g. 0 and 1, respectively. Individuals are then asked to locate intermediate health states H_i on this scale so as to convey their evaluation of each health state relative to the two polar states and to each other, with distances between points on the scale reflecting an individual's preferences between the various health states, in the sense that if H_2 is placed midway between H_1 and H_3 it reflects the respondent's judgment that the difference between being in state H_1 and being in state H_2 is the same as the difference between being in H_2 and being in H_3.

Standard gambles also identify two end-point states (as above, these are often, but not always, death and normal good health). Individuals are then asked to consider a choice between:

(a) the certainty of an intermediate health state H_i for t years; or
(b) undertaking a risky treatment, offering a probability p of

raising the individual's health to the better end-point state for the following t years, but also involving a probability $1 - p$ that the individual's health will fall to the lower end-point state.

Individuals are asked to state the value of p that would make them indifferent between (a) and (b). If the end-point states are assigned values of 1 and 0, the indifference value of p may be taken as an individual's index of preference for H_i. If an individual's preferences are consistent with the axioms of von Neumann–Morgenstern expected utility theory, it is widely expected that standard gambles and visual analogue methods will tend to generate the same interval scales for any given set of health states.

Time trade-offs present individuals with a different form of choice problem. Here the alternatives are:

(a) living in intermediate state H_i for t years, followed by death; or
(b) living in normal good health for x years (where $x < t$), followed by death.

If x_i is the value of x which produces indifference between (a) and (b), then x_i/t is taken as the measure of preference for H_i. If an individual's preferences obey the von Neumann–Morgenstern axioms and if that individual regards any one year of life in a particular health state as being of equal value to any other year of life in the same state, then it may be hoped that time trade-offs will produce the same interval scale as standard gambles or rating methods.

However, several studies concerned with measuring the utilities of a variety of health states have reported evidence which suggests that the different methods of eliciting those indices may produce systematically different results.

For example, Torrance (1976) plotted the mean values obtained from a category rating technique against the mean values for the same health states elicited from the same people using his time trade-off method. He concluded that 'although not equivalent, the two techniques exhibit a systematic relationship . . . (that) can be approximated by a number of different functions. Two that fit well . . . are a logarithmic function and a power function' (1976: 134).

In that study Torrance also observed significant differences between the values produced by the rating technique compared with the standard gamble method, but found no significant differences between the standard gamble and the time trade-off method and concluded that 'we can tentatively accept the hypothesis that, for the measurement of population mean values, the two techniques are equivalent' (Torrance 1976: 134).

A later study by Bombardier *et al.* (1982) did not share Torrance's view about the equivalence of standard gambles and time trade-offs. In common with Torrance, they found a substantial and systematic difference between the standard gamble and the visual analogue rating method, but they suggested that the time trade-off results lay somewhere between the two. They plotted the various sets of mean values against each other (i.e. time trade-off against visual analogue, standard gamble against visual analogue, and standard gamble against time trade-off) and estimated linear relationships in each case. They concluded that 'there is much more similarity between the values obtained using the visual analogue and the time trade-off techniques than between either of these two and the standard gamble' (Bombardier *et al.* 1982: 152).

Llewellyn-Thomas *et al.* (1984) also reported systematic differences between standard gambles and a visual analogue scale, although by that time such a finding had ceased to cause much excitement: 'This difference has been noted previously by others (reference to Torrance), and because it is not the primary focus of this paper, we will not discuss it further' (1984: 547).

However, such disparities *are* the primary focus of the present paper. I shall consider the explanations that have been offered by some of the authors mentioned above, and suggest an alternative explanation which, if correct, may have substantial implications for the ways in which health state indices are derived, and the uses to which they are put.

POSSIBLE EXPLANATIONS

Let us denote the indices for H_i derived from standard gambles, time trade-offs and visual analogue scaling as S_i, T_i and V_i respectively.

In his paper, Torrance explained the non-linear relationship between his V_i and T_i values as follows. He claimed that 'the time trade-off technique can be viewed as a magnitude estimation of disutility or badness' and pointed to work in the field of psychophysical measurement which showed that 'the category scale, when plotted as a function of the magnitude scale, tends to be related to the magnitude scale by a concave power curve'. He found this explanation reassuring: 'This discovery that the results of the study are consistent with a large body of psychometric literature is quite exciting to the investigator, and certainly adds further credibility to the whole project' (1976: 136 n. 2).

However, Bombardier *et al.* had evidence which suggested a somewhat different pattern, and they offered a different explanation. They suggested that their results 'can perhaps best be interpreted as a general aversion to gambling with one's health, a "gambling aversion" which must be distinguished from the "risk aversion" familiar to students of decision analysis' (1982: 152). This kind of explanation has much in common with the distinction made by Gafni and Torrance (1984) between a quantity effect, QE (i.e. diminishing marginal utility of additional units) and a gambling effect, GE (i.e. fear of gambling itself, requiring an additional risk premium). Gafni and Torrance suggested various ways in which such a gambling effect might be identified, including an approach like the one used by Bombardier *et al.* which allows some estimate of the difference between S_i values (which are supposed to involve both QE and GE) and the V_i values (which should only involve QE). At first sight, this appears to be a plausible explanation borne out by the evidence: linear regressions of S_i on the two non-gambling values V_i and T_i both give estimates of an intercept of about 0.3, which might be regarded as a measure of GE.

However, there is an alternative way of looking at the data. Instead of linear relationships, let us estimate power functions along the lines suggested by Torrance, restricted so that the fitted curves pass through (0,0) and (1,1). On the basis of table 2 of Bombardier *et al.* (1982), we get:

$$V_i = 1 - (1 - S_i)^{0.44} \qquad R^2 = 0.80 \qquad (1)$$
$$V_i = 1 - (1 - T_i)^{0.55} \qquad R^2 = 0.88 \qquad (2)$$

which can be compared with the relationship estimated in Torrance (1976):

$$V_i = 1 - (1 - T_i)^{0.62} \qquad R^2 = 0.80 \qquad (3)$$

These three functions are depicted in Fig. 9.1, from which it is clear that the non-linear relationship between T and V in (2) is even more pronounced than the relationship estimated by Torrance

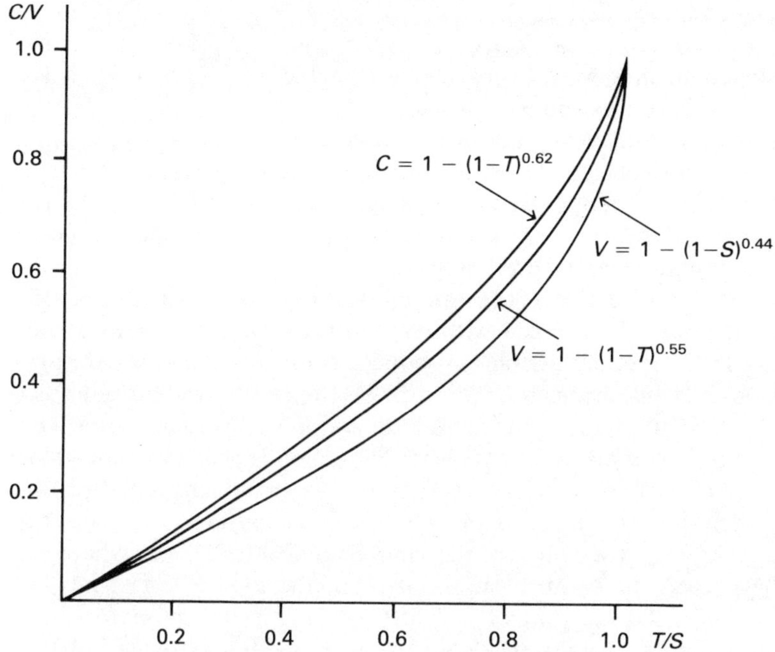

Figure 9.1 Non-linear relationship between *C*/*V* and *T*/*S*

between *T* and *V*; moreover, specified in this way, *T* seems closer to *S* than to *V*, contrary to what Bombardier *et al.* suggested on the basis of linear specifications.

Despite the restrictions imposed, (1) and (2) appear to fit the data just as well as the unrestricted linear functions estimated by Bombardier *et al.*, suggesting that an explanation couched in terms of systematic non-linear relationships may be no less plausible than a gambling effect interpretation. So can we provide another more unified account of the data?

The explanation considered in this paper is based upon an alternative model of decision-making known as regret theory. The origins of this model can be found in papers by Bell (1982), Fishburn (1982) and Loomes and Sugden (1982), but the version used here will be the more general form proposed by Loomes and Sugden (1987).

Regret theory was initially developed as a model of decision-making under risk and uncertainty, and has been applied and tested mainly in that context. However, in the present paper I shall suggest how the model may be quite naturally extended to decisions involving choice under certainty and how, when extended in that way, it provides a possible explanation of all the data referred to above.

In its present form, regret theory is concerned with actions: that is, *n*-tuples of state contingent consequences, where the consequence of action A_i under state S_j is denoted by x_{ij}. In the context of risk and uncertainty, the probability that S_j will occur is denoted by p_j, where $\Sigma p_j = 1$.

The term 'action' does not imply that individuals necessarily have to act to be faced with some *n*-tuple of consequences. For example, a set of possible consequences might be imposed, or may be due to 'natural causes', or may be the result of a gift: a lottery ticket given to you by a friend is an action in this sense. However, regret theory proposes that when an action is acquired other than by choice, the experience of any particular consequence will be associated with some level of 'choiceless' utility. This was the terminology used in Loomes and Sugden (1982); elsewhere we have used the term 'basic' utility, but the idea is the same – to focus on the element of satisfaction or dissatisfaction which an individual derives from a consequence independently of how the individual came to experience that consequence. This is represented by a function, $C(.)$: for convenience, $C(x_{ij})$ is written c_{ij}.

It is then suggested that when a consequence is experienced *as a result of choice*, the 'choiceless' utility may be modified. Consider a choice between the following two actions: A_1 gives a 50–50 chance of £2 or £20 depending on whether a fair coin lands heads (state S_1, consequence £2) or tails (state S_2, consequence £20). Alternatively, A_2 offers £10 for certain. When contemplating whether to choose A_1 (and therefore reject A_2), you know that if the coin lands heads you will receive £2; but you also know that, as a result of your decision, you will have missed out on the £10 you would have had if you had chosen differently. If this gives rise to a painful sensation – a decrement of utility – due to decision regret, you can anticipate that your overall level of satisfaction with the outcome will be less than C(£2). On the other hand, you also know that if you choose A_1 and the coin lands tails, C(£20) will be augmented by an increment of utility due to *rejoicing* at having made the choice which turned out best. Representing regret–rejoicing by a function $R(.,.)$, and weighting each outcome by the probability of that state occurring, we can derive expressions for the expected modified utilities associated with each course of action:

Choose A_1 and reject A_2: $0.5[C(2) + R(2, 10)] + 0.5[C(20) + R(20, 10)]$
Choose A_2 and reject A_1: $0.5[C(10) + R(10, 2)] + 0.5[C(10) + R(10, 20)]$

More generally, we can define a function

$$\psi(x_{ij},x_{kj}) = c_{ij} - c_{kj} + R(c_{ij},c_{kj}) - R(c_{kj},c_{ij}) \tag{4}$$

which expresses the overall net advantage of choosing A_i rather than A_k in the event that S_j occurs. Denoting the relations of strict preference, weak preference and indifference by $>$, $\geqslant$ and $\sim$ respectively, the maximization of expected overall satisfaction can be expressed compactly as follows:

$$A_i \gtrless A_k \Leftrightarrow \Sigma\, p_j\, (x_{ij}, x_{kj}) \gtreqless 0 \tag{5}$$

Loomes and Sugden (1987) discuss a small number of conditions on $\psi(.,.)$ which give the model its predictive power. For the purposes of this paper, two properties are of particular relevance. First, $\psi(.,.)$ is skew-symmetric: that is, $\psi(x_{ij},x_{kj}) = -\psi(x_{kj},x_{ij})$ for all x_{ij},x_{kj}. This follows from the definition in (4), and the main reason for drawing attention to it here is because of its convenience in deriving some of the results below. The second property is regret aversion if x_3,x_2 and x_1 are three consequences such that $c_3 > c_2 > c_1$, then $\psi(x_3,x_1) > \psi(x_3,x_2) + \psi(x_2,x_1)$. This contrasts with the case in which $\psi(x_3,x_1) = \psi(x_3,x_2) + \psi(x_2,x_1)$ where the predictions of the model would be identical to those derived from von Neumann–Morgenstern expected utility theory. However, if regret aversion holds, regret theory entails a variety of departures from the conventional axioms, including certain 'violations' of first-order stochastic dominance preference, transitivity, reduction of compound lotteries and the weak form of the independence axiom. But how does the model account for the data on health state indices, and the discrepancies described earlier?

Consider first the discrepancy between the results generated by standard gambles and those produced by rating methods. During the rating method, respondents are asked to evaluate the experience of being in some health state between full health and death. Note that they are not asked to make any choice or decision, but simply to locate the utility of *being in* health state H_i. It is suggested that what such questions tend to elicit may be something close to the 'choiceless' utility of H_i, hereafter denoted by h_i: it is much like asking someone how far 'the utility of being in possession of an extra £10' takes them along the line towards 'the utility of being in possession of an extra £20'.

By contrast, the standard gamble explicitly poses a decision problem. A_1 is a treatment with two possible consequences: either full normal health for t years (with probability p), or immediate death (with probability $1 - p$). A_2 is the certainty of living in H_i for t years. Respondents are asked to set p at the level which makes them indifferent between the two alternatives. As noted earlier, if the two consequences of A_1 are also the two end-points on the rating scale (assigned values of 1 and 0), it may be expected that $p = h_i$. However, suppose that instead of expected utility theory we apply regret theory, using the decision rule given by expression (5):

$$A_1 \sim A_2 \Leftrightarrow p\psi(1, h_i) + (1 - p)\psi(0, h_i) = 0 \qquad (6)$$

Using the skew-symmetry property, we can rearrange the right hand side of (6) to give the condition for indifference as

$$p = \psi\,(h_i, 0)/[\psi(1, h_i) + \psi(h_i, 0)] \qquad (7)$$

In the special case where $\psi(1, h_i) + \psi(h_i, 0) = \psi(1, 0)$ – that is, in the special case which corresponds to expected utility theory – we could normalize by setting $\psi\,(1, 0) = 1$ and indifference would be achieved when $p = h_i$. But if there is regret aversion, $[\psi(1, h_i) + \psi(h_i, 0)] < 1$, so that $p > h_i$. What is more, the extent of the deviation between p and h_i will vary according to the extent to which the term in square brackets falls below 1. Without knowing more about $\psi\,(.,.)$ we cannot say precisely which value of h_i will minimize the term in square brackets, but we can say that the term in square brackets will tend towards 1 as h_i tends towards either 1 or 0, so that the discrepancies will tend to increase then decrease as h_i falls from 1 to 0, giving the kind of curvature approximated by the functional form of equation (1) as shown in Fig. 9.1. Thus regret theory provides a possible explanation for the non-linear relationship between S and V.

Of course, it may be argued that the gambling effect offers an alternative explanation of the disparity between S and V. However, it would not appear to be able to account for two other observed disparities.

First, if the GE explanation were correct, the absence of any gambling element in time trade-offs means that we should expect to observe the same GE in comparisons between S and T as in comparisons between S and V; and we should expect the effect to disappear when comparing T with V.

Bombardier *et al.* believed that this was precisely what their evidence showed. However, as we have seen, Torrance found a significant non-linear relationship between T and V, and such a relationship can also be estimated on the basis of the evidence in Bombardier *et al.* as in equation (2). Moreover, when viewed as non-linear functions, T is still 'between' V and S, but now appears to be rather more similar to S.

To explain this, we need to go beyond regret theory as it currently stands and extend the model to encompass choices under certainty. In the context of the time trade-off method, we might proceed as follows.

Figure 9.2 displays a choice matrix in which 'states of the world' are replaced by periods of time – remaining years of life, 1 to t. As before, A_2 offers the certainty of H_i for t years. But now, with the time trade-off method, respondents are asked to consider an alternative treatment A_1 which would give them full health for time $x < t$, and to identify the value of x that makes them indifferent between A_1 and A_2.

The key question is whether under these choice circumstances the utility of the consequence of one action may still be modified according to how it stands in relation to the consequence of the alternative action. There are many examples in economics and psychology where it seems that comparative considerations may be important, even for decisions under certainty. However, rather than list examples, let us specify a hypothesis which is consistent with the evidence under consideration, and which can be tested further in future work. The hypothesis is that the utility derived from the consequence of a particular action depends not only upon the nature of the consequence itself, but also upon how it compares with the corresponding consequence(s) of alternative action(s) in the choice set; and that this may be represented by a function $\phi(.,.)$ which has essentially the same properties and plays the same role as $\psi(.,.)$ in regret theory.

In the context of time trade-off decisions as represented in Fig. 9.2, the 'corresponding consequences' are the different health states that would be experienced in any period, depending on the

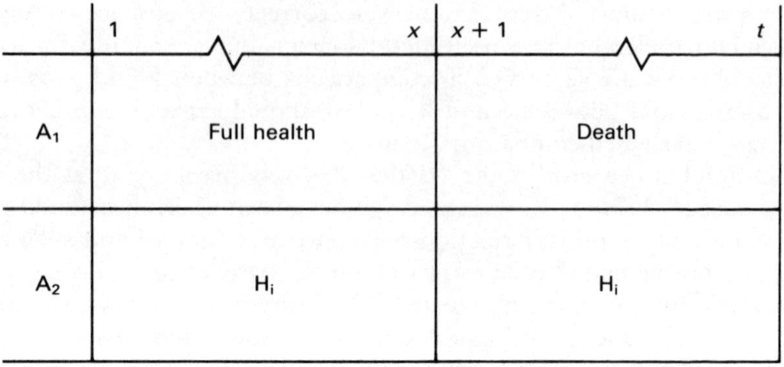

Figure 9.2 Choice matrix for time trade-off method

choice made. Thus in year 1, A_1 would give full health while A_2 would give state H_i, so that the net advantage of choosing A_1 and rejecting A_2 for that year would be $\phi\,(1, h_i)$. Instead of weighting $\phi(.,.)$ by probabilities, other decision weights w_j must be used. In the time trade-off case, if all years are given equal weight, the indifference condition will be:

$$A_1 \sim A_2 \Leftrightarrow (x_i/t)\phi\,(1, h_i) + [(t - x_i)/t]\,\phi\,(0, h_i) = 0 \tag{8}$$

Alternatively, if we consider a very simple version of time preference employing a discounting factor d, where $0 < d < 1$, we can rewrite (8) as follows:

$$A_1 \sim A_2 \Leftrightarrow [(1 - d^x)/(1 - d^t)]\phi(1, h_i) + [(d^x - d^t)/1 - d^t)]\,\phi(0, h_i) = 0 \tag{9}$$

Thus for $0 < d < 1$, x_i/t (that is, T_i) will, in general, be less than p (that is, S_i). The extent of the difference between x_i/t and p will vary with both d and t. However, for any given d, $x_i/t \rightarrow p$ as $t \rightarrow 0$, and this may help to explain why Bombardier *et al.* found a more significant difference between S and T than Torrance observed. Torrance's (1976) comparison between S and T was based on scenarios where t was really quite small – just 3 months – whereas the scenarios used by Bombardier *et al.* typically involved rather bigger values of t. Other studies (e.g. Sackett and Torrance, 1978; McNeil *et al.*, 1981) provide further support for the idea that the indifference value x_i/t is sensitive to the magnitude of t, in the direction suggested above.

Some further evidence not accounted for by the gambling effect explanation was reported by Llewellyn-Thomas *et al.* (1982). They observed disparities *within* the standard gamble procedure. They used three variants of the standard gamble (referred to as Methods 1, 2 and 3) to obtain utilities for five intermediate health states labelled A to E. Method 1 took full health (assigned utility 1) and death (assigned 0) as the two outcomes of the gamble, and for each health state in turn asked respondents to set the probabilities necessary to produce indifference between the gamble and the certainty of that health state. This produced the 'reference utilities' for the other two methods.

Method 2 kept death as one of the outcomes of the gamble, but made the other outcome the health state ranked just above the state being evaluated. Thus if (as was the case) state A had previously been ranked second and state D third, then respondents were asked to set the probability of A (and thus the residual probability of death) which would produce a gamble equivalent to the certainty of D; and so on. Method 3 inverted the procedure by fixing full health as the best outcome of the gamble and taking as the other outcome the health state just below the one being evaluated, i.e. Method 3 asked for the probability mix of full health and state D which respondents regarded as exactly as good as the certainty of A.

What they found was that the three different methods yielded systematically different sets of utility indices. This is reminiscent of the 'utility evaluation effect' discussed by Machina (1987: 131–2), and clearly runs counter to standard expected utility theory. However, regret theory offers a possible explanation, along the following lines.

Suppose that Method 1 produces reference utilities p_A and p_D for the two states. Now suppose that Method 2 is used to evaluate D, and that indifference is produced when the gamble involves a probability q that state A will occur and a $1 - q$ probability of death:
expected utility theory entails:

$$p_D = qp_A + (1 - q)0; \text{ that is, } q = p_D/p_A \qquad (10)$$

However, this equality will not hold in general under regret theory. Let the choiceless utilities of the two health states be denoted by h_A and h_D. Then we can adapt equation (7) to give

$$p_A = \psi(h_A, 0)/[\psi(1, h_A) + \psi(h_A, 0)] \qquad (11)$$

$$p_D = \psi(h_D, 0)/[\psi(1, h_D) + \psi(h_D, 0)] \quad (12)$$
$$q = \psi(h_D, 0)/[\psi(h_A, h_D) + \psi(h_D, 0)] \quad (13)$$

From this it can readily be seen that equation (10) will not in general hold. For example, even if – by chance – the term in square brackets in (11) takes the same value as the term in square brackets in (12), so that $p_D/p_A = \psi(h_D, 0)/\psi(h_A, 0)$, this will not be equal to q unless $\psi(h_A, 0) = [\psi(h_A, h_D) + \psi(h_D, 0)]$, which is ruled out by regret aversion.

A similar argument applies to Method 3, and to any other variant which involves taking different pairs of outcomes for the gamble. In other words, even if we confine ourselves to the standard gamble procedure, we cannot expect to find a unique utility associated with any particular state of health other than those to which we arbitrarily assign values of 1 and 0.

In summary, then, the regret model, extended to encompass relevant choices under certainty, appears to be able to provide a unified account of the data cited above. In particular it explains:

(a) why there is a non-linear relationship between S and V even though these are often regarded as alternative ways of eliciting the same interval scale;
(b) why there is a non-linear relationship between T and V, even though there is no 'gambling' involved;
(c) why $S \approx T$ when t is close to zero, whereas for larger values of t, T produces results which lie somewhere between those generated by S and V; and
(d) why the standard gamble method may produce different values for the same H_i, depending on which reference states are used.

DISCUSSION AND IMPLICATIONS

Since S, T and V produce systematically different results, it is natural to ask which one(s) should be used. Torrance is inclined to take S as the 'gold standard' against which the other methods may be judged. On this basis, he suggests (1986: 27) that the time trade-off technique is 'relatively valid' while the rating method is not. Bombardier *et al.* acknowledge the theoretical elegance of S, but concern about the practical difficulties of using standard gambles together with what they perceive as the bias due to 'gambling aversion' leads them to suggest that 'perhaps both the time trade-off and visual analogue methods should continue to be used' (1982: 158). However, they believe that 'direct estimation by a visual analogue or any comparable technique can lead respondents to overestimate the seriousness of disability' and on balance they conclude that 'if a choice has to be made, the time trade-off technique, which demands a less abstract decision, would seem to represent the more promising approach' (1982: 158).

However, all the authors express various degrees of concern and doubt. For example: 'Given the uncertainties still surrounding the reliability, validity and precision of utility values, it is important to perform sensitivity analysis on them' (Torrance 1986: 27). Or again, referring to a comparison between *S* and *V*: 'It is, of course, possible that these two valuation techniques are not even comparable, that either or both may be inadequate means of measuring the underlying utility associated with disability states' (Bombardier *et al.*, 1982: 155).

Llewellyn-Thomas *et al.* considered that their results

> suggest that it may be naive to think of any state of health as possessing a single utility or value. . . . Even when a widely accepted and theoretically sound method of value assessment is employed, such as the von Neumann and Morgenstern standard gamble, the variant of the method used to elicit responses, the outcome of the gamble, and the nature of the stimulus may have a substantial effect upon the measured value. We believe that efforts should be made to understand the nature of these influences rather than to ignore them or to attempt to devise methods that will eliminate them.
>
> (Llewellyn-Thomas *et al.* 1984: 550)

This is certainly one of the implications of a model such as regret theory. Efforts to improve and refine the various methods in an attempt to reduce imprecision and correct for biases appear commendable, but may be missing the main point. Although imprecision exists, and biases undoubtedly occur, no part of regret theory's account of the data makes any appeal to imprecision or systematic bias. Quite the opposite: the differences within and between the various methods of eliciting values are consistent with the regret model in its non-stochastic form. So if, as suggested above, variants of *S* produce a range of 'utilities' for each health state primarily because expected utility theory is the wrong model, this range will not be eliminated by applying more sophisticated versions of the standard gamble methodology. And if the differences between the V_i, T_i and S_i are meaningful – that is, they reflect important real factors, such as the distinction between choice and choiceless situations, and the impact of a time discount factor – then to treat them as biases and to 'correct' for them may actually introduce distortions.

In short, restricting attention to further efforts along conventional lines may be an inefficient allocation of scarce research time and resources, which might be better spent exploring and testing alternative approaches for which the existing data seem to provide *prima facie* support. If it turns out that alternative models such as regret theory do not provide a better account of the evidence, we can return to the task of refining the existing instruments armed with more data and greater confidence. On the other hand, if alternative models substantially outperform expected utility theory, we might redirect our efforts to explore methods and measures consistent with those alternative models.

This is not a minor, pedantic, purely academic point. It is not difficult to think of a number of important areas where there may be substantial implications for individual behaviour, clinical practice and health care policy in general.

For example, consider the case of coronary artery bypass grafting (CABG), which has been studied by researchers using different approaches: for instance, Pliskin *et al.* (1980) used standard gambles, while Williams (1985) employed a scale derived from questions asking for more direct (choiceless) estimates of the value of various states of health. However, in this case, both approaches may be inappropriate. The usual alternative to CABG surgery is to continue with medical management. Undergoing the surgery involves making a decision in the form of giving informed consent to an operation which may improve the individual's health relative to what medical management could achieve, but also involves the possibility of worsening the position – including a definite probability (perhaps 0.03) of perioperative death. Since the individual must (formally) make a decision, measures of choiceless utility are not appropriate; but neither are the values generated by standard gambles, if they fail to take due account of any regret and rejoicing that may be involved.

Given the importance of consent and compliance, considerations of decision regret may enter into many other areas of health care: besides surgery, one can think of examples of drug therapy which involve the risk of unpleasant or dangerous side-effects (e.g. the use of some anti-hypertensives or non-steroidal anti-inflammatory drugs) and diagnostic tests and preventive measures which carry some risk (e.g. amniocentesis, whooping cough vaccination). To what extent considerations of decision regret may affect the evaluation of such treatments, and/or the degree of take-up or compliance, is an open question – but one which may profitably be investigated.

Of course, considerations of regret may not be limited to the sufferers themselves. Doctors (or others) acting as agents may try to anticipate such considerations on a patient's behalf – but may also be influenced by similar considerations on their own account. Hershey and Baron (1987) have discussed some of the possible implications of regret in health care decision-making, including the issue of the circumstances under which regret ought to be taken into account. They suggest that although it may be reasonable for individuals to anticipate regret–rejoicing when making decisions for themselves, 'when we make decisions for others, it is the consequences of our decisions for *them* that ought to be paramount, and our own regret should not be a consideration'. However, they acknowledge in a footnote that if physicians fear being sued for malpractice if things turn out badly, only a saint could put such considerations aside. In fact, even if there is little likelihood of legal action, the 'caring agency relationship' and/or a desire to avoid sensations of guilt or responsibility, may also be sources of decision regret. Again, to what extent such considerations do/should affect behaviour is still an open question, but it is not difficult to identify a number of possible areas where it may play a role: for example, how parents act on behalf of their children; recommendations about surgical procedures, e.g. lumpectomy or mastectomy; family doctors' apparent unwillingness to support home deliveries; and the variability in family practitioners' patterns of referral, ordering of tests, etc. The impact of considerations such as decision regret in these and many other areas may also be an issue which is ripe for further research.

FRESH EVIDENCE AND FURTHER QUESTIONS

The previous three sections were written for a MacArthur Foundation Workshop which took place in January 1991. That Workshop gave me the incentive to review and reorganize some ideas that had been developing over two or three years, based on the existing literature and published evidence available to me at the time. But just prior to the Workshop I had an opportunity to gather some fresh evidence; and during the Workshop I benefited from ideas and suggestions by other participants. This section reports the fresh evidence and presents some additional thoughts stimulated by that evidence and by the discussions during and after the Workshop.

Additional evidence

During 1990 I joined Michael Jones-Lee and Peter Phillips from the University of Newcastle upon Tyne to conduct a pilot study commissioned by the Transport and Road Research Laboratory on behalf of the UK Department of Transport (DTp). The purpose of the pilot study was to explore the ways in which a large-scale survey might elicit from a representative sample of citizens the values they placed on reductions in the risks of fatal and non-fatal injuries resulting from road accidents.

Part of the pilot study involved the use of visual analogue scales and standard gambles. The results, in terms of sample means, were quite consistent with the earlier evidence of a decidedly non-linear relationship between V and S. However, there were grounds for having some reservations about the quality of the data. In particular, the interviews were conducted by (five different) interviewers who worked for a commercial opinion poll organization: the kind of questionnaire used on this occasion was outside their normal experience, and some felt they had not been given sufficient training in all the techniques involved. On the other hand, four of the five interviewers returned a number of perfectly usable completed questionnaires which showed broadly similar patterns of response, so that perhaps the reservations should not be exaggerated too much. Nevertheless, when an opportunity arose to conduct further piloting under more controlled conditions, I took it. The procedures used and their results are described below.

The respondents were thirty graduate students following a Masters course in health economics at the University of York. Some had a background in economics, others had clinical or other health care professional experience. All could be expected to be more than averagely numerate, but many had received only a rudimentary introduction to the idea and techniques of health state measurement. Their participation in further piloting for the DTp study was a precursor to a more detailed and comprehensive discussion of that topic as part of their course.

The term 'serious non-fatal injury' as defined by the DTp covers a wide spectrum. On the advice of a senior clinician working on a related study, we had devised eight different 'injury description cards' ranging across that spectrum. Two further cards, representing normal health and death, were added to the set. The ten cards are reproduced (in alphabetical order) in Appendix 1.

Each respondent received a set of these cards (not in alphabetical order). They were asked to take the top two cards, read through both, then place them on the table in front of them, putting the description they regarded as worse below the other – or putting the two cards side by side if they regarded them as equally bad. Then they took the third card, read it through, and located it on the table relative to the other two; and so on, until all ten cards had been read and ranked from best (or least bad) to worst, according to their personal preferences.

They were then each given a visual analogue scale (Appendix 2) calibrated from 100 to 0. After locating the (equal) best description(s) at 100 and the (equal) worst description(s) at 0, they were asked to locate the other descriptions along the scale, using the intervals between locations to indicate how much better or worse they felt one health state was than another. (Further details of the procedure used are given in Appendix 2.) This phase of the exercise also had the effect of causing respondents to re-read the descriptions and perhaps consider their initial rankings more carefully, altering the ordering if they wished.

Once they had completed the scaling exercise, they were asked to consider a subset of four of the injury description cards (R, S, X and W) and respond to four standard gamble questions involving a choice between the certainty of a particular non-fatal injury and a risky treatment with 'normal health' and 'death' as the possible outcomes. In each case, respondents were asked to use ticks, crosses and an asterisk to show, respectively:

(a) the highest risk of death where they were sure they would choose the risky treatment rather than the certainty of the intermediate health state;
(b) the lowest risk of death that would surely cause them to reject

the treatment and instead accept the certainty of the intermediate health state; and

(c) the level of risk that would make it most difficult to decide which alternative to choose.

Appendix 3 shows the way the first standard gamble question, involving injury description R, was presented. The other three questions were identical, except that R was replaced successively by S, X and W.

Table 9.1 reports the results. Each individual is identified by a number (ID) 1–30, and each row shows an individual's set of

Table 9.1 Visual analogue scores and standard gamble indices

ID	*vR*	*R**	*vS*	*S**	*vX*	*X**	*vW*	*W**
1	0.10	0.950	0.15	0.990	0.57	0.999	0.75	1.000
2	0.06	0.500	0.22	0.800	0.56	0.980	0.69	0.999
3	0.29	0.800	0.76	0.970	0.95	1.000	0.99	1.000
4	0.29	0.500	0.47	0.650	0.73	0.960	0.81	0.995
5	0.32	0.950	0.42	1.000	0.68	1.000	0.84	1.000
6	0.49	0.900	0.61	0.950	0.74	0.980	0.90	0.998
7	0.20	0.400	0.55	0.800	0.85	0.992	0.95	1.000
8	0.24	0.650	0.61	0.850	0.87	1.000	0.97	1.000
9	0.47	0.825	0.71	0.850	0.84	0.935	0.95	0.985
10	0.16	0.750	0.47	0.920	0.58	0.990	0.79	1.000
11	0.39	0.400	0.60	1.000	0.90	1.000	0.97	1.000
12	0.50	0.800	0.70	0.995	0.80	1.000	0.90	1.000
13	0.24	0.910	0.46	0.975	0.75	0.996	0.80	1.000
14	0.06	0.500	0.32	0.935	0.48	0.960	0.79	0.992
15	0.05	0.800	0.10	0.999	0.47	1.000	0.70	1.000
16	0.49	0.980	0.90	0.998	0.95	0.999	0.98	1.000
17	0.26	0.250	0.32	0.920	0.68	1.000	0.47	1.000
18	0.21	0.500	0.34	0.750	0.58	0.600	0.74	0.900
19	0.44	0.850	0.49	0.990	0.78	0.990	0.90	0.995
20	0.67	0.990	0.89	0.999	0.94	1.000	0.97	1.000
21	0.53	0.970	0.74	0.995	0.86	1.000	0.95	1.000
22	0.21	0.920	0.74	0.998	0.87	1.000	0.95	1.000
23	0.15	0.700	0.50	0.950	0.85	0.998	0.95	0.999
24	0.33	0.500	0.67	0.900	0.95	0.995	0.97	0.999
25	0.25	0.850	0.50	0.920	0.75	0.998	0.83	1.000
26	0.18	0.750	0.34	0.850	0.59	0.920	0.80	0.970
27	0.21	0.700	0.47	0.910	0.81	0.990	0.92	1.000
28	0.18	0.650	0.32	0.800	0.46	0.950	0.67	0.980
29	0.20	0.850	0.35	0.992	0.70	0.995	0.80	0.998
30	0.35	0.850	0.70	0.999	0.82	1.000	0.95	1.000
Mean	0.29	0.731	0.51	0.922	0.75	0.974	0.85	0.994
Median	0.25	0.800	0.49	0.950	0.76	0.997	0.90	1.000

responses. In columns *vR*, *vS*, etc. the visual analogue score is shown, rescaled (for those who considered descriptions L and/or N to be worse than death) so that death is assigned a score of 0 and normal health is 1. *R**, *S**, etc. show the utilities (again on a scale from 0 to 1) derived from the standard gamble responses, based on the asterisks used to indicate the level of risk where a respondent found it most difficult to decide which alternative to choose. A utility of 1.000 signifies that a cross was placed against a 1/1,000 risk of failure, i.e. the respondent would certainly not accept treatment at that level of risk of death.

Plotting visual analogue scores on the vertical axis, and standard gamble utilities on the horizontal axis, we find that 18 of the 30 respondents give answers which are completely consistent with the kind of non-linear relationship illustrated earlier in Fig. 9.1: that is, each plotted point lies on, or to the south-east of, the straight line joining the two points on either side of it, and all four points corresponding to R, S, X and W lie strictly to the south-east of the 45° line from (0, 0) to (1, 1).

Of the other twelve respondents, most generally follow that same pattern, usually with only a single observation that doesn't conform. The number of major departures from the pattern is very small. Only one observation out of 120 – (*vR*, *R**) for individual 17 – lies to the north-west of the 45° line. Individual 17 also records another unusual observation, scoring W as worse than X on the visual analogue scale. Perhaps the only other significant 'abnormality' lies in individual 18's responses: a lower standard gamble utility index for X than for S, although S was rated significantly worse than X on the visual analogue scale. However, the number of non-conformist observations is so small that removing them would make little difference to the mean values which, if superimposed on Fig. 9.1, would lie substantially to the south-east of even the most pronounced non-linear relationship shown there.

To sum up, the aggregate pattern is not driven by a few outliers, but is representative of the individual behaviour of the majority of a sample of numerate graduate students of health economics who could generally be expected to understand the concepts of interval scaling and standard gambles. There were very few signs of obviously aberrant responses – substantially fewer than in the DTp pilot study – and every effort was made to give the two techniques as good a chance as possible of producing similar indices for each of the four injury descriptions. Yet the result was a non-linear pattern even more pronounced than those observed previously.

Regret – or something else – or a bit of both?

Earlier I described and extended a formal model which is capable of organizing much of the published data. However, in the form in which it was published, much of the earlier evidence was aggregated, and the point of the experiment to generate the fresh evidence described above was to see how far the pattern was reproduced at the individual level. At first sight, it seems to be a robust and pervasive phenomenon which appears to be consistent with the regret model. But is this actually the case?

At the MacArthur meeting, Baruch Fischhoff acted as discussant of the paper in its earlier form, and subsequently provided, or guided me towards, further written material. In particular, I have been struck by the distinction (discussed in more detail in Fischhoff 1991) between basic and articulated values. In Fischhoff's words, the

> philosophy of basic values . . . holds that people lack well-differentiated values for all but the most familiar of evaluation questions – where they have had the chance, by trial, error and rumination, to settle on stable values. In other cases, they must derive specific valuations from some basic values through an inferential process.
>
> (Fischhoff 1991)

This is contrasted with the 'philosophy of articulated values', expressed most succinctly by the proposition that 'If we've got questions, they have answers.' In other words, it assumes that most people have comprehensive, well-specified preferences and values which can be readily accessed by asking sufficiently clear and precise questions.

Fischhoff also writes:

> Between the philosophies of articulated values and basic values, lie intermediate positions. These hold that, while people need not have answers to all questions, neither need they start from scratch each time an evaluative question arises. Rather, people have stable values of moderate complexity, which provide an advanced starting point for

> responding to questions of real-world complexity. Where a particular version of this perspective falls on the continuum defined by the two extreme philosophies depends on how well developed these partial perspectives are held to be.
>
> (Fischhoff 1991)

In his commentary on the earlier version of the paper, Fischhoff suggested that I have implicitly adopted an articulated values perspective. Certainly, both expected utility theory and the formal regret model assume that people act as if their values are highly articulated. But in practice it is doubtless the case that most people operate at intermediate positions on the spectrum. By taking a sample of graduates with knowledge/experience of health care matters, a good level of numeracy and a greater-than-average facility for abstract/analytical thought, and presenting them with a small set of fairly tightly circumscribed decision tasks, the experiment provided conditions which were favourable to the articulated values perspective. On the other hand, since the decisions involved thinking about the impact upon themselves of health states outside their regular experience, and since they were given only a rather limited amount of time to consider these implications, it would not be surprising to find signs of only partially articulated values. Let us consider the data in that light.

Suppose we start from a position close to the articulated values end of the spectrum, taking the regret theory explanation to be generally correct, but allowing for a modicum of (unbiased) imprecision/random error in people's responses. From this perspective, the most striking feature of the data is the apparent strength of the 'regret effect'.

For example, consider the upper half of Table 9.2, which reproduces those cases where respondents scored states R or S from 0.45 to 0.55 inclusive. According to the regret theory interpretation, these are cases where, in choiceless utility terms, the difference between being in the particular state and being in normal health is about the same as the difference between being in the state and being dead, so that h is approximately equal to $1 - h$. If there were no regret effect, this should translate to people being indifferent between the intermediate health state for sure and treatment offering a roughly 50–50 chance of normal health or death. If a regret effect is incorporated, this need no longer be the case; and if (as seems quite plausible) the comparison between intermediate health and death evokes a stronger effect than the contrast between intermediate health and normal health, we may not be surprised to find standard gamble responses suggesting that $\psi(h, 0)$ is somewhat larger than $\psi(1, h)$. But what does seem surprising is how much larger $\psi(h, 0)$ is than $\psi(1, h)$, if the standard gamble responses are to be interpreted in this way. The right hand column of the upper part of Table 9.2 shows how many times greater $\psi(h, 0)/\psi(1, h)$ is compared with $h/(1 - h)$. Of the thirteen cases identified, the smallest ratio is greater than 2, and the largest ratio is greater than 100, with the median being 11.5. This either means that the regret effect is very powerful indeed – or else that something other than, or in addition to, regret is at work.

Table 9.2 Measures of disparities – selected cases

ID	*Injury*	*v*	*	*Ratio*
4	S	0.47	0.650	2.09
7	S	0.55	0.800	3.27
12	R	0.50	0.800	4.00
9	R	0.47	0.825	5.32
6	R	0.49	0.900	9.37
27	S	0.47	0.910	11.40
25	S	0.50	0.920	11.50
10	S	0.47	0.920	12.97
23	S	0.50	0.950	19.00
21	R	0.53	0.970	28.67
13	S	0.46	0.975	45.78
16	R	0.49	0.980	51.00
19	S	0.49	0.990	103.04

ID	*Injury*	*v*	*Min* *	*Min ratio*
9	W	0.95	0.970	1.70
24	X	0.95	0.980	2.58
16	X	0.95	0.990	5.21
6	W	0.90	0.990	11.00
19	W	0.90	0.990	11.00
23	W	0.95	0.998	26.26
3	X	0.95	0.999	52.58
7	W	0.95	0.999	52.58
21	W	0.95	0.999	52.58
22	W	0.95	0.999	52.58
30	W	0.95	0.999	52.58
20	X	0.94	0.999	63.77
27	W	0.92	0.999	86.87
11	X	0.90	0.999	111.00
12	W	0.90	0.999	111.00

This impression appears to be reinforced throughout the data. For example, consider those cases – listed in the lower half of Table 9.2 – where states X or W are scored from 0.90 to 0.95 inclusive. Here the column second from the right shows the lowest risk of failure where respondents were sure they would reject the risky treatment. Using these figures to calculate the absolute minimum values of $\psi(h, 0)/\psi(1, h)$ consistent with the standard gamble responses, and comparing these minimum values with the corresponding $h/1 - h$ values, gives the right-hand column ratios, which in the majority of cases exceed 50. In other words, the majority of respondents who, according to the scoring exercise, rated states X or W as constituting a loss of something between 5 and 10 per cent of utility on the scale from normal health to death, were willing to accept the certainty of that state rather than contemplate a treatment involving no more than a 0.001 chance of death and at least a 0.999 chance of being restored to normal health. It is difficult even for one of the authors of regret theory to believe that regret alone can do that much work.

An alternative, or supplementary, explanation which takes us somewhat away from the highly articulated end of the spectrum and more into the territory of partial perspectives runs as follows. When presented with the task of ranking the injury descriptions and then locating them on the calibrated scale, there may be a tendency for respondents' attention to be taken by the worst features of the experience, or those which are most immediate or imaginable. For those who try to enter into the spirit of the exercise in the relatively short time available, it is likely that they will be able to think most easily and quickly of the major sources of pleasure they currently enjoy that would be most obviously lost, damaged or disrupted. The things that would remain least affected, or the new sources of pleasure that would be found to (partially) substitute for those that are lost or damaged, may not come so readily to mind. In the case of temporary injuries such as those described in X and W, the experience of being in the injured state may receive disproportionate weight, and the fact that respondents will live most of the rest of their lives in normal health may be somewhat neglected – until they are presented with a scenario, like the standard gamble, which prompts them to pay more attention to all that normal life which would be lost if the treatment should fail. Even in cases such as R and S where there is some (and in the case of R, quite significant) permanent disability, the introduction of the possibility of losing everything may help to shift attention somewhat from the most negative to the more positive aspects of the situation: 'O.K., so I may not be able to go rock climbing any more, but that's not the end of the world: there are bound to be lots of other things I could do instead.'

The impact of regret may still be an important factor, especially in the cases of X and W: 'What a fool I'd be to take a chance and end up dead when I only have to wait a few months/couple of years and I'll be back at full strength.' But my belief is that the very pronounced disparities between the measures generated by the scaling task and the indices produced by the standard gambles are not produced by regret alone, but are at least partly – and perhaps quite substantially – due to the fact that the different elicitation procedures may cause people with less than fully articulated values to distribute their attention, and therefore their decision weights, differently between characteristics which are all *formally* present to an identical extent throughout.

CONCLUDING REMARKS

During the time between completing the earlier draft of this paper and embarking on the last section, I was exposed not only to other researchers' perspectives on value elicitation but – perhaps even more potent – the experience of helping to construct and apply several different elicitation procedures, briefing and debriefing interviewers, receiving verbal feedback from respondents and analysing the data generated by them. It has been both a stimulating and an unsettling experience, resulting in rather less formal hypothesis-testing and rather more speculation than those of us with a background in the discipline of economics feel altogether comfortable with. Some may condemn the second part of the last section as '*post hoc* theorizing', but I think it should rather be regarded as 'alternative hypothesis identification'. The task of more thoroughly exploring and testing these (and other) hypotheses still lies ahead. At present the account offered by regret, or more generally, the influence on valuations of comparisons between juxtaposed alternative consequences, remains a contender for explaining at least part of the systematic disparities between different health state measurement techniques. What proportion of the disparities are due to regret, what other considerations (or omissions) affect people's judgments, and how far the relative weights of different factors alter with context – these are all still open questions and may never be answerable in precise quantifiable terms which can be generalized across individuals. Nevertheless, if we wish to understand better how to incorporate individuals' values and preferences into personal and social decision-making, there is clearly room to discover more than we currently know about the influences that lie behind the systematic disparities we have observed.

NOTE

1 Some of the ideas in this paper grew out of earlier collaborative work with Robert Sugden and Lynda MacKenzie. The paper benefited further from the opportunity to present it at a MacArthur Foundation Workshop in La Jolla in January 1991. I am grateful to participants in that Workshop, and particularly to Baruch Fischhoff who provided first a verbal, and later a written commentary. I also wish to acknowledge the support of ESRC Award No. R000231194, and the value of collaboration with Michael Jones-Lee and Peter Phillips on a pilot study for the UK Department of Transport.

REFERENCES

Bell, D. (1982) 'Regret in decision making under uncertainty', *Operations Research* 20: 961–81.

Bombardier, C., Wolfson, A. D., Sinclair, A. J. and McGreer, A. (1982) 'Comparison of three preference measurement methodologies in the evaluation of a functional status index', in R. Deber and G. Thompson (eds) *Choices in Health Care: Decision Making and Evaluation of Effectiveness*, Toronto: University of Toronto.

Fischhoff, B. (1991) 'Eliciting values: is there anything there?', in L. Cooper and M. Hechter (eds) *Values*, Stanford: Stanford University Press.

Fishburn, P. C. (1982) 'Nontransitive measurable utility', *Journal of Mathematical Psychology* 26: 31–67.

Gafni, A. and Torrance, G. W. (1984) 'Risk attitude and time preference in health', *Management Science* 30: 440–51.

Hershey, J. C. and Baron, J. (1987) 'Clinical reasoning and cognitive processes', *Medical Decision Making* 7.

Llewellyn-Thomas, H., Sutherland, H. J., Tibshirani, R., Ciampi, A., Till, J. E. and Boyd, N. F. (1982) 'The measurement of patients' values in medicine', *Medical Decision Making* 2: 449–62.

—— (1984) 'Describing health states: methodological issues in obtaining values for health states', *Medical Care* 22: 543–52.

Loomes, G. and Sugden, R. (1982) 'Regret theory: an alternative theory of rational choice under uncertainty', *Economic Journal* 92: 805–24.

—— (1987) 'Some implications of a more general form of regret theory', *Journal of Economic Theory* 41: 270–87.

Machina, M. J. (1987) 'Choice under uncertainty: problems solved and unsolved', *Journal of Economic Perspectives* 1: 121–54.

McNeil, B. J., Weichselbaum, R. and Pauker, S. G. (1981) 'Speech and survival: tradeoffs between quality and quantity of life in laryngeal cancer', *New England Journal of Medicine* 305: 982–7.

Pliskin, J. S., Shepherd, D. S. and Weinstein, M. C. (1980) 'Utility functions of life years and health status', *Operations Research* 28: 206–24.

Sackett, D. L. and Torrance, G. W. (1978) 'The utility of different health states as perceived by the general public', *Journal of Disease* 31: 697–704.

Torrance, G. W. (1976) 'Social preferences for health states: an empirical evaluation of three measurement techniques', *Socio-Economic Planning Sciences* 10: 128–36.

—— (1986) 'Measurement of health state utilities for economic appraisal', *Journal of Health Economics* 5: 1–30.

Williams, A. (1985) 'Economics of coronary artery bypass grafting', *British Medical Journal* 291: 326–9.

APPENDIX 1: INJURY DESCRIPTION CARDS

H

In hospital

- 1–4 weeks with burns/cuts
- Moderate to severe pain

After hospital

- Some pain/discomfort for several weeks, possibly months
- After healing no permanent loss of physical/mental abilities
- But prominent scarring permanently damages your appearance – you may feel self-conscious in some, possibly many, situations involving other people

J

Your normal state of health

K

Injuries resulting in death

L

In hospital

- Several weeks, possibly several months
- Head injuries resulting in severe permanent brain damage

After hospital

- Mental and physical abilities greatly reduced for the rest of your life
- Dependent on others for many physical needs, including feeding and toileting

N

In hospital

- Several weeks, possibly several months
- Loss of use of legs and possibly other limbs due to paralysis and/or amputation

After hospital

- Confined to a wheelchair for the rest of your life
- Dependent on others for many physical needs, including dressing and toileting

R

In hospital

- Several weeks, possibly several months
- Moderate to severe pain

After hospital

- Continuing pain/discomfort for the rest of your life, possibly requiring frequent medication
- Substantial and permanent restrictions to work and leisure activities

S

In hospital

- 1–4 weeks
- Moderate to severe pain

After hospital
- Some pain gradually reducing, but may recur when you take part in some activities
- Some restrictions to leisure and possibly some work activities for the rest of your life

T

- Sudden jarring/'whiplash' injury which does *not* require admission to hospital

After effects
- Frequent pain/discomfort in neck and/or back
- Some restrictions to work and/or leisure activities due to neck/back pain
- After 1–3 years, return to normal health with no permanent disability

W

In hospital
- 2–7 days
- Slight to moderate pain

After hospital
- Some pain/discomfort for several weeks
- Some restrictions to work and/or leisure activities for several weeks/months
- After 3–4 months, return to normal health with no permanent disability

X

In hospital
- 1–4 weeks
- Slight to moderate pain

After hospital
- Some pain/discomfort, gradually reducing
- Some restrictions to work and leisure activities, steadily improving
- After 1–3 years, return to normal health with no permanent disability

APPENDIX 2

After ranking all ten cards, each respondent was asked to write the letter(s) of the (equal) best card(s) against 100 on the scale opposite, and write the letter(s) of the (equal) worst card(s) against 0.

The respondent was then asked to consider the full ranked set of cards and see if any card contained a description that s/he regarded as about halfway between the best and worst cards in terms of badness. That is, was there any description such that the subjectively judged difference in badness between that description and the one regarded as best was about the same as the difference between that description and the one regarded as worst? If so, the letter of that card was to be located at or near 50. If not, could the respondent divide the ranked cards into two groups: those above the 50 level, i.e. closer to best than to worst; and those below 50, i.e. closer to worst than to best? In this case, s/he was asked to locate the lowest-ranked of the first group at an appropriate point above 50, and the highest-ranked of the second group at an appropriate point below 50.

S/he was then asked to consider the first group and try to identify a mid-point *within* that group – again, either a particular card or else a dividing line between two adjacent cards. This procedure was repeated for the second group. Having by that time located (approximate) mid- and quarter-points, the respondent was asked to locate the remaining cards, using the intervals between to indicate subjective judgments of relative badness.

Finally, respondents were invited to consider the scale as a whole and make any further adjustments which they felt might more accurately reflect their subjective judgments.

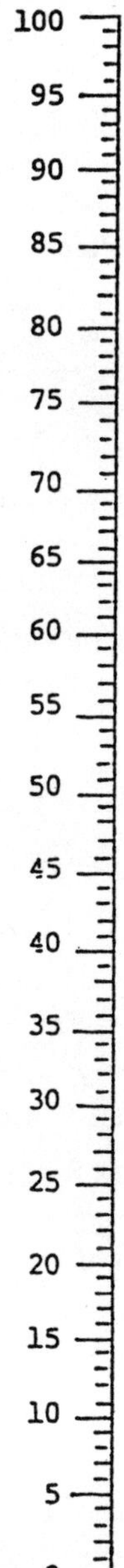

APPENDIX 3

EITHER: THE CERTAINTY OF THE INJURIES DESCRIBED ON CARD R

OR: TREATMENT – FAILURE RESULTS IN YOUR DEATH
– SUCCESS RETURNS YOU TO NORMAL HEALTH

Please put a √ against all cases where you are CONFIDENT that you would CHOOSE the treatment,

put a × against all cases where you are CONFIDENT that you would REJECT the treatment and accept the injuries on card R

put a ★ against the case where you consider the alternatives to be most finely balanced

Chances of Failure	Chances of Success
1/1000	999/1000
2/1000	998/1000
5/1000	995/1000
1/100	99/100
2/100	98/100
3/100	97/100
5/100	95/100
8/100	92/100
10/100	90/100
15/100	85/100
20/100	80/100
25/100	75/100
30/100	70/100
40/100	60/100
50/100	50/100
60/100	40/100
75/100	25/100
90/100	10/100

Death preferred

10

BOUNDED RATIONALITY IN ACTION[1]

The German submarine campaign, 1915–18

Avner Offer

There are two approaches to an economic interpretation of war. One is to regard the war as a problem of management by focusing upon the endowment of factors – including population, capital and natural resources – and the way in which this endowment affected the war's preparation, conduct and outcome. The procedure resembles business history, and involves a study of personalities, institutions, contingencies and constraints. The second method is to try to specify the variables in an analytical model. The approach can be macro-economic, regarding war as the unintended consequence of economic change, or micro-economic, taking warriors to be economic men who act rationally to optimize outcomes (Choucri and North 1975; Bueno de Mesquita 1981). Economic explanation is not normally concerned with the behaviour of specific individuals. But in war, as in business and political management, individuals are often crucial, and we need to probe the rationality that underlies the actions of a small group. In this chapter, the concept of economic rationality is explored and then applied to an interpretation of a crucial episode of economic warfare during the First World War. This episode is then set in a wider context of the relationship between resource endowment and military doctrine, with examples taken from the Second World War and from the Vietnam War.

I

Rationality is not always benign, but the notion of rationality does imply a desirable outcome. Most of the countries that participated in the First World War were much worse off when they emerged from the conflict. For many, if not most, of them the war was a deliberate choice, pondered long in advance during years of peace. When outcomes are undesirable, it is worth asking why. As Jon Elster says: 'it is only by close consideration of the reasons for failure that it will be possible to construct a more general account of human behaviour in which the concept of rationality will have a privileged, but not exclusive role' (1986: 27). The assumption of irrationality is not very helpful, since it places motives and actions outside the realm of explanation. Self-defeating action is not always arbitrary and random – on the contrary, it can be consistent and coherent.

Rationality does not exclude unfavourable outcomes. In the game theory device of 'prisoner's dilemma' unfavourable outcomes can flow from rational behaviour, but the merit of rationality is also its defect: it allows for almost any outcome. Another reason for sub-optimal outcomes is that when initial conditions such as perfect knowledge and perfect competition are not satisfied, outcomes are less than perfect as well.

Rational choice is a behavioural norm. Since the term is often employed rigorously, I shall use the term 'reasoning' instead. Formal reasoning implies the explicit exercise of reason and choice. It may be loosely defined as follows: 'When ends are given, formal reasoning is the process of choosing the means to achieve these ends, by collecting information, subjecting it to methodical analysis, and selecting the most appropriate form of action after weighing the alternatives, within the constraints of available resources.' A familiar deviation from this norm is encompassed by Herbert Simon's notion of 'satisficing' – a result of 'bounded rationality'.[2]

Simon's argument can be summarized in the following propositions. First, most practical projects are simply beyond our capacity to compute: 'For most problems that Man encounters in the real world, no procedure that he can carry out with his information processing equipment will enable him to discover the optimal solution, even when the notion of "optimum" is well defined' (Simon 1982, vol. 2: 430). This notion of bounded rationality is especially appropriate for explaining individual behaviour. Second, uncalculating mental states – including emotion, drive, instinct and impulse – get in the way. Such responses belong to the world of action, even economic action: they are acknowledged by advertising in peacetime and propaganda in wartime. Third, knowledge is almost always incomplete. Data are insufficiently available, and our command of rational procedures is imperfect. Fourth, people differ in their accceptance of uncertainty and risk. Fifth, delay can alter the nature of problems between the time they are perceived and the time they are tackled. Sixth, there is uncertainty about the behaviour of others, both allies and opponents. Seventh, goals are not always well-formulated; indeed there may not be a single unique rational solution to a problem.

A set of behavioural deviations from formal rationality have been identified and classified by social psychologists. A good deal of empirical research in that field has uncovered an 'intuitive reasoning' which deviates in persistent and predictable ways from 'formal reasoning'. Such deviations pervade the world of action and are an important reason why things do not turn out the way they are meant to. Some of the most pervasive pitfalls of intuitive reasoning include the following responses.[3] First, the methods chosen are those that happen to be available and familiar, not those most suitable to the task: an economist prefers to apply economic theory, a soldier military force, and so on. One persistent error is to use theories outside their domain of application. Data are also selected from those that happen to be available. Second, objects are assigned to the category they resemble. For example, a military problem must have a military solution. Third, vivid rather than boring data are preferred. One memorable anecdote can carry more conviction than a table of statistical data. Fourth, explanations are easily formulated, and, once established, theories and beliefs are held tenaciously, even in the face of strong evidence to the contrary. Confirming evidence is unconsciously preferred, and disconfirming evidence neglected. Fifth, there is a tendency to attribute behaviour to dispositions rather than situations – bad decisions are attributed to stupidity, and not to circumstances. Sixth, there is a whole sequence of failings to make proper inferences from quantitative data and from probabilities. People have a very faint notion of what constitutes a proper sample and of how it relates to a population; they find it difficult to identify correlations between variables, and do not sufficiently recognize that exceptional events will normally be followed by more familiar ones (regression to the mean) (Kahneman *et al.* 1982). Seventh, people have misplaced confidence in their own judgment, their own capabilities and their own luck. Military men are especially prone to this kind of delusion. With egos already inflated by deference and flattery, where bluster is the norm, it is easy for soldiers to lose their sense of reality (Dixon 1976). Eighth, people rarely have a good understanding of their own motives.

To make things clear, these patterns of action are not a norm, but a description. In the real world, decision-makers fall back on intuitions and rules of thumb. Instead of maximizing, people make do. Decisions and outcomes fall well short of the best that are attainable in principle. Instead of collecting data, analysing according to the best statistical procedures, and making an orderly assessment of possible action, decision-makers take short-cuts. They look for a good alternative rather than the best one; they rely on experience they have accumulated rather than seeking new information. Nevertheless, a great deal turns out acceptably. Not knowing what the best might be, people are satisfied with the good. The adversary is equally hampered. Given the complexity of many problems, intuitive reasoning is economical. In certain conditions it can be shown to be more efficient, or more rational, than formal reasoning (Nisbett and Ross 1980: ch. 11). Yet another deviation from formal reasoning is determined by the need for approbation and status. Behaviour is strongly conditioned by the expectations of others and the norms of society or of some smaller reference group.

These concepts do not amount to a rigorous theory, but they help to form a more realistic notion of how decision-makers perceive and pursue their interests. They also underpin the following account of the German submarine campaign during the First World War.

II

The decision to begin unrestricted submarine warfare on 1 February 1917 was Germany's most critical action during the First World War. Occurring on the very threshold of the Russian Revolution and of Britain's impending bankruptcy, it fortified the Allied side with all the wealth and power of the United States. In its consequences for Germany, it was likened by the German Chancellor to a 'second decision for war'.[4] Economic considerations were not marginal in this decision: economic warfare was the decisive strategy. The central question is: how did the Germans come to choose it?

German submarines began to attack merchant ships in October 1914, in response to Britain's declaration of large parts of the Channel and the North Sea as 'war zones'. In November 1914 the Minister of Marine, Admiral Tirpitz, told an American journalist that Germany had the means to intercept the bulk of Britain's food imports. The German press picked up this hint and began to agitate for deployment of the new weapon. Businessmen and academics also pressed the navy to use the submarine. 'Britain', two German professors wrote, 'with brutal frankness, has established the starvation of our population as a war aim.' If German reprisals were going to violate international law, Britain had set the precedent. These thoughts, addressed to the commander of the fleet, were endorsed by some of the most distinguished professors at the University of Berlin. The scholars pointed out how much Britain depended on imports, and recommended a combined air and undersea attack, with U-boats to destroy shipping and Zeppelins to attack food warehouses in the ports. Among the signatures on this document were those of two leading economists, Max Sering and Gustav von Schmoller. Professor Sering was certain that Britain would comply within a few weeks.[5]

Germany was inhibited both by the small number of submarines available and by their short range and limited endurance. At the end of January 1915 only twenty-one boats were available, eight of them obsolete. Raw numbers do not signify a great deal, since there were different classes of boats with different capabilities, and all of them required long periods of maintenance in port. This was not sufficiently appreciated by the naval command (Spindler 1960: 5–7).

The first submarine campaign, of February 1915, began as a tactical rather than a strategic venture. Britain's trade was the target, but the economic effect was not worked out. The sinkings began as a reprisal against the British blockade and as an experiment in the use of a new weapon. The success of the U-boats and the sinking of the *Lusitania* in May 1915 revealed their potential power, and also the risks that their use courted. It was not until March 1915 that the German Naval Staff began to collect data on British trade. This was undertaken in Department B1 by Reserve Lieutenant Dr Richard Fuss, a bank manager in peacetime. A second expert, whose role eventually came to match the one played by Fuss, was Dr Herman Levy, Professor of Economics at Heidelberg. Levy's reputation was based on a series of publications in the German tradition of historical economics: he wrote about the development of economic institutions, and had no aptitude for quantitative or analytical work. Among Levy's many published works was a book on English agriculture. His energy also found an outlet in a number of novels, some published under his own name and others under an assumed one. Although one of Levy's monographs was translated into English before the war, that should not be taken as a measure of his authority. His study of English landownership was unfocused, lacking in rigour, thin on data and dubious in its judgments.[6]

In January 1915 Levy wrote a short paper for the Admiralty on Britain's policy of economic specialization. Using data from the 1905 report of the British Royal Commission on the Supply of Food and Raw Material in Time of War, Levy cited the high rate of imports and the low level of stocks.[7] He noted that England, for commercial reasons, preferred to supply itself 'from hand to mouth' and that, in consequence, prices were already rising to record heights. A shortage of raw materials would also affect British manufacturing industry and give rise to unemployment; the English working classes would be badly affected (Spindler 1932, doc. 19: 225–8). In August 1915 he wrote another paper for the Admiralty Staff which examined the prospects of economic warfare against British trade. Levy divided the consequences into three. First, he considered the direct effect of sinkings on reduction of tonnage, rise of prices, shortage of goods and contraction of trade. Second, he outlined the indirect effects of disrupting the flow of trade, clogging up harbours and raising insurance costs. Third, Levy examined the impact on vulnerable sectors of the economy.

In its quest to transform its U-boats into strategic weapons, the German navy faced a crucial problem: how to deliver a decisive blow with limited means. If the navy were to have a decisive impact on the war, it needed to identify a sector that was both vital to the British economy and exposed to attack. Levy identified such a sector: England's supply of wheat. Grain prices in Britain were already much higher than in Germany, proof of difficulties in sustaining the flow of imports. Here was a target small enough for the submarines to destroy, and yet critical for Britain's survival. The target would be even smaller at a time when British stocks were low.[8]

Levy's views formed the core of economic reasoning that

supported the submarine campaign. A more developed version of his ideas appeared in a published pamphlet (Levy 1915). As a writer on English agriculture, Levy was familiar with the decline of Britain's grain production and its reliance on wheat. Levy took his ideas directly out of the work of the Royal Commission on the Supply of Food of 1903–5. According to Levy, the British bread supply was open to successful attack because of the system of staggered importation of grain from all over the world. In Germany and other large grain-producing countries, domestic stocks lasted for most of the year. Britain relied on an 'uninterrupted stream' of grain, and did not hold much of it in storage. At their highest, stocks amounted to seventeen weeks' supply; at their lowest, they would last for only six and a half weeks.

The Royal Commission on the Supply of Food also provided Levy with a mechanism to convert grain shortage into political crisis. He referred to a passage from the Commission's report which argued that if wheat imports were cut off when domestic stocks were already exhausted, there would be a rise in prices, a dangerous panic and a shortage so serious that war could not be sustained. German Admiralty Staff files contain a printed flow-chart (from August 1915) that describes twenty-five different ways in which the U-boat war would raise costs within the British economy. Levy also had a notion of the direct and indirect linkages of blockade, but for him the rising price of corn and meat was to be the crux. He expected this mechanism to drive Britain into defeat.[9]

On 30 August 1915 the Admiralty Staff printed a memorandum that advocated a submarine campaign not for limited objectives, but for a decisive one: to force Britain to sue for peace by means of economic warfare. To secure such a prize submarines should disregard international law and sink without warning, even at the cost of bringing America into the war.[10]

III

August 1915 marked the start of the Naval Staff's effort to promote economic warfare as a strategy to win the war. The case was expounded in full in the Chief of the Admiralty Staff's memorandum of 12 February 1916. More than 500 copies of this thirty-eight-page pamphlet were circulated in naval and military circles, launching a 'battle of memoranda' that continued until the end of the year. The papers were prepared by Dr Fuss, who was joined by Levy in July; he was advised by the grain merchants Weil and Newman, and by other experts from business, finance and agriculture. The sequence of naval papers (one in July, another in August) culminated in the Chief of the Naval Staff's memorandum of 22 December 1916. The case for economic warfare as a decisive weapon is best considered in this long tract, which crowned about sixteen months' work.[11]

The Admiralty's strategic problem was to identify a target that was both critical and capable of destruction before the United States could place its full weight on the Allied side. The paper of 22 December identified two such targets: the British wheat supply, and the merchant tonnage that carried it.

One constraint on the project was the capacity of Germany's submarines to sink merchant ships. In the first few months of 1916 sinkings amounted to some 200,000 tons of shipping a month, and were still at this level in August. But in October and November they rose to 400,000 tons. These results were achieved with conventional cruiser warfare, which required the submarines to approach merchant vessels on the surface and let their crews take to the lifeboats. The Admiralty promised that if restrictions were lifted, a monthly sinking rate of 600,000 tons could be achieved, coming down to 500,000 tons as the traffic became thinner. An oft-repeated figure was 4 million tons in six months, or 667,000 tons a month. The actual sinkings for the first six months of the unrestricted submarine campaign almost matched this forecast and reached an average of 643,000 tons.[12]

Unrestricted submarine warfare would raise the kill by 50 per cent, but it introduced a time constraint.[13] This question of time (the *Terminfrage* as it later became known) was the result of several factors, some of which the planners may not have considered. Few soldiers or statesmen in Germany had any doubt that unrestricted submarine warfare would bring America into the war. The U-boats had to finish their work before American intervention became decisive. That is why there was no room for half-measures. The navy had to promise victory because if it failed the outcome was certain defeat.

When the navy put the proposal to the army in January 1916, the time-scale for victory was given as two months. A few days later the time had risen to four months. In the navy's paper of 12 February 1916, it was six months. Thereafter, the figure fluctuated:

six to eight months, then five months, four, and in December 1916 five to seven months.[14] This suggests that the time constraint was not entirely derived from economic calculations, but was a prior constraint on the plan.

There was a feeling that time was working against Germany. A note of desperation recurs in the battle of notes and memoranda. Up to August 1916 the argument was that Germany's allies, and possibly also the German people, could not survive another winter of war. In December 1916 the prospect of another year of war could be faced no longer. In a war of attrition an already exhausted Germany was bound to lose, because it had fewer resources than the Allies. Both the Naval Staff and the army High Command declared that submarine warfare was a desperate measure, the last remaining chance for victory (*Beilagen, Aktenstücke*: 146, 155, 177, 241–2, 284–7).

Wheat was almost the sole ingredient of bread in Britain, and some 80 per cent was imported. Furthermore, the quantities imported (about 6 million tons a year) corresponded quite closely with the U-boats' sinking capacity. In the summer of 1916 a new factor emerged. Professor Levy reported that overseas harvests were poor (Stegemann 1970: 56). North America, which had provided 90 per cent of British imports in 1915, would not have a surplus for export, and Britain would have to look to India, to South America and especially to Australia for the rest. A ton of shipping could carry 5 tons of grain from North America, but only half that amount from the southern hemisphere or India. It would take double the tonnage to import the same amount of grain, thus employing a much higher proportion of the merchant fleet. Out of this estimate there came a curious calculation, that every 100,000 tons of shipping destroyed signified a deficit of 240,000 tons of grain, or twelve days of English consumption. It is curious because not all shipping carried grain; because some of the grain would still come from North America; and because other things (e.g. countermeasures) would not remain equal. Even under the best possible assumptions the figures did not add up. It is difficult to pin down a single statement of the tonnage required to ship the grain, but one that comes closest puts it at 1.4 million tons, which was about one-seventh of the tonnage available to Britain for civilian purposes (including neutral ships) (Memorandum of 22 December 1916, *Beilagen, Aktenstücke*: 248–53, 261–2). Other cargoes were also vital: fats, pit-prop timber and ores were carried from Spain and Scandinavia. Nevertheless it was the poor harvest overseas that seemed to determine the critical period. Working backwards from the beginning of the new harvest in August, the campaign would have to begin no later than 1 February 1917 (*Beilagen, Aktenstücke*: 239–41, 264).

The cargo space available to Britain was a far more unwieldy target. It was estimated in December 1916 at some 20 million tons, which was about five times the six-month sinking capacity of the U-boats. So the primary task of Department B1 was to show how the sinking of some 4 million tons could create a situation sufficiently critical to force Britain to sue for peace.

One step, as we have seen, was to inflate the tonnage required for carrying grain, by assuming supply from more distant producers. The second move was to lower the estimate of tonnage available to the Allies, in order to make it a more plausible target. In broad outline it was done this way. Out of 20 million tons of shipping available, some 8 million tons were committed to the supply and transport of troops and their equipment. Another 4 million tons were involved either in refitting, in carrying the imports of Britain's allies or in coastal shipping. That left some 8 million tons of shipping (*Beilagen, Aktenstücke*: 264–7). Of 3 million tons of neutral shipping, 40 per cent would be scared away. The effective monthly traffic to England was no more than 6.14 million tons. After six months of submarine warfare, Department B1 claimed that this trade would be cut by 39 per cent (*Beilagen, Aktenstücke*: 273–4). In this event, the paper implied, the grain supply would be cut in the same proportion. The resulting rise in prices, and then the actual shortages of bread, would create such panic and outcry that Britain would not be able to continue the war. Accordingly, in its memorandum the Admiralty Staff stressed that compliance with international law should be suspended in order to bring about the terror and panic which were necessary for success (*Beilagen, Aktenstücke*: 278–9).

A large part of the December 1916 paper was devoted to demonstrating that the process of collapse was already in progress: freight, insurance and commodity prices had risen enormously, with bread prices much higher than in Germany. Labour unrest was already spreading, together with anti-war agitation, demonstrations and other symptoms of panic (*Beilagen, Aktenstücke*: 254–7). Another part of the paper dealt with possible British countermeasures and adaptations. For ships to sail in convoy would not provide a practical solution, since convoys took time to assemble, sailed at the speed of the slowest and would also present a large target to submarines. Their irregular arrival would congest the harbours and the railways. It would not be easy to release ships from military duties or Allied support. The English lacked the aptitude to organize an efficient system of rationing and the fortitude to endure shortages. Some captured German ships might be pressed into service, but these would be more than offset by the desertion of the Dutch and Danish neutrals. American intervention could not make a critical difference within the time-span projected. American financial support could not increase the flow of goods to the Allies, who already used all of America's capacity. Time would be too short for America to raise, train and dispatch a significant number of troops, whose quality was dubious anyway (*Beilagen, Aktenstücke*: 275–6, 266–76, 279–83).

From the very start the naval programme encountered strong resistance, most effectively from Chancellor Bethmann Hollweg and Interior Minister Helfferich, who attacked its more obvious fallacies. This amounted to a rejection of the Admiralty's time-limit, of the idea that a decisive blow could end the war in a few months. Indeed, Bethmann Hollweg regarded war-weariness (on both sides) as the only chance of a peace settlement, and was certain that American entry would stiffen the Allies and make such a peace impossible. He argued that England would be able to adapt. New construction and captured enemy tonnage would augment the fleet; naval countermeasures would reduce the sinkings; shipping would be shifted from military to civilian requirements – the 'sideshow' Allied expedition to Salonika might be recalled. Rationing and other organizational measures would effect economies. As blockade could never be total, and the essential grain cargoes were quite small, it was not possible to starve Britain out. England had 18 million tons of shipping. Who believed that it could no longer fight with 14 million (*Beilagen Aktenstücke*, pt 4, Bethmann Hollweg, docs 149, 150, 152; 29 February 1916, 5 March 1916, 13 March 1916)?

In August 1916 Helfferich also pointed out that Germany stood to lose a substantial overseas trade, which was vital to provision the army, the occupied territories (by means of the American relief commission) and the large towns. Furthermore, he claimed that the tonnage figures were incorrect. With 12 million tons available for trade, the loss even of one-third would not compel

England to surrender (*Beilagen, Aktenstücke*, docs 157, 167; 31 August 1916, 6 October 1916).

Both the Chancellor and the Minister of the Interior warned very strongly of the danger of ignoring American political, financial, productive and military potential. German envoys in America agreed. The statesmen saw the project as a dangerous gamble. Even within the navy the calculations were regarded with suspicion, and an army study produced a more pessimistic forecast.[15] Helfferich even argued that the campaign would actually increase British food supplies (as proved to be the case). An allied America would make sacrifices to provide for Britain on a scale that it would not make as a neutral (*Beilagen, Aktenstücke*: 228).

Other fallacies eluded the critics. The key to these errors is found in a phrase in the December 1916 memorandum. Admiral Holtzendorff, Chief of the Naval Staff, wrote: 'The economy of a country resembles a masterpiece of precision mechanics; once it falls into disorder, interference, frictions and breakages continue incessantly' (*Beilagen, Aktenstücke*: 245). It is difficult to imagine a less appropriate simile. A war economy resembles a self-repairing organism, not a machine. Fuss and Levy simply assumed that very little could be done to counter the submarines. They made the most favourable assumptions, and refused to consider British adaptations. They had neither the tools, the understanding, nor, probably, the will to undertake an analysis that took into account the British responses and adaptations. Their form of argument was essentially anecdotal and historical. Instead of probing the possible causes of price inflation they simply took rising prices as evidence of material shortages, without ever considering either the effect of monetary expansion or the full employment of both labour and plant. There was no attempt to calculate real wages. Their blockade economics were intuitive, and showed no grasp of how the price mechanism enables an economy to substitute commodities and factors for each other. Mancur Olson has described these adaptations concisely and well: as prices change, the economy adapts by substitutions among its inputs and output. Home production, which had not been profitable before, now becomes viable. As freight costs rise, many commodities cannot be carried economically, thus freeing tonnage for other goods – and so on (Olson 1963: ch. 4).

The largest single constraint turned out to be congestion at the ports and on the railways, and not the submarine. Decisive action could – and did – clear much of it away (Doughty 1982: ch. 1). German blockade economics showed the same neglect of the price mechanism as did the rationing efforts within Germany which had exacerbated the domestic food crisis (Skalweit 1927: pts 4 and 5). The 1 February deadline was also misguided since the end of the six-month period coincided with the English harvest, which was likely to stiffen resistance. Other things being equal, an earlier date might have been a better time to begin.

At the end of August 1916 a new team was appointed to the army High Command; Ludendorff, a relatively junior officer who combined high professional competence with almost maniac zeal, became the single most powerful man in Germany, although his powers fell short of dictatorship. With his partner Hindenburg, Ludendorff pressed the naval case for unrestricted submarine warfare with renewed vigour. Their support was decisive. On 9 January the Kaiser yielded to the combined influence of military and naval pressure, and decided to launch the campaign on 1 February, over the misgivings of his civilian advisers.

IV

In war the lack of information is pervasive. Information is itself a weapon, the stakes are very high, and both uncertainty and stress loom large. But the norms of reasoning remain the same. On the face of it, the decision to begin unrestricted submarine warfare was an economic one: it took the form of a rudimentary analysis of costs and benefits. The outcome was failure. With so much uncertainty, and with an intense personal commitment to the outcome, the economists and their masters were both walking into the pitfalls of intuitive reasoning.

The 'theory' for the campaign came out of the work of the Royal Commission on Food Supply, as modified by the new capabilities of the U-boats. The German Admiralty went through the motions of normative reasoning: it took advice from experts, and collected statistics to build up its case. But the experts were actually selected for their bias. In the face of powerful objections, the Admiralty demonstrated a typical failing of intuitive reasoning. It clung to its preconceptions. The Admiralty had caught a glimpse of economic victory early in the war, and was extremely reluctant to give it up. Like scientists stuck in a 'degenerating research programme', they could not be swayed by argument or evidence.[16] As intuitive reasoners, Levy and Fuss blocked out evidence that would not fit the theory. The research paradigm of historical economics was not very suitable for modelling the dynamic effects of blockade. But no elaborate analysis was required. After all, the civilian statesmen were able to present a good counter-case. It was not the method that was necessarily unsuitable, but those who applied it. They also made the error of focusing upon evidence that was close at hand: America was far away, and its intervention in the war a remote prospect, so the admirals gave it insufficient weight in their reasoning. Pride was implicated. Both the experts and the admirals had staked their egos on the submarine plan. There was a strong undercurrent of impotent anger, a quest for an effective reprisal for the deepening material deprivation in Germany.

It is tempting to ascribe behaviour to dispositions rather than situations, but the admirals, and the generals who supported them, were not stupid. They were competent men who had reached the top of their professions. They acted like typical intuitive reasoners by seeking guidance from a doctrine they knew and understood. They preferred the familiar doctrine of military leadership to the alien one of economic analysis. This is not to deny that the military code is appropriate in its own sphere, and that it diverges from economic egotism for excellent reasons. The commander of a destroyer or an infantry battalion must be prepared for sacrifice, even self-sacrifice, as part of a larger design. A naval or military officer is trained to run much greater risks, even with his own life, than are acceptable in peacetime. Action in war is surrounded by imponderables and, other things being equal, victory goes to the stronger will. Will-power and an unshakable belief in ultimate victory are themselves weapons. A soldier is trained to go on fighting to the last bullet, in the hope that something will turn up – and to accept fate if it does not.

The officer's code is adapted to the needs of military command. But, as intuitive reasoners, the German commanders applied this code to problems that it could not resolve. The proper frame of reference was a political and economic assessment of benefits and costs. Bethmann Hollweg was far from a model of normative reasoning: his role in the war decisions of July and August 1914 shows that he was capable of making wild leaps in the dark. But in this case his reasoning was much more rational. Not that he was any less resolute than his military counterparts. He simply had a clearer view of the balance of risks and opportunities. This comes out in his attitude to international law. Although he stressed the danger of breaking international law, he did not regard it as a matter of principle. Legal proprieties would not be an obstacle if there was a prospect of success. What he would not support was a gamble.[17]

In the language of political science, the submarine campaign was an 'expressive' and not an 'instrumental' course of action. Action itself became the end. More was at stake for the soldiers than for civilians. War is a professional undertaking, and professional competence and pride were implicated. The soldiers' perception of themselves as the élite of an expanding empire required territorial gains in the west. Bethmann Hollweg regarded these acquisitions in Belgium and France as desirable, but not vital (Jarausch 1973: ch. 7). Since naval inaction was bound to result in their loss anyway, the admirals and generals regarded a short, decisive campaign (with a chance of success) as the lesser evil. Their civilian supporters expressed this preference for action when they said: 'Rather war with America than starvation' (Jarausch 1973: 287). After the war Bethmann Hollweg explained why he did not resign:

> To my mind, the technical point of the calculations with regard to economics could not of itself be conclusive. . . . To sit absolutely passive, staring into the future, and to endure that defeat in war which lay before us, according to the judgement of the military branch, and, at the same time, to have in one's hand an instrument of warfare which had not been tried out, and which, when all was said and done, held out certain prospects of success – well, we had to make use of this instrument; it was not to be avoided.[18]

The submarine campaign falls into a pattern with other great decisions of war: with August 1914, with Verdun (1916) and with Ludendorff's Spring Offensive in 1918. In all four cases Germany embarked on an offensive against overwhelming material odds, almost, it seems, for the sake of the struggle itself. It attempted to break a political impasse with a military gamble, with little regard for the odds. It pitched professional zeal and the intensity of desperation against superior material forces.

The dominance of this mind-set was confirmed when the naval campaign failed to achieve its goals. Sinkings continued in 1918, although it was no longer clear what they could achieve. The success rate declined steeply. More than 6 million tons were sunk in 1917, and only 2 million in 1918. But the Naval Staff was prepared to jeopardize the peace negotiations in October and November 1918 in order to continue the anti-shipping campaign. Naval fatalism was expressed in the intention of the High Seas fleet to sail out for battle on the very point of Germany's collapse, in late October 1918 (Salter 1921: 356–7; Rudin 1944: 244–9).

The U-boat captains did not disappoint the Naval Staff's expectations. Sinkings more than matched the forecast in the first six months, and continued to be a serious drain on the British war economy until the very end of the war. In the spring of 1917 and several times later they gave British leaders a great deal of anxiety (Fayle 1924: chs 6, 11). Adaptations and countermeasures, however, carried Britain through. German naval planners failed to appreciate the decisive importance of American financial support for a Britain that was almost bankrupt. They underestimated British organizational capacity. Tonnage losses were not an appropriate measure of success. The real target was the grain supply, and here the U-boats did not even remotely approach their target. At the end of November 1916 the British wheat stock stood at less than sixteen weeks' supply, with only eleven days' supply in government hands.[19] The food controller, however, demanded six months' reserve, and the Royal Commission on Wheat Supplies (the supply agency) took this requirement into account, and also allowed for a 10 per cent loss to the submarines. The average losses of the Commission up to August 1917 amounted to only 6 per cent, far short of the 40 per cent or so implied by German expectations.[20] Only once, in March 1917, did the monthly losses exceed 10 per cent, and in 1918 they rose only once above 2 per cent.[21] During the decisive first six months of the campaign British grain reserves more than doubled. By giving grain cargoes higher priority, government and millers' stocks (excluding bakers and retailers) increased from a five-and-a-half-week supply at the end of March to a fourteen-week supply at the end of July.[22]

V

The German military code may appear to be an irrational body of doctrine to apply in this context, but it was an appropriate adaptation – an economizing adaptation to Germany's resource endowment. In the first place, the system of military indoctrination and discipline can be regarded, in a prisoner's dilemma framework, as a social adaptation required to overcome the rational survival impulse of the individual soldier, in order to ensure the survival of the community (Brennan and Tullock 1983).

At the level of resource endowment, Germany's geopolitical, diplomatic and strategic posture made it inferior in both manpower and economic resources to its rivals France and Russia. The *entente cordiale* added the prospect of British and possible Italian intervention against Germany. In contemplating a war on two fronts, Germany invested considerable effort in developing the most efficient tactical and logistical framework, so as to make the most of its restricted manpower resources. A cursory examination of casualty statistics suggests that Germany used its manpower more efficiently than did Britain and France. The total casualties of the Allies were about one-third higher than were those of the Central Powers, despite the Allies' large advantage in firepower. A detailed breakdown of casualties by fronts is not available, but Germany lost fewer men (2.04 million) than did France, Britain, the United States and the Dominions combined (2.3 million, excluding Indian and South African losses). The fact that the Germans sustained much heavier losses on the Eastern, Balkan and Italian fronts than did the Western Allies on their side-shows (Palestine, Gallipoli, Salonika, Mesopotamia), suggests that – in terms of this simple criterion, and given their material and numerical inferiority – man-for-man the German army was a more effective killing machine (Winter 1985: 75).

Other countries, with different resource endowments, had different priorities and developed different military structures. Research into other wars throws some light on the interplay between economic and military rationality. A comparison of fighting power – of the productivity, so to speak, of fighting resources – has been carried out on the United States and the German armies in the Second World War. In that war, too, the German army was more efficient. In a study of seventy-eight engagements between the German and American armies – taking into account numbers, terrain, posture, the effect of airpower – the actual outcome could be predicted only on the assumption that the Germans were 20–30 per cent more effective than were the British and American forces facing them: 'On a man for man basis the German ground soldiers consistently inflicted casualties at about a fifty per cent higher rate than they incurred from the opposing British and

American troops under all circumstances' (Creveld 1982: 5–6, citing Dupuy 1977).

The same unbreakable will, the same tactical military excellence, was applied with such disastrous results to the decision for the submarine campaign. For all its tactical excellence, the German army had a talent for winning battles and losing wars. The German objective of tactical efficiency was achieved at the expense of strategic realism. Having an efficient army proved too much of a temptation to German statesmen. A more rational course for Germany might have been to seek peaceful ways of advancing the national interest. In terms of the definition of formal reasoning adopted in this article, the ends were given. But rational choice needs to consider ends as well as means. The ends that are suitable at one level of action form the means at a higher level. German military doctrine was focused on battlefield efficiency. At the level of international relations, military efficiency was not an end in itself, but merely one out of many instruments available to secure power and plenty. When military commanders assumed responsibility for national policy, they failed to make the transition from one set of ends to another. The norms instilled by their professional training were too strong to transcend.

It is instructive to consider the sources of German tactical excellence. With manpower limitations, the Germans developed a tactical doctrine that stressed the quality of their human capital. This approach had two aspects. One was the tactical doctrine of *Auftragstaktik*: at every level of command, operational orders took the general form of defining the objectives and leaving the details to be worked out by the subordinate commanders. Control was decentralized, and both the local knowledge and the initiative of subordinate commanders were given full play (Creveld 1982: 35; Holborn 1986: 291). This approach, which was taken down to the level of the smallest unit, was a feature of German military doctrine before the First World War. As the military regulations put it in 1906: 'combat demands thinking, independent leaders and troops capable of independent action'. The regulations of 1908 stated 'from the youngest soldier upwards, the total independent commitment of all physical and mental forces is to be demanded. Only thus can the full power of the troops be brought into action' (Creveld 1982: 35–6). This approach maximized individual military skills, and 'learning by doing' on the battlefield. Given the rudimentary state of battlefield control, which relied on rigid, low-capacity telegraph and telephone lines, the system of delegating authority also gave the army tactical flexibility. The Germans were able to turn this flexibility to advantage in their Spring Offensive of 1918, where infiltration tactics finally broke the deadlock of the Western Front. This was in stark contrast to the rigid discipline which disabled the frontal assaults of the other side (Creveld 1985: 172–84).

There was another key feature in German military organization. They realized – without the benefit of social science research, which has later confirmed this understanding – that the main source of motivation on the battlefield is the approbation of fellow soldiers. In order to promote the social cohesion of the fighting unit, the German army in the Second World War recruited its regiments on a territorial basis, and made a rule of preserving the integrity of its units, maintaining a large number of small formations, regardless of casualties, and rotating units frequently between the front and the rear. For officers, career progress was bound up with operational success. The German approach to war has stressed the primacy of human resources, of motivation and leadership. In contrast, the American armies of the Second World War gave the fighting arm – the infantry – the lowest priority for manpower quality. The American approach to war has stressed logistics: firepower rather than manpower, and quantity rather than quality. It has carried a higher proportion of support and headquarters personnel than has the German army; its form of command was more centralized and left less for the junior commander to decide. Most importantly, despite the findings of their own social scientists, the Americans had little understanding of the importance of unit cohesion and peer approbation as military resources. American combat units were constantly kept in the line, allowing experienced veterans to be killed off or to collapse with combat fatigue, and were reinforced by manpower drafts sent as individuals, with no previous bonding. This led to serious problems of motivation and combat performance (Creveld 1982). Given the nature and abundance of American resources, and the norms of American society, this approach reflected American comparative advantage.

This argument does not imply that formal reasoning is always more appropriate than military doctrine or other forms of intuitive reasoning. America has also lost a war, against an enemy inferior in resources even to the Germans. A suggestive example is provided by American management in the Vietnam War. In that war an effort was made by the American government to apply formal reasoning to the management of war. The heart of this effort was in the Office of Systems Analysis at the Department of Defence – a group of economists who attempted to apply the scalpel of rationality to military decisions. In a book written during the conflict, the leaders of this group complained that not enough formal rationality had been applied. 'Systematic analysis was a major missing element in understanding what the United States was doing in and to Vietnam.' Their own office was only allowed to carry out a limited effort, part of which consisted of developing and maintaining a 'single, authoritative plan for manpower, logistics, procurement and financial planning' (Enthoven and Smith 1971: 270–1).

Formal reasoning was a powerful tool. Without any benefit of hindsight, the economists concerned were able to point to their own analysis to show that a military strategy in Vietnam based on manpower attrition rates could not be successful. The economists were fully aware of the difference between the military and the economic ethos, but regarded military conventions as obstacles, without acknowledging their role in motivation. Thus their manpower management system was based on a 'debit/credit account' of 'personnel spaces' that encouraged commanders to disband units in order to draw reinforcements. They concluded: 'This system worked well, and we believe it helped to save millions of dollars in the support of U.S. combat operations' (Enthoven and Smith 1971: 276). There is no consideration of whether such quantitative indicators were a good measure of fighting power, or whether the scarce factor in American operations in Vietnam was dollars or combat efficiency. This may be unfair, as more information is needed for a proper judgment to be made. But the book, which is written with impressive intelligence, underlines the gap between the priorities of soldiers and economic analysts. In the First World War the Germans applied intuitive reasoning, where formal reasoning would have been appropriate. The American experience in Vietnam suggests how formal reasoning, when applied inappropriately, can become another instance of intuitive reasoning.

It is a foolish historian who tries to fight wars retrospectively. What this paper has attempted to show is the interaction, in wartime, of two different ends of rationality, both of them functional, both of them designed to optimize the use of resources. The problem of wartime leadership is to know, in a situation fraught with uncertainty and stress, which one to heed.

NOTES

1 This paper was first published under the title 'Economic interpretation of war: the German submarine campaign, 1915–1918' in the *Australian Economic History Review* 24 (1989): 21–41. It develops the ideas contained in chapter 24 of the author's book *The First World War: An Agrarian Interpretation* (1989).

2 I have drawn on Ermini (1986), Simon (1982), Elster (1986) and Sen (1987). All contain extensive bibliographies.

3 What follows draws mainly upon Nisbett and Ross (1980).

4 Jarausch (1973: 281). Britain was no longer able to finance its purchases in North America (see Burk 1981: 36).

5 A collection of documents is in Spindler (1932, vol. 1: 177ff). The professors' memorandum is dated 26 January 1915 (doc. 24: 234–42 and 241; 'a few weeks' 234). See also Spindler (1960: 1–14), Ritter (1972: 124–5) and Stegemann (1970: 23–4).

6 I discovered this when consulting it for my own book on English landownership. See Levy (1911). Levy's *nom de plume* was Hermann Lint.

7 Royal Commission on Food Supply. For the antecedents of this Commission see Offer (1985: 204–12).

8 Levy, 'Wirtschaftliche Strategie in U-Bootkrieg' (19 August 1915), Admiralstab, roll T1022/905, PG/75952, vol. 20.

9 'Der U-Bootkrieg und die englische Volkswirtschaft (in graphischer Darstellung)', p. 3 (printed August 1915); Admiralstab, roll T1022/905, PG/75952, vol. 20; Levy (1915: 6, 38).

10 Untitled memorandum on economic warfare, 30 August 1915, Admiralstab, roll T1022/905, PG/75931.

11 For an account of the department's work see Stegemann (1970: 51–64). Some of the papers are printed in *Beilagen, Aktenstücke*; others (including the 12 February 1916 memorandum) are in Admiralstab, roll T1022/905. I have not seen the originals in Freiburg.

12 'England und der U-Boot-Krieg' lecture by Fuss read on 31 March 1917 at the Industry Club in Düsseldorf (printed Berlin 1917): 11–12, Admiralstab, roll T1022/905, PG/75931, vol. 1; Stegemann (1970: 58); Holtzendorff, memorandum of 22 December 1916, *Beilagen, Aktenstücke*: 247; tonnage sunk February to July 1917, Olson (1963: 83).

13 There is a little puzzle here: although unrestricted sinkings were meant to be 50 per cent higher, the navy asserted that they would be twice as effective. See the Admiralty memorandum of 22 December 1916, *Beilagen, Aktenstücke*: 240 and 278.

14 These estimates are all in the *Beilagen, Aktenstücke*: 143, 146, 165, 177, 204 and 264.

15 *Beilagen, Aktenstücke.* See also Stegemann (1970: 57, 74); Simon,

'Die Fiktion des Frachtraummangels' (1 September 1916), Admiralstab, roll T1022/1019, PG/76094.

16 The point is that scientists do not readily abandon a position even in the face of disconfirming evidence and more powerful theory (see Lakatos 1978: 113, 116–17).

17 For Bethmann Hollweg's regret that a total blockade was impossible, see *Beilagen, Aktenstücke*, doc. 152: 171; doc. 158: 182. Gamble: *Beilagen, Aktenstücke*, doc. 149: 161.

18 Evidence of Bethmann Hollweg, 5 November 1919, *Stenographischer Bericht*: 294 and 295. Translation from Carnegie Endowment, *Official documents*: 472.

19 Total stocks – 'Wheat supplies – importing countries' (January 1917), Anderson Papers PRO 30/68/7, fos 15–16; government stocks, Royal Commission, Wheat Supplies Report, App. 13: 40.

20 J. F. Beale, 'Memorandum by the Wheat Commissioner for consideration by the Food Controller', No. 9 (March 1917), Anderson Papers PRO 30/68/8, fo. 91.

21 J. F. Beale, 'Memorandum by the Wheat Commission for consideration by the Food Controller', No. 23 (18 September 1917), fo. 9. See Wheat Supplies Report, App. 10: 37, for monthly losses through enemy action. Average losses for February to December 1917 were 6.73 per cent.

22 Wheat Supplies Report, App. 13: 40. Retail and bakers' stocks (another 10–17 days' supply) bring the figure to sixteen weeks, comparable to November 1916.

REFERENCES

Admiralstab der Marine, Akten betreffend Handelskrieg mit U-Boote, Washington, DC: United States National Archives.

Beilagen, Aktenstücke (1920) Verfassunggebende deutsche Nationalversammlung, *Untersuchungsauschusses . . . über die Friedensaktion Wilsons, Beilagen zu den Stenographischen Berichten, Aktenstücke zur Friedensaktion Wilsons, 1916/17, pt 4–5*, Berlin.

Brennan, G. and Tullock, G. (1983) 'An economic theory of military tactics: methodological individualism at war', *Journal of Economic Behaviour and Organization* 3.

Bueno de Mesquita, B. (1981) *The War Trap*, New Haven.

Burk, K. (1981) 'The mobilization of Anglo-American finance during World War I', in N. F. Dreisziger (ed.) *Mobilization for Total War: The Canadian, American and British Experience, 1914–18, 1939–45*, Waterloo, Ontario.

Carnegie Endowment for International Peace (1923) *Official German Documents Relating to the World War*, New York.

Choucri, N. and North, R. C. (1975) *Nations in Conflict: National Growth and International Violence*, San Francisco.

Creveld, M. Van (1982) *Fighting Power: German and U.S. Army Performance, 1939–1945*, Westport, Conn.

—— (1985) *Command in War*, Cambridge, Mass.
Dixon, N. (1976) *The Psychology of Military Incompetence*, London.
Doughty, M. (1982) *Merchant Shipping and War: A Study in Defence Planning in Twentieth-Century Britain*, London.
Dupuy, T. (1977) *A Genius for War*, London.
—— (1979) *Numbers, Prediction and War*, New York.
Elster, J. (1986) 'Introduction', in J. Elster (ed.) *Rational Choice*, Oxford.
Ermini, L. (1986) 'A survey of recent contributions to the criticism of classical rationality', unpublished mimeo, University of California at San Diego.
Enthoven, A. C. and Smith, K. W. (1971) *How Much is Enough? Shaping the Defence Program 1961–69*, New York.
Fayle, C. E. (1924) *History of the Great War. Seaborne Trade*, vol. 3.
Holborn, H. (1986) 'The Prusso-German School: Moltke and the rise of the General Staff', in P. Paret (ed.) *Makers of Modern Strategy*, Princeton.
Jarausch, K. (1973) *The Enigmatic Chancellor: Bethmann Hollweg and the Hubris of Imperial Germany*, New Haven.
Kahneman, D., Slovik, P. and Tversky, A. (eds) (1982) *Judgement Under Uncertainty: Heuristics and Biases*, Cambridge.
Lakatos, I. (1978) *The Methodology of Scientific Research Programmes*, Cambridge.
Levy, H. (1911) *Large and Small Holdings: A Study of English Agricultural Economics*, London.
—— (1915) *Die Neue Kontinentalsperre. Ist Grossbritannien Wirtschaftlich Bedroht?*, Berlin.
Nisbett, R. and Ross, L. (1980) *Human Inference: Strategies and Shortcomings of Social Judgement*, Englewood Cliffs, NJ.
Offer, A. (1985) 'The working classes, British naval plans and the coming of the Great War', *Past and Present* 107.
—— (1989) *The First World War: An Agrarian Interpretation*, Oxford.
Olson, M. jr (1963) *The Economics of the Wartime Shortage*, Durham, North Carolina.
Ritter, G. (1970) *The Sword and the Scepter*, vol. 2, Coral Gables, Florida.
—— (1972) *The Sword and the Scepter*, vol. 3, Coral Gables, Florida.
Royal Commission (1905) Supply of Food and Raw Material in Time of War, Minutes of evidence. Cd. 2643, 2644 XXXIX.
—— (1921) Wheat Supplies, First report with appendices. Cd. 1544 XVIII.
Rudin, H. (1944) *Armistice 1918,* New Haven.
Salter, J. A. (1921) *Allied Shipping Control: An Experiment in International Administration*, Oxford.
Sen, A. (1987) *On Ethics and Economics*, Oxford.
Simon, H. A. (1982) 'Rational decision making in business organizations', in H. A. Simon, *Models of Bounded Rationality*, vol. 2, Cambridge, Mass.
Skalweit, E. (1927) *Die Deutsche Kreigsernährungswirtschaft*, Stuttgart.
Spindler, A. (1932) *Der Handelskrieg mit U-Booten*, vol. 1, Berlin.

—— (1960) *Wie es zu dem Entschluss zum Uneingeschränkten U-Boots-Krieg 1917 Gekommen Ist*, Göttingen.
Stegemann, B. (1970) *Die Deutsche Marinepolitik 1916–1918*, Berlin.
Winter, J. M. (1985) *The Great War and the British People*, London.

INDEX

Abraham, K. 118
action 83; calculation and habits 2, 45–8; intuitive reasoning and 181–2; regret theory and 154
adaptation: selection and 43; war economy and 190, 194
advertisements 81
Alchian, A. A. 40
Allais, M. 9, 20, 29
altruism, universal 43
anonymity condition 139
anxiety 113
application-related language skills 25
arbitrage 84
Arrow, K. J. 147; impossibility theorem 4, 133; IIA condition (independence of irrelevant alternatives) 133, 137–42, 144–5
art 73–4
articulated values 168–72
Auftragstaktik 196–7
Austrian theorists 46
available information set 155–8
axioms of choice 14–17, 20, 22–3; evolution and 47–8; logical theory 54–5; social choice 132–3; testing SEU 29–33; *see also* maintained hypotheses; rules

bargaining games 78
Baron, J. 29, 163
basic values 168
battlefield efficiency 195–7
beliefs 8–9; Keynes and rational 92–103; maintained hypothesis 12, 13, 17, 21; measure theory 22; post-modernity 71
Bell, J. 115–16
Benthamism 104
Bergson–Samuelson social welfare functions 142, 144
Bethmann Hollweg, T. von 189, 192–3
betweenness 15–16; *see also* completeness
binary preference relations 123–4
Binmore, K. 82–3
blockade economics 184–5, 187–91, 192
Bombardier, C. 151, 152, 153, 157, 158, 160–1
bootstrapping 27–8
bounded rationality 1; German submarine campaign 4, 179–99; and information overload 37–40, 60–1
bounded vision 65
Britain 182–94 *passim*
business cycles 118

calculation 36, 40, 48; habits and economic evolution 45–8; information overload 37–40
Camic, C. 47
capital assets, prospective yields from 106–13
capitalism 104–5

Cartesian philosophy 45–7
casualties, wartime 195
category rating scales *see* visual analogue scales
centipede game 82–3
centralists 135–6
certainty 57–8, 157–60
change, radical 65, 112, 119
changing evaluation criteria 30, 30–1
chess 39, 61
choice 1; axioms of *see* axioms of choice; creative 82, 84–6; generalizing the theory of 59–65, 66; logical theory of 53–9, 65–6; public 4, 123–47; *see also* preference ordering
coalition governments 126
common rationality assumption 82–4
competence-difficulty gap 39
completeness 23, 54, 124
complexity 60–2
computational limitations 37–40
confidence 63–4
consciousness 46–7, 48
consistency 7–9, 12–13, 18, 33
consumer demand 128–9
consumer surplus measures 141–2
consumption 105–6
contradictory desires 85–6
conventions 80–2, 108; *see also* rules
co-ordination games 76–84
coronary artery bypass grafting (CABG) 162
cost of social choice 126
creative decision-making under uncertainty 82, 84–6
Creveld, M. Van 196–7
cycles 118

Darwin, C. 42, 43
Darwinian analogy 2, 36–7, 40–5, 48, 59
decision-making *see* choice
decision regret 162–3; *see also* regret theory
deconstruction 70, 84
deliberation *see* calculation
demand estimation 128–9
Department of Transport (DTp) 164, 165
desires, contradictory 85–6
dictatorship 126–7, 136
direct acquaintance: Keynes's early beliefs 92–6, 113; Keynes's mature beliefs 96–9, 113
direct intuitive observation 97–8
doctors 163
'dogmatic fallacy' 98
doubt 72–4, 74, 76, 77–9, 86; *see also* uncertainty
Douglas, M. 48, 84–5
dualistic philosophy 45–7
Dupuy, T. 196

economic warfare 185–94
economics 36; moral science 100; post-modernity and 3, 73, 74–86, 87–8; religious problem 8–9
efficiency: military 195–7; survival and 42–4
Elster, J. 43, 85–6, 180
enigmas 72
Enthoven, A.C. 198
entrepreneurship 84–5
environment, evolution and 44–5, 46–7
Epimethean self 86
epistemology 96
equivalence, marginal rate of (MRE) 142–6
ergodic stochastic processes 58
ethics 80
eugenics 104
evolutionary selection 2, 36–7, 40–5, 48, 59
expectations: Keynes and investment decision 63–4, 106–13, 117–18; rational 74–6, 81; short-term 117
experiments, scientific 8
explanatory power 58–9, 60, 66
extremal restrictedness 135–7

falsification 29–33
feasible choice set 53

feedback, environmental 44–5
firms 40–1, 42
Fischhoff, B. 168–9
Fishburn, P. C. 23, 153
fishing 131–2
Folk theorems 77
forecasting 109–13, 118
formal language skills 25
formal reasoning 180, 198
frequency theory of probability
101–2, 112, 115
Friedman, M. 29; evolution 40, 41–2, 42; information overload 37–8; logical theory of choice 58, 59
Fuss, R. 183, 190, 192

Gadamer, H. G. 91
Gafni, A. 152
gambling effects 152, 156–7; *see also* standard gambles
game theory 2, 76–84
generalized expected utility theory 15–16
German Admiralty 4, 185–6, 188, 191–3
Germany 198; military code 194–7; submarine campaign 4–5, 182–94
Gould, S. J. 42, 43
governments 126
grain blockade 184–5, 186, 187, 194
Grisley, W. 32

habits 37, 42, 48–9; economic evolution and 45–8
Hahn, F. 78
harvests, poor 187, 188
Hayek, F. A. von 41, 46, 91
health state measures 4, 149–78; explanations for disparities 151–60; implications of disparities 160–3
Heiner, R. 39–40
Helfferich, Interior Minister 189–90
hermeneutics 91, 114
Hershey, J. C. 163
Hey, J. D. 38
Hicks, J. R. 140, 142, 147
hierarchy 47–8, 49
Hindenburg, P. von B. und von 191
Holtzendorff, Admiral 190

imitation 42
immunizing stratagems 2, 29–33
impossibility theorems 4, 133, 142
'incentive-compatible' compensation schedules 31–2
independence 16–17, 23, 54
'independence of irrelevant alternatives' (Arrow's IIA) condition 133, 137–42, 144–5
indifference: individual curves 136–7; social 125
individual, post-modernity and 70, 85–6, 87–8
individual indifference curves 136–7
individual preferences 140–2; ordinal 142–6, 146
individualism, Keynes and 102
induction 95–6
information: available set 55–8; complexity and 60–2; overload 37–40, 46
injury description cards 165–8, 174–6
instability 125–6, 127
instrumental rationality 69, 74–80, 86–7
intention *see* calculation
interpersonal comparisons 139
intuitive reasoning 181–2, 191–2, 198
investment decision 3, 63–4, 66, 94, 106–13
irrationality: Keynes and 3, 94–5, 99, 100–1, 102–3, 103–13, 114; social 125–9

Januzszack, W. 73–4
Jevons, W. S. 105

Kellogg, E. D. 32
Keynes, J. M. 3, 62–4, 91–119; investment decision 3, 63–4, 66, 94, 106–13; irrationality and economic motivation 103–13; nature of rational belief 92–103

knowingness 81
knowledge: direct acquaintance and 93, 95–6, 97–8, 99; doubt and 72; partiality of 61–2
Koestler, A. 47
Kuhn, T. S. 24, 65

Lakatos, I. 24
language 96–7, 98–9
language game 24–34; evaluating utility theory 29–33; persuasion 26–7; science as 24–6; theory use 27–9
Laudan, L. 24
Lawson, T. 94, 106, 107, 108
Levy, H. 183–4, 184–5, 187, 190, 192, 199
Lewontin, R. 43
liquidity 106
Llewellyn-Thomas, H. 151, 161
logic, human 97, 98–9
logical theory of rational choice 2–3, 52–66; criticism 58–9; generalization from 59–65
Loomes, G. 86, 153, 154, 155
Ludendorff, E. von 191

Machina, M. J. 15–16, 29, 33, 159
maintained hypotheses 1–2, 8–17, 20, 21
majority voting 124–5, 125, 134–7, 139
marginal rate of equivalence (MRE) 142–6
marginal rate of substitution 140–2
market valuation 109, 118
Marxism 103
Masterman, M. 24
mathematical language community 2, 27–8
May, K. O. 139, 140
Mayston, D. J. 131, 140, 143, 144, 145, 147
meaning 70, 96–7, 98–9
measure theory 22–3
merchant shipping, Britain's 186, 187–8, 189, 193–4
military rationality 4–5, 192–3, 194–9
Mill, J. S. 37
Mises, L. von 46
modernity 73; *see also* post-modernity
money-motive 105, 106, 113, 114
Moore, G. E. 96, 101, 101–2
moral sciences 100
Morgenstern, O. 26, 29
motivation: battlefield 197; economic and irrationality 103–13, 114
multiple equilibria models 75
multiple-exit models 56, 61
Muth, J. 74

Nash equilibria 76–8
natural language community 2, 27–8
Nelson, R. 42
neoclassical economics 13
Neumann, J. von 26, 29
non-stochastic choice 57–8
normative economics 1, 7, 17–20, 21

obedience 101–2
objective functions 69, 128; normative economics 1, 17–20, 21
objectivity: information set 56–7; post-modernity 70–4, 75; values 100–1
Olson, M. 190
'one person, one vote' 139
ontology, Keynes and 99–103, 113
optimization objective 53
ordinal individual preferences 142–6, 146
organic interdependence 99–100, 101, 102, 107
outcomes, rationality and 179–80
overfishing 131–2
overlapping generations models 75

Paci, E. 99, 115
paradigm change 23–4, 24
Pareto efficiency 128
Pareto principle 129–32
path dependency 127–8, 141–2

perception 20–1, 93
'perfect dictionary, fallacy of' 98
perfect equilibria 76–7, 82–4
perfect information 57
Peters, T. 85
phenomenology 99, 114, 115
photographs 72
physics 8, 24–5
'play' 70
politics 125–7, 133–7
population forecasting 110, 118
positive economics 1–2, 7–17, 21
post-modernity 3, 68–88; defining 69–70; economic resonances 74–86
power functions 150, 152–3
precautionary motive 64
preference functions, levels of 45
preference ordering 53–5; individual 140–6, 146; public choice 123–5; single-peaked preferences 133–4; social irrationality 125–9; *see also* choice
preference reversal experiments 30–1
prices 188, 190–1
prisoner's dilemma 131–2, 180
probability 3, 62, 63, 92–3; frequency theory 101–2, 112, 115; subjective 26; weight and 63–4
procedural rationality 3, 60–1, 66, 79–80
Promethean self 86
prospective yields 106–13
psychological factors 94, 105–13, 114–15, 118
public choice 4, 123–47
puritanism 105, 116–17
purpose *see* calculation

quasi-ordinalism 140–2, 146

Ramsey, F. P. 26, 96–7
rational expectations 74–6, 81
rationality: concept 1–2, 6–21; definition 14; meaning 22
realism 58–9, 59, 66
reference groups 25–6, 34
reflexivity 54–5, 124; self- 80–1
regret behaviour 19
regret effects 169–72
regret theory 86, 153–5; health state measures 4, 155–60, 161–3, 168–72, 172–3
reinterpreting evidence 30, 31–2
relativism 70–4; *see also* subjectivity
religion 8–9, 12, 13, 17, 21
repeated games 77
representation theorems 22
require alternative theory (RAT) 29–30
risk 14–17, 57–8, 62
road accident studies 164–8, 174–8
Rorty, R. 80, 82, 85
routines *see* habits
Royal Commission on the Supply of Food 184, 185, 191
Royal Commission on Wheat Supplies 194
Rubic's cube 39–40
rules: information overload 39–40, 61; obedience to moral 101–2; *see also* axioms of choice; conventions
Rymes, T. K. 110–11

satisficing 38–9, 42, 180
Savage, L. J. 20, 26
saving 105–6
Schmoller, G. von 183
scholasticism, excessive 96, 98
science 34; changing objectives of 32–3; as language game 24–6; maintained hypothesis 8, 21
secessionists 135–6
selfishness 43
self-reflexivity 80–1
self-respect 85
self-sacrifice 102, 115–16
selves, multiple 85–6
Sen, A. K. 6–7, 135, 139
sensationalism 98
Sering, M. 183
Shackle, G. L. S. 106, 107
short-term expectations 117

Simon, H. A. 3, 47; procedural rationality 60–1, 66, 79; satisficing 38–9, 180
single-peaked preferences 133–4
Smith, K. W. 198
social conditioning 37, 48–9
social indifference 125
social rationality 4, 123–47
Spencer, H. 41, 42
Spindler, A. 183, 184
stability 65, 133–7
standard gambles 149–50, 178; compared with other health state measures 150–72 *passim*
stochastic choice 57–8
stock markets 108–9
subjective expected utility (SEU) theory 9, 12, 16–17, 22–3; *see also* utility theory
subjective probability theory 26
subjectivity 56–7; *see also* relativism
submarine campaign, German 4–5, 182–94
substitution, marginal rate of 140–2
Sugden, R. 78, 86, 153, 154, 155
'survival of the fittest' 36–7, 40–5
systematic errors 30–1, 74–5

tax policy 128
theory, role of 10–13; *see also* maintained hypotheses
time trade-offs 150; compared with other health state measures 150–63 *passim*
Tirpitz, Admiral 183
Torrance, G. W. 149; health state measure comparisons 150–1, 151–2, 152, 157, 158, 160, 161
tractability 58, 59–60, 66
trade blockade 183–5, 187–91, 192
transitivity 23, 55, 124; evaluation of SEU theory 32, 33; social rationality 124–9
translation theorem 32

uncertainty 1, 130; generalizing theory of choice 61–5, 66; Keynes 107, 118–19; maintained hypothesis 9, 14–17; post-modernity 3, 72–4, 76, 78, 83–6; *see also* doubt; risk
uniformity 63, 64
uniqueness theorems 22
United States of America 182, 186, 189, 190, 192, 194; Vietnam War 197–8; World War II fighting power 195–6, 197
utility evaluation effect 159
utility theory 2, 22–34; generalized expected 15–16; language game 24–9; theory evaluation 29–33; *see also* subjective expected utility theory

validation process 58–9, 60, 66
valuations 108, 109, 111, 118
values 100–1, 168–72, 172–3
Vietnam War 197–8
visual analogue scales 149, 177; compared with other health state measures 150–72 *passim*
votes, allocation of 139–40; *see also* majority vote; social rationality

war 179; *see also* Vietnam War; World War I; World War II
Waterman, R. 85
weight, probability and 63–4
welfare economics 147
wheat blockade 184–5, 186, 187, 194
Whitehead, A. N. 96, 97, 119; direct acquaintance 97–9; frequency theory of probability 101, 112, 115
Wiltshire, D. 41
Winslow, E. G. 96, 99, 107, 113
Winter, S. 42
World War I 4–5, 179–80, 182–94, 198
World War II 195–6, 197

yields, expected 106–13